A JUDAISM FOR THE TWENTY-FIRST CENTURY

Rabbi Pete Tobias

Adapted for Australia and New Zealand
by Rabbi Jonathan Keren-Black

A Judaism for the Twenty-First Century
by
Rabbi Pete Tobias
Revised for the Southern Hemisphere by
Rabbi Jonathan Keren-Black

with the endorsement of the
Union for Progressive Judaism
Australia, New Zealand and Asia
and with the permission of Liberal Judaism UK

ISBN 145-6-307576

First published in 2010
2nd, 3rd and 4th Edition 2011
5th Edition 2012
6th Edition 2013

UK Edition first published in 2007 as
'Liberal Judaism: A Judaism for the Twenty-First Century'

by
Liberal Judaism
(Union of Liberal and Progressive Synagogues)
The Montagu Centre, 21 Maple Street
London W1T 4BE United Kingdom

Rabbi Pete Tobias

All rights reserved.

www.upj.org.au
www.lbc.org.au
www.liberaljudaism.org
www.rabbipete.co.uk

No part of this publication may be reproduced
in any form or by any means, except as the law allows,
without the written permission of MHM Publications
mhmpublications@dodo.com.au.

A Judaism for the Twenty-First Century

DEDICATION

This book is dedicated to the late Rabbi John D. Rayner *z'l* who wrote, among many other things, the 'Affirmations' that form the chapters of this book. Initially, I did not write the chapters sequentially, and the last one to which I came was chapter 26, detailing the contribution of individual leaders to the development of Progressive Judaism. I felt it would be appropriate to include at the end of that chapter a brief summary of John Rayner's enormous contribution to Progressive Judaism, following the brief biographies of other key figures he had identified. On September 19th 2005, I completed the first draft of the book, save for the paragraphs about John. I turned to my e-mails to find one announcing the sad news of his death that very day. That John never had the chance to read this book saddens me; it would have benefited from the observations that would surely have followed the word 'However...' in the second paragraph of his appraisal. He was a teacher, a scholar, a gentleman and a source of inspiration to so many. I hope that he would have approved of this book.

Rabbi Pete Tobias

As well as being Senior Rabbi at the Liberal Jewish Synagogue and Chair of the European Region of the World Union for Progressive Judaism, John Rayner taught Rabbinics at the Leo Baeck College in London for over 40 years, and both Pete Tobias and Jonathan Keren-Black were amongst the students he taught and deeply influenced.

CONTENTS

Acknowledgements — p. vi
Introduction — p. 1
Introduction to this version — p. 3
Transliteration — p. 4

Part 1: Common Ground

1. Judaism — p. 5
2. The Jewish view of God — p. 9
3. The Jewish view of humanity — p. 16
4. The Jewish view of human history — p. 21
5. *B'rit* ('Covenant') — p. 26
6. The Jewish People — p. 31
7. Jewish history — p. 36
8. The State of Israel — p. 44
9. Jewish literature — p. 51
10. Torah ('Teaching') — p. 59
11. *Mitzvah* ('Commandment) — p. 64
12. Talmud Torah ('Study of Torah) — p. 69
13. Ethical values — p. 74
14. The Jewish home — p. 80
15. The synagogue — p. 85
16. Prayer and worship — p. 90
17. Jewish liturgy — p. 98
18. The Sabbath — p. 108
19. The Calendar and the Days of Awe — p. 114
20. The Three Pilgrimage festivals — p. 123
21. Chanukkah and other days of celebration and mourning — p. 134
22. Jewish rites of passage — p. 144

CONTENTS

Part 2: Distinctive Approach

23. The dynamic, developing character of Judaism	p. 152
24. The diversity of Jewish tradition	p. 157
25. Respect for conscientious options	p. 163
26. Progressive Judaism	p. 169
27. A synthesis of Judaism and modernity	p. 178
28. Bible scholarship	p. 184
29. The Messianic Age	p. 188
30. The Synagogue has permanently replaced The Temple	p. 193
31. Sincerity in worship	p. 198
32. The equal status of women and men in synagogue life	p. 204
33. The equal status of girls and boys in Jewish education	p. 209
34. The equal status of women and men in marriage law and ritual	p. 215
35. Children are not to be held responsible for the actions of their parents	p. 222
36. Children of mixed marriages are to be treated alike	p. 227
37. Inclusive attitude to Jewish identity	p. 233
38. Ethical emphasis of the Prophets	p. 238
39. Sincerity in observance	p. 245
40. Individual autonomy	p. 253
41. Rabbinic Law and the modern world	p. 258
42. Respect for other religions	p. 262
Glossary	p. 268
Index	p. 274

ACKNOWLEDGEMENTS

Many people have helped with the production of this book. It would probably never have seen the light of day had I not found myself temporarily immobilised with a snapped Achilles tendon in the summer of 2005, so I must thank my son Adam for the tennis game that was the occasion of that injury, which enabled me to compose the first draft on a laptop while watching England regain the Ashes. Thanks also to Rosita Rosenberg, who saw it in its first and final stages, and to Rabbi Andrew Goldstein who has been present at every stage of its (and my) development. Colleagues and friends too numerous to mention took time to read and comment on it at subsequent stages, but special thanks go to Rabbi David Goldberg for two lunches and a parking ticket. Many people at Liberal Judaism have helped see the project through to fruition: thanks to Penny Beral and, most especially, to the long suffering Selina O'Dwyer. A mention must go to Vincent Harding who patiently bore the constant demands of changes in design. Particular gratitude is due to John Eidinow, without whose diligent reading of the various versions, accompanied by advice, guidance and encouragement (usually provided over coffee at Puccino's) the book would be much poorer. And finally to Robbie, who has so patiently put up with my moodiness, absent-mindedness and constant need to rewrite a sentence or two at the most unlikely hours.

PT April 2007

I am delighted that the Progressive movement in Australia, the first synagogue of which was founded in Melbourne with much support and encouragement from Lily Montagu in London back in 1930, celebrated its eightieth anniversary in 2010 and continues to develop and thrive. My colleague Rabbi Jonathan Keren-Black, assisted by the careful eye of Philippa McMahon, has produced this version, tailored for use in that region, which continues the connection originally forged so many years ago between London and Melbourne by Lily Montagu.

PT December 2010

INTRODUCTION

This book seeks to set out the principles of Progressive Judaism and apply those principles to contemporary society and culture, the world of today in which Progressive Judaism and its adherents must find their moral bearings.

Reconciling their beliefs with an ever-changing world is not a new experience for Jews. One of this book's fundamental assertions is that Judaism has constantly adapted itself to meet the challenges posed to it by the need to survive in evolving societies – had it not done so, this ancient religion would long since have been written out of history. As we enter a third millennium (according to one particular method of counting time), the need for religion to live up to its potential as a positive force in human development has never seemed more urgent. In its purest form, religion encapsulates humankind's most noble aspirations in the search for life's meaning and purpose. In practice, sadly, it often seems that, amid claims of divine preference, religion has lost its way in a maze of particularistic ritual that does no justice to the human spirit or its Creator.

'A Judaism for the Twenty-First Century' and its original UK version, 'Liberal Judaism, A Judaism for the Twenty-First Century' are grandchildren. Their parent is 'Judaism for Today', written in 1978 by Rabbi John D Rayner and Rabbi Bernard Hooker. Their grandparent is 'The Essentials of Liberal Judaism', by Rabbi Israel Mattuck in 1947. The family in which it proudly and humbly takes its place (proudly since it is an honour to make a contribution to that family, humbly because of the greatness of its predecessors) is The World Union for Progressive Judaism, the movement that was established in London in 1926, whose headquarters are today in Jerusalem.

In 1809, in Seesen, Germany, the first Jewish services were held where men and women were able to sit together, use was made of the everyday language, and the prayers were somewhat shortened and modified. Over the following two hundred years, Progressive Judaism has sought to discern and emphasise the universalistic concerns and the messianic purpose of Judaism, both enshrined in the visions of

Israel's ancient prophets. In this regard, its emphasis sometimes differs from what might be called mainstream Judaism. Although Progressive Judaism shares its heritage with all Jews around the world, it values sincerity and integrity even above ritual and tradition. Therefore it emphasises the demand for justice implicit in the establishment of biblical laws more than adherence to the tiniest details of laws and customs that have been derived from them over the generations. Much of present-day Judaism, it would seem, is more concerned with these laws and customs, rituals and traditions than with the ethical and moral imperatives that inspired them and that underpin them.

Progressive Judaism strives to rediscover and emphasise the underlying principles that have been at the heart of this ancient faith since its inception more than three thousand years ago.

It is this emphasis, placing the prophetic demands for justice ahead of acknowledging Judaism's age-old traditions for their own sake, that makes Progressive Judaism unique. This stance is reflected in another, central document, 'Affirmations of Liberal Judaism', written by Rabbi John D Rayner in 1992 (the two constituent movements of the World Union for Progressive Judaism operating in Britain are the Liberal Movement and the Reform Movement). Re-edited in 2006, it lists forty-two propositions about Progressive Judaism. The first twenty-two map out the ground shared with other branches of Judaism. The second twenty list those aspects that give Progressive Judaism its unique character.

Each of the forty-two affirmations inspires a chapter of this book. Building on Rabbi Rayner's 1992 work, the complete text offers an overview of Judaism from this Progressive perspective. It is written both in the expectation that it will, in due course, be superseded, and in the hope that this will be the case. A Judaism that does not develop is not a living Judaism. What follows, then, is a picture of where Progressive Judaism stands at the beginning of the twenty-first century. To quote from its predecessor, it is an ancient faith with a modern message. That message, and this work, tells how Progressive Judaism is at the cutting edge of a religion constantly evolving. As readers will discover, Progressive Judaism challenges the assumptions that modern-day Judaism makes about itself, insists that its adherents confront today's major issues with the honesty and integrity our age demands, and brings to that confrontation the ethical and spiritual awareness that inspired the earliest creators of Judaism and the founders of Progressive Judaism itself.

This is Progressive Judaism: A Judaism for the Twenty-First Century.

Rabbi Pete Tobias
Elstree, April 2007

INTRODUCTION TO THIS VERSION

Progressive Judaism is a rich and wonderful framework for Jewish life in the modern world. There is no shortage of excellent prayerbooks and Torah commentaries, reading and study material about contemporary Progressive Jewish issues, philosophy and thought, but contemporary and accessible introductions are fewer on the ground. Indeed, since Rabbi Dr John S Levi's '30 Questions' booklet went out of print, there has been nothing specifically available for the Australian community to meet this need.

When I read Rabbi Pete Tobias' book 'Liberal Judaism, A Judaism for the Twenty-First Century', it clearly demonstrated once again the huge amount that the Progressive Jewish Movements, members of the World Union for Progressive Judaism around the world, share, but also that in some areas there is local nuance and variation. Realising that, with its clarity and breadth, it would make an excellent introduction and fill a pressing need for us also, I sought permission from Rabbi Tobias and from Liberal Judaism in the UK to produce our own version. Permission was most generously granted, and this book is the result.

Thanks to modern 'Print-on-demand' technology, the book is regularly updated to reflect the latest positions and thinking, and to suit the UPJ's 'Introduction to Judaism' courses.

Rabbi Jonathan Keren-Black
Melbourne, June 2013

TRANSLITERATION

Transliteration is intended to familiarise the reader with the pronunciation of Hebrew words and terms. Any in-depth study of Judaism, and especially any intention to practise as part of a Jewish community, would benefit greatly from the ability to read Hebrew, the teaching of which is beyond the scope of this book, but see 'Hebrew From Zero' featured at the end pages of this book for one good system.

The transliteration scheme used in this book is designed to be easy to pronounce. Nevertheless, the reading of transliteration is an acquired skill, and some rules need to be learnt.

PRONUNCIATION
- a   as in *are*
- e   as in *get*
- i   as in *bit*
- o   as in *on*
- u   as in *rule*
- ai as in *aisle*
- ei as in *eight*
- tz as in *pizza*
- ch as in *Bach**
- '   as in *G'day***

* This is the guttural *kh* sound that has come into English from Hebrew via Yiddish, as found in common terms such as *challah, Chanukah, chuppah* and *chutzpah*.

** The apostrophe acts as a brief syllable break and usually indicates a *sh'va*, or may be used to visually separate combinations of consonants.

When letters or vowels are silent, they are not usually represented.

Capital letters are used as in English (to begin sentences and for proper nouns), even after a prefix, as in *kEloheinu* and *biYrushalayim*.

Part 1: Common Ground

1

JUDAISM

We affirm our commitment to Judaism, the cultural heritage of the Jewish People, and the centrality within that heritage of the Jewish religion, which, since the time of Abraham and Sarah, has proclaimed the sovereignty of the One God.

A Judaism for the Twenty-First Century

The beginning of the twenty-first century may seem an unlikely time for a book about religion to be written – especially a religion that is well over three thousand years old. There are those who would argue that many of the difficulties with which our world is confronted today are a consequence of religion and therefore are unlikely to be solved by it. But every religion began as an attempt by human beings to understand their place on this earth and give meaning and purpose to their lives. Subsequent development and (mis-) interpretation of religious doctrine has led to conflict, it is true, but the nature and the role of religion remain unchanged. It is the attempt to provide answers to life's questions, comfort through life's uncertainties and meaning to human existence.

If this is the yardstick for a religion, then Judaism, stretching back across countless generations, can certainly claim to have worked towards fulfilling that role. The fact that it has survived for this length of time would suggest that it has, in some measure, succeeded. It has done so by developing and changing, by adapting itself to new challenges and new environments at all stages of its history. Progressive Judaism today represents one broad stream of this adaptation and development, the specific characteristics of which will be more fully explored in the second half of this book. This opening section will explore those elements of Judaism that are agreed upon and shared by all strands of this four thousand year old tradition.

Judaism has long been regarded as being more than a religion. One of the most popular descriptions of Judaism is that it is a 'way of life'. But which way of life is being referred to in such a statement? Is the reference to devout ultra-Orthodox Jewish men praying earnestly at the Western Wall in Jerusalem? A Jewish family gathered around a table watching mother light candles at a *Seder*[1] or a *Shabbat*[2] meal? Or bagels filled with smoked salmon and cream cheese? How do these elements go together to define the cultural heritage of the Jewish religion?

The very fact that Judaism has such a long history and that the world has changed so immeasurably since the days of Abraham and Sarah, traditionally regarded as its founding patriarch and matriarch[3], confirms Judaism's recognition of the constantly developing nature of the world. This religion continues to ask and assess, re-form and re-evaluate those questions about life to which Judaism seeks to provide the answers. As such, on a theoretical level, certainly, Judaism can be seen as a framework from within which its adherents can continue to search for answers to those fundamental human questions about the meaning and purpose of life.

In practical terms, of course, Judaism is so much more than this. It is a culture, with literature, traditions, beliefs and practices, which have developed and grown in all the places where Jewish communities have made their home. All of these elements of Judaism are precious and we cherish and value them as reminders of our past, even if we do not always make them part of our present. In the end, it comes back to that need to ask questions, to find meaning and purpose in our lives, which lies at the heart of this ancient faith and which gives Judaism the opportunity to give meaning and relevance to our lives as it has in so many previous generations. Judaism is an engagement in and a commitment to a four thousand year old process that traces its roots back to its very first generation, to the story of Abraham and Sarah as related in the biblical Book of Genesis.

---

[1] The family meal celebrated on the first night of the festival of *Pesach* (Passover)
[2] Sabbath: the Jewish Sabbath commences with the lighting of candles at sunset on a Friday
[3] Genesis 12 ff

Here, in his developing relationship with God, Abraham sets the tone for the experience and the attitude that will shape Judaism for all its future generations. Abraham makes a commitment to the One God, listens to the words of this God (as presented by the biblical author), obeys, challenges and argues with this God. This attitude is exemplified and refined in Abraham's biblical grandson, Jacob, whose name is changed to Israel[1] – which translates as 'he (*or* one) who struggles with God'.

And that is Judaism. It is the result of hundreds of generations of Jews following the examples of their ancestors such as Jacob; struggling with God, seeking answers to those eternal questions about how we should find meaning and purpose in our lives, our relationships with others and with our world. Jewish history is the experience of that struggle; Jewish literature is the record of it. And each generation of the Jewish people adds its own chapter, each individual Jew his or her own story to the heritage, to the process called Judaism.

---

[1] Genesis 32:29

2

THE JEWISH VIEW OF GOD

We affirm the Jewish conception of God: One and indivisible, transcendent and immanent, Creator and Sustainer of the universe, Source of the Moral Law, a God of justice and mercy Who demands that human beings shall practise justice and mercy in their dealings with one another.

A Judaism for the Twenty-First Century

At the heart of Judaism is the recognition and acknowledgement of a divine source of power and inspiration, the embodiment and focus of all religious quest: God. The most significant element of the Jewish understanding of God, explicitly declared in the *Sh'ma*, one of the central elements of Jewish liturgy, is the affirmation that there is only one God. This concept, which emerged against a background of the idolatrous worship of many gods, has been a central feature of the Jewish religion since its earliest days. The awareness of an invisible and indivisible divine presence has shaped and sustained Judaism throughout the ages.

Proving God's existence, a favourite pastime of philosophers of all generations, has never been a concern of Judaism's. As the Psalmist wrote 'Only the fool says in his heart "There is no God."'[1] Judaism's attitude to the existence of God, then, is not so much a question of belief as one of awareness. We may, at certain times in our lives feel more or less aware of God's presence, but the starting point for Judaism is that there is a God.

For many, particularly in our modern technological age, this assertion presents a major problem. The feeling is, perhaps, that our ancient ancestors, living in an uncertain world, had a much greater requirement for the belief in the existence of a divine power to explain all those things that they did not understand and to which they could turn in times of danger, need or gratitude. Unlike them, we are generally much better protected from the vicissitudes of nature and have a greater understanding of the workings of the universe. This, coupled with the secular values of the age in which we live and the scepticism born of our rational approach to the world, means that God is far less apparent in our time than was the case in the world of our ancestors. In particular, science has created an environment in which we are unlikely to believe anything to be

---

[1] Psalm 14:1, 53:1

the case unless it can be proven empirically. This approach, which pervades more of our modern lives than we are perhaps prepared to acknowledge, seems to make belief in God appear irrelevant or anachronistic to many.

In the end, though, human beings can never truly know or define God – such a suggestion is, by its very definition, absurd. This has not, however, prevented Jews, in all ages and from a variety of perspectives, from making statements and assumptions about the nature and the role of God. We cannot know God but we can make certain assertions about God's existence. Already mentioned is the key Jewish belief that there is only one God, a basis from which can be derived other elements of the Jewish conception of the divine power and the universe.

The Jewish belief that there is one God leads to the conclusion that the universe is also a unity and God is its Creator. While Progressive Judaism acknowledges that the six-day creation story in the opening chapter of Genesis is a myth that does not tally with the scientific understanding of our own age that favours the theory of the universe as having started with a 'Big Bang', the suggestion in the creation story, that light suddenly emerged out of darkness, has some parallels with modern cosmology. Ultimately, although science can tell us what happened milliseconds after the Big Bang, it is unable as yet to offer an explanation as to what caused the explosion and – more significantly – why it happened. Such speculation belongs to the sphere of religion, which regards this miracle of creation as being a manifestation of the divine.

Having set in motion whatever were the forces that caused the universe to come into being, God – as their source – also sustains the universe at every moment. This ongoing role of God in organising the natural powers that are present at every level of creation is acknowledged in Jewish liturgy, which praises God who *m'chadeish b'chol yom tamid ma-aseh v'reishit* – 'You daily renew creation.'[1] This implies the presence of God in the works of nature, the organisation of physical forces that was set in place at the very instant of creation, which can be destructive as well as creative.

We frequently see examples of the destructive potential of nature. Earthquake and tsunami, hurricane, drought and fire are as much a part of the fabric of nature as hot summer days and winter rains. Crippling diseases and horrific cancers exist alongside healthy, fully functioning bodies. Our biblical ancestors believed that their words and offerings could influence the divine power to alter the pattern of nature. In our time, we tend to look upon natural catastrophe or devastating illness as a proof of the non-existence of God when, in fact, they are a manifestation of nature: they occur because destructive forces must necessarily also be present in a system in which creative forces are at work. God's role in such cases is not to intervene and suspend or change the laws of nature but rather to imbue human beings with the capacity to respond to, deal with and try to overcome or protect against their effects. This divinely bestowed human attribute will be considered at greater length in the next chapter.

Such an approach to nature and God's role within it raises problems when one considers the question of miracles. The earliest commentators on the Hebrew Bible were the scholars who began their work of contemplating these texts in the second century before the Common Era.[2] These commentators were troubled by the events preceding the biblical Exodus, for

---

[1] *Mishkan T'filah* ('Tabernacle of Prayer'), World Union Edition, is the Sabbath and daily prayerbook of Progressive Judaism in our region, as well as an excellent resource for studying Progressive Judaism. This prayer, '*Yotzeir or*' is found on p.60 (and in traditional Jewish liturgy)

[2] Judaism refers to the periods of time commonly known in Western tradition as BC and AD as 'Before the Common Era (BCE) and 'Common Era' (CE) respectively.

example, where God sought to punish the Egyptians for enslaving the Israelites. In order to achieve this, so the biblical text relates, God suspended the natural course of events and introduced a series of apparently supernatural – and very brutal – occurrences that only the Egyptians suffered.[1] The explanation the scholars offered, faced with the 'biblical fact' of these miracles, was that God had pre-programmed these events into nature at the moment of creation in order that they would occur at the pre-ordained time. The alternative, namely that God had indeed intervened to alter nature at a specific point in history, raises a simple but inevitable question: if God was able to change nature on that occasion, why have similar interventions not been made at other times of catastrophe, whether in the lives of nations or individuals? A third option, of course, available to us but not to the scholars committed to the literal 'truth' of the Torah, is to accept that miracles as intentional 'acts of God' simply do not take place; that nature invariably behaves according to the laws of physics. The issue is then how human beings receive and respond to manifestations of nature, which, although they obey the laws of physics, still have the capacity to surprise or even hurt us.

The creative (and sometimes destructive), immensely powerful aspect of God is necessarily and inevitably beyond human power to explain or comprehend. God is, by definition, greater than and separate from the created universe, as well as being present in every aspect of it. Any attempt to describe God will be only that: an attempt, a description of something that cannot fully be described, a vague apprehension of something that cannot fully be comprehended. Nevertheless, human beings, in seeking to describe God, will naturally ascribe to God features with which they are familiar in order to make such descriptions more accessible to listeners and readers, though, as generations of Jewish scholars have been at pains to point out, these are only metaphorical. Anthropomorphisms (references to God as

---

[1] Exodus chapters 7-14

A Judaism for the Twenty-First Century

having human features or characteristics) cannot be taken literally; their role is to help the understanding and appreciation of God. In the end, though, we must accept God's transcendence with the words of the prophet Isaiah: '"My thoughts are not your thoughts, neither are My ways your ways," says the Eternal One. "For as the heavens are higher than the earth, so are My ways higher than your ways, and My thoughts than your thoughts."' [1]

Although Judaism is adamant that God is transcendent and exists within and beyond the universe in ways we cannot explain or understand, it equally emphasises God's immanence: the perception and appreciation of the divine presence that is available to every individual. The seeming contradiction between these two aspects of God is addressed in the hymn *Adon Olam*,[2] a hymn sung in many synagogue services. It begins by describing how God existed before the universe was created and will continue to exist after it has ended, yet concludes with the words, 'Into Your hands I entrust my spirit, when I sleep and when I wake, and with my spirit my body also; the Eternal One is with me, I shall not fear.' Here we find the basis of the personal relationship that Judaism believes can exist between individuals and God; a closeness experienced by Abraham, Rebecca,[3] Jacob and Hannah,[4] for example, and available to all their descendants.

One aspect of this relationship that Judaism has always emphasised is the nature of the demands that God makes of human beings within that relationship. As well as being the power that organises and sustains the creative forces of the universe, God is the source of that drive within all creation to

---

[1] Isaiah 55:8f
[2] World Union Edition of *Mishkan T'filah* p.625
[3] See Genesis 25:22-23. There is less recorded in the case of the matriarchs and other women, and consequently less awareness that they too relate directly and personally to God on significant occasions and in pivotal ways.
[4] See 1st Samuel 1:11

survive and to grow. For human beings, that growth is not just a case of physical development and evolution; it also carries a moral aspect. God is the source of the attributes of justice and mercy that human beings are expected to practise in their dealings with one another.

Before moving to that aspect of the relationship between God and human beings, however, it is necessary to return to a question that was alluded to at the beginning of this chapter. If belief in the existence of God is at the heart of Judaism, how then can those who find themselves unable to believe in God count themselves among its ranks? It would be easy – and perhaps insulting – to suggest that it may be the human inability to comprehend God that lies at the heart of some people's refusal to recognise or acknowledge a divine presence. But it is hard to deny that there are many aspects of our modern world that might persuade us of the improbability of the existence of a benevolent Creator who seeks to guide and protect us. However, the plea of Progressive Judaism to a person who might be struggling with doubts about the existence of God is that they should persist with the struggle. Just as Abraham and Jacob argued and struggled with God, so too should their descendants continue that process.

Given that one can never truly know or understand God or fathom God's ways, those who are wrestling with their doubts are likely to have a more meaningful relationship with the divine power than those whose faith is blind and lacks challenge. Progressive Judaism aims to offer a spiritual home to those who are searching for, as well as to those who believe they have found, a meaningful relationship with God – Progressive congregations probably contain many members who consider themselves to be staunch atheists alongside those whose relationship with God may be one of mutual challenge rather than benign acknowledgement. Such a congregation truly reflects Judaism's attitude towards the Divine.

3
THE JEWISH VIEW OF HUMANITY

We affirm the Jewish conception of humanity: created in the Divine Image, endowed with free will, capable of sublime goodness but also of terrible evil, mortal yet with a sense of eternity, able to enter into a direct personal relationship with their Creator, and to restore that relationship, when it is broken, through repentance **(t'shuvah)**.

It is a feature of Judaism that its adherents are in a relationship with God, and that this relationship is an ongoing one. Just as Judaism has its understanding of the divine, so too does it offer a definition of humanity. 'Eternal God, what are human beings that you have made us, humankind that you are mindful of us? For you have made human beings little less than divine and crowned us with glory and honour.' [1]

These well-known verses from the eighth Psalm confirm the Jewish conception of humanity: that human beings are the pinnacle of God's creation and that we have, in ways that are not clear to us, been created in the divine image. This cannot mean, of course, that we look like God; rather that there is, implanted within us in some mysterious and intangible way, a spark of the divine and the possibility of our establishing and maintaining a connection to it. This awareness of God within us is something we can acknowledge or ignore; it is always there but recognition of it varies from individual to individual, from generation to generation, according to situation or circumstance.

This emphasises one of the most important elements of the Jewish understanding of humanity: the fact that we have been given free will. Our ability to decide our own actions – and by extension to carry responsibility for them and their consequences – is the basis of our evolution and development. Without that capacity, humanity would never have embarked upon its journey from prehistoric ignorance to uncover the potential upon which our present society has been built and towards the fulfilment of which it is still journeying.

Of course, the development of that human society has come at a price. The cost of free will is the potential to destroy as well as to create, to demonstrate cruelty and hatred as well as love and compassion. According to the Rabbis, every human being is

---

[1] Psalm 8: 4-5

endowed with a good inclination and an evil inclination (*yeitzer ha-tov* and *yeitzer ha-ra*) – forces within us that vie at all times for our allegiance. There is merit in both. The Rabbis assert that if it were not for the evil inclination, people would not have sufficient determination to build a house or demonstrate any ambition whatsoever.[1] It is also the source of human creativity. Judaism is convinced that our natural human inclination is towards the good and the positive, despite the countless bloody events in history that stand as proof of our regular failure to choose good over evil.

This is the consequence of free will – and occasionally the devastating and destructive manifestations of humanity's will might cause us to question the very existence of God. How can God permit human beings to behave with such callous cruelty and neglect towards fellow human beings? The answer lies in our understanding of God. As has already been suggested[2], God cannot interfere with or alter manifestations of nature, having established the universe according to a particular set of physical laws. The same applies to human nature. Having implanted free will within us, God must leave us to respond to that ability to choose.

Of course, God can influence our choices. That is the nature of the divinely inspired potential that has been implanted within us. God has given us the freedom to choose but wishes us to follow our good inclination. Human beings have an innate awareness of right and wrong: it is upon this awareness that the potential for human development and progress is based. We have, sadly, all experienced tragedy and injustice in our lives and, thanks to modern technology, we now have the ability to see into remote and strife-torn areas of the world, exposing us to more images of suffering and misery inflicted by nature and human beings than any previous generation. Although this

---

[1] *Midrash* Genesis *Rabbah* 9:7
[2] See p.12

may deaden our senses, charitable and humanitarian responses to global tragedies suggest that the natural human instinct is to do what we can to assist people in desperate need. There is within us an ability to empathise with the suffering of fellow human beings and a desire, welling from somewhere deep inside us, to do whatever we can to help. This is a manifestation of the Divine within us, that sense of responsibility and duty towards our fellows and a wish to give assistance and support in times of suffering. No-one can say from where this wellspring of compassion draws its source. All we can do is acknowledge it as God-given, recognise it as being part of our human duty and respond to it accordingly with acts of kindness and love.

This exposure to human suffering all around the globe reminds us constantly of our own mortality. This recognition that we are on this earth for only a brief span can encourage our *yeitzer ha-ra* and make us selfish, determined simply to attend to our own needs. As indicated above, a degree of self-interest is necessary for individual survival and improvement   However, set against this is a sense of eternity, an inexplicable awareness that whatever we give to life does not come to an end when we depart from the planet and that whatever good we bring into the world does not perish.

It is one of the paradoxes of God that the divine presence can be perceived both as an indescribable, impenetrable force that transcends the universe and as an immanent personal presence with whom it is possible to have an individual relationship. Such a relationship is not experienced by all human beings, but those who are able to establish such a connection with the Divine find that their lives can be enriched in ways not immediately apparent to those for whom no such connection exists.

A Judaism for the Twenty-First Century

Judaism has always emphasised the possibility of such a relationship with God, however God may be perceived or understood by an individual. This awareness of the divine presence should encourage a person to choose good over evil, to follow the correct path – the path that is dictated by one's *yeitzer ha-tov*. Human fallibility means that this is not always possible, but Judaism affirms the capacity of human beings to recognise their own failings and, moreover, to perceive this recognition as an apprehension of God, whether working within them as a manifestation of conscience or as an external force.

This recognition of human failing and the desire to correct it is known as *t'shuvah*. This is usually translated as 'repentance' but has more to do with returning, finding one's way back to the right path. So convinced is Judaism of the possibility – and necessity – of correcting one's failings and so repairing one's relationship with the Divine, that an annual period of time, culminating in the Day of Atonement, is set aside for this to be considered and attempted.[1] *T'shuvah* can be made at any time, however, whenever human beings recognise their failings and seek to atone for them. This possibility, to correct the imbalance between the evil and good inclinations, is built into every individual. Ultimately, this ensures that a humanity that has been given free will can, despite its many terrible failings, make progress towards fulfilling the divine potential that has been implanted within it, and thereby work to bring goodness into the world.

---

[1] See chapter 19, 'The Days of Awe'.

4

THE JEWISH VIEW OF HUMAN HISTORY

We affirm the Jewish conception of human history: a drama of progress and setback, triumph and tragedy, yet divinely destined to lead to an age when all worship the One God, good will triumph over evil, and the reign of freedom, justice, love and peace will be permanently established throughout the world.

Although accounts of human development in the Bible can hardly be described as historically accurate (and nor were they really intended to be), what they do demonstrate is that their authors were keenly aware of humanity's failings as well as its capacity for good.

The biblical book of Genesis opens with an account of the beginning of the world and by the time we are a quarter of the way through the eleventh chapter, we have seen deception and murder, wickedness and arrogance. This culminates in God disposing of human beings with the Flood and then confounding their attempt at building a tower to reach the sky by causing them to speak a variety of languages: not a particularly auspicious beginning for a species that, as noted in the previous chapter, has been created in the divine image.

But these stories in the early part of Genesis are seeking to depict and explain aspects of human life rather than represent factual historical experience. They demonstrate to us the wisdom and insight of our ancient ancestors: their authors were no less aware than are we of the shortcomings of humankind, and they felt compelled to write stories depicting those shortcomings. But the accounts of such failings tell only half the story of humanity. Perhaps the most intriguing of the early legends in Genesis is the story of the Tower of Babel in chapter eleven. Although its purpose was presumably to explain why different cultures speaking different languages existed in the Ancient Near East, the idea that God should deliberately seek to confuse human beings and create obstacles that prevent them from communicating with one another tends to fly in the face of what Judaism perceives as humanity's task. If the process and progress of human history is meant to be humanity's journey towards self-awareness and self-fulfilment, then the theology behind the story of the Tower of Babel either represents a cruel divine joke or a desire by the divine power to make humanity's task all the more difficult. Or perhaps, as the story in Genesis itself suggests, it was the motivation behind the construction of the Tower of Babel that was the problem: human co-operation in this venture was based upon arrogance rather than a desire to work in partnership with God.

The emergence of different cultures – more numerous than the author of Genesis 11:1-9 could have imagined – coupled with human arrogance has meant that humanity's journey in search of that mythical level of co-operation has been long and painful, but also one of enormous progress. Mighty empires have come and gone, often leaving devastation in their wake, but also testimonies to the human ability to build societies of great complexity, as reflected in the archaeology, art and literature they produced. Every successful empire, however flawed may have been its philosophy, however misguided and brutal its efforts to impose its will upon others and however vociferous the opposition to it and how undignified its ultimate collapse, has made a contribution to history and to the progress of humanity.

The modern world in which we live, for all its glaring faults, owes immeasurable gratitude to the efforts of past generations. In the past two centuries, revolutions in scientific knowledge and its technological application have ensured that, for many, life today is more sophisticated and structured, better protected from nature and disease and better understood than has ever been the case in the past. These developments show humanity's progress from its earliest days of uncertainty and superstition.

But the task is not complete and nor has the journey been one of uninterrupted progress. The human failings highlighted in those early chapters of Genesis have manifested themselves with horrific consequences at frequent intervals in human history. Arrogance has led one society or culture to imagine itself superior to another and to seek to impose its will over its rivals, developing ever more sophisticated methods of killing fellow human beings to impose and enforce that will. These human tendencies ensure that we cannot deny the reality of the human potential to do evil and to wreak havoc as well as to create and to build.

At the risk of appearing to emphasise a particularly Jewish perspective on history, perhaps the best modern example of this contrast in human history and development is nineteenth and early twentieth century Germany. The cultural developments in so many different scientific and artistic fields in Germany during the nineteenth century – not least among them the emergence of the modern version of our ancient faith that underpins Progressive Judaism – were immense. Yet this cultured society was the breeding ground for the horrors of the Holocaust, one of the most chilling examples of how humanity's technological developments have been used to bring destruction to other human beings. Of course, there are many other examples of human cruelty. Our age has witnessed genocide in Rwanda and ethnic cleansing in the Balkan states, while the development of weapons of mass destruction casts a chilling shadow over the new millennium as divisions between cultures emerge and peoples continue to confront each other with hostility and loathing.

But Judaism firmly believes – as all religions surely should – that humanity's journey from its earliest days is one which leads inexorably, if somewhat haltingly, towards a time when such mutual mistrust and its consequences will lie in the past. No matter how much evidence may suggest that human beings are destined always to confront one another with hostility, there are also enough examples in human history to suggest the development of a maturity that will eventually triumph. We live in a world more aware of itself – its diversity, its shortcomings and its potential – than has ever been the case before. This is the consequence of human development, the unfolding of history as it continues its journey towards a recognition and realisation of humanity's destiny: to live in harmony with itself, its world and its Creator. Judaism is committed to playing its part in mapping out the path and encouraging its adherents to make that journey, along with the rest of humankind.

5

B'RIT ('COVENANT')

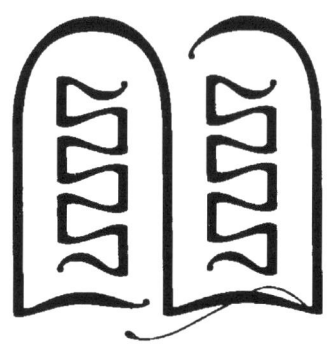

We affirm the Jewish concept of* B'rit *('Covenant'): the special relationship that came to exist between God and our Hebrew and Israelite[1] ancestors, and the responsibility that therefore devolves on their descendants, to be God's witnesses and servants.

---

[1] The title 'Hebrew' is used to refer to a Canaanite people, possibly derived from the Hebrew word meaning 'to cross' (the people crossed the Tigris, the Euphrates and the Jordan rivers to leave Mesopotamia and enter Canaan). 'Israelite' refers to those people claiming to be descended from the patriarch Jacob (whose name was changed to Israel) or who dwelt in the biblical Kingdom of Israel. Generally, however, these two titles refer to the ancestors of the Jewish people (though the later term 'Jew' actually derives from the inhabitants of the biblical kingdom of Judah).

Brit ('Covenant')

Judaism's commitment to that journey and its perception that it is co-operating with God in seeking to undertake it, suggests a specific and perhaps unique partnership with the Creator. Central to ancient Israelite religion and its offspring, Judaism, is the covenantal nature of the relationship between its people and their God. A brief historical exploration of the nature of covenants in the Ancient Near East will help to explain this relationship.

Around three thousand years ago, the inhabitants of the land of Canaan lived in varying social and political circumstances. The Canaanites lived in cities that were ruled over by local kings – who were themselves invariably subject to more powerful rulers of major empires such as Egypt or Assyria. The Israelites, on the other hand, were semi-nomadic groups who dwelt on the land outside the walls of the Canaanite cities but were often subject to the power of the local Canaanite rulers.

The nature of the relationship between rulers and their subjects at this time was that of a covenant. The ruler made certain demands upon the subject – the provision of tithes or taxes as well as loyalty – and, in return, the powerful ruler promised to protect and defend the interests of the subjects. Where such relationships were formally defined and documented (and many such Babylonian covenant documents have been found) they took the form of a list, detailing what the ruler would provide for those subjects who kept their side of the covenant – and what would befall them if they did not.

There are many examples of such covenants in the Hebrew Bible and Jewish tradition: God's promise to Noah in Genesis chapter 9, never to send another flood is, according to rabbinic interpretation, balanced with seven laws that are demanded of the whole of humankind, including prohibitions against theft and murder. Just a few chapters later, we find Abraham making a covenant with God, and circumcision *(b'rit milah* – the covenant of cutting) is established as a sign of that mutual agreement.

This common biblical model of contract is reflected most precisely in the biblical Book of Deuteronomy. This book, unique among the Five Books of Moses for its unity and consistency, begins by detailing God's demands and requirements for the Israelite people and, having done so, then sets out the consequences of observing or failing to observe them. Chapter 28 of the Book of Deuteronomy begins with the words *'V'hayah im shamo'a tish'ma b'kol Adonai elohecha lish'mor v-la'asot et kol mitzvotav'* – 'If you diligently listen to the voice of the Eternal your God to observe and carry out all God's commandments…' and there follow fourteen verses of all the blessings that God will bestow upon the people. Verse 15 begins in identical form, save for the insertion of the Hebrew word *lo* – 'If you do not listen, observe and carry out…' etc. There then follow more than fifty verses describing the most appalling suffering – famine and war, siege and starvation – that will be the consequence of failing to observe God's commandments.

This formulation reflects precisely the structure of the covenant relationship that existed between a ruler and his subjects in the Ancient Near East. Those who developed the ancient Israelite religion demonstrated great ingenuity in adapting a very earthly, political relationship into a symbolic covenant between the Israelites and their God.

This particular covenant was sealed at Mount Sinai[1] (or Mount Horeb according to the Deuteronomy version[2]) and it is a covenant to which, according to an interpretation of that biblical text, all the Israelites' descendants were committed at that awesome moment. In Chapter 30 of Deuteronomy (shortly

---

[1] Exodus chapters 19-20
[2] Deuteronomy chapter 5

Brit ('Covenant')

after the 'terms' of the covenant listed in chapter 28), we read 'This covenant and this contract is not being made only with those of you standing here today before the Eternal One your God, but also with those who are not standing here with us today.' [1]

The Rabbis interpreted this as meaning that every member of the future generations of the Children of Israel was – as it were – present at Sinai and therefore committed to the conditions of the covenant. Rabbi Shimon bar Yochai, however, added a daring observation that carries great theological weight as well as confirming the interdependent nature of both parties committed to a covenant relationship. In relation to Isaiah 43:12, which reads, 'And you are My witnesses, says the Eternal One, and I am God,' he taught that God is saying, 'If you are my witnesses, then I am God but if you are not my witnesses then I am not, as it were, God.' [2]

This gives an indication of the role of the Jews – their side of the agreement – in relation to God. A failure to acknowledge God will have consequences not just for the Jewish people but also for God. In order for God's influence to be able to be effective, God has to be recognised by the people. The covenant is very much a two-way relationship that has responsibilities – as well as benefits – for both parties.

This reality also serves to counter an oft quoted but rarely properly understood suggestion that the Jews are a 'chosen' people. This notion is often put forward in a critical way, suggesting a sort of elitism that the Jews either claim or, more often, others accuse the Jews of claiming for themselves. The very nature of a covenant relationship precludes this.

---

[1] Deuteronomy 30:13-14
[2] *Pesika d'Rav Kahane* 102b

Although we will never know what mysterious force it was that initially attracted our ancient ancestors into a relationship with the One God while those around them were still worshipping idols, the difference between the demands of this divine figure and those of contemporary objects of human worship is quite clear. Moreover, as the prophet Amos points out, if Israel has been selected or chosen in any way, this is as much a burden as it is a privilege. 'Hear this word the Eternal One has spoken against you, O people of Israel - against the whole family I brought up out of Egypt: "You only have I chosen of all the families of the earth; therefore I will punish you for all your sins."'[1] Having made this point, Amos also recognises that God has a relationship with other nations: 'True, I brought Israel up from the land of Egypt, but also the Philistines from Caphtor and the Arameans from Kir,'[2] Amos recognises that all humans are equal in the eyes of God: 'To Me, O Israelites, you are just like the Ethiopians.'[3]

Whatever else the covenant between the Jewish people and God symbolises, there can be no doubt that it is primarily a responsibility, a duty. It is a duty to recognise that human beings have a role to play in apprehending the will of God and a responsibility to join in the task of endeavouring to establish that will on earth. That is the side of the mysterious covenant that Judaism's ancient ancestors made with God when they stood at the foot of the mountain and, metaphorically, all Jews were there with them.

---

[1] Amos 3:1-2
[2] Amos 9:7
[3] *ibid.*

6

THE JEWISH PEOPLE

We affirm our commitment to the Jewish People, bearer of the Jewish religious and cultural heritage, and our duty to defend the civil rights, and to seek the material and spiritual welfare, of Jews and Jewish communities everywhere.

A Judaism for the Twenty-First Century

It is an awareness of and a commitment to that covenant of more than three thousand years ago that has shaped the Jewish people. The question still remains, however: who or what, exactly, are the Jewish people? This is not a question about Jewish status - an important issue in Judaism, to be sure - but this question is more abstract. It is an attempt to define what it is that links the Jewish people; what it is that, in the words of one of the readings in the prayerbook (*Siddur*), '...unites and sanctifies the House of Israel in all lands and ages.' [1]

It is significant, perhaps, that the reading from which these words are taken is one that precedes the lighting of the candles to welcome *Shabbat*. The Sabbath is an extraordinary and unique institution, one of the things that has indeed held the Jewish people together 'in all lands and ages' but Sabbath observance is not, in the end, the measure of what constitutes membership of the Jewish people.

The fact that there have been Jews 'in all lands and ages' also gives the lie to a misguided and now out-dated theory, propounded as scientific 'fact' by those whose motives may be somewhat suspect, that the Jewish people are a 'race'. The geographic and cultural diversity among Jews around the world mean that there are, in addition to the English-speaking Jews of Australasia, the UK, the USA and other countries with which we are most familiar, Indian Jews and Chinese Jews, South American Jews and black African Jews – each with their own histories and cultural traditions that owe as much to their geographical location as they do to their Jewish roots.

Of course, there are areas where the Jews are particularly concentrated – this is especially true of the more Orthodox

---

[1] *World Union Edition of Mishkan T'filah* p.119. House of Israel here means 'The Jewish people' and Israel is often used in the prayerbook in this way, as in '*Sh'ma Yisrael*, Hear, O Israel', or colloquially, 'Listen, you Jewish people'.

32

branches of Judaism where geographical proximity to the centres of the community is important. But within Progressive Judaism in our region, for example, there are communities in areas in which there is no major Jewish presence such as Hobart or Dunedin, and efforts are made to encourage Jews in such locations to find their place in the Jewish community.

Moreover, in areas such as Eastern Europe, Judaism is currently enjoying a renaissance. With the collapse of the Soviet Union and the lifting of the 'Iron Curtain', the new freedom has permitted large numbers of people to attempt to re-engage (or engage for the first time) with a Jewish heritage that for so many was little more than a memory or a rumour. Significant numbers of these Jews have now left the former Soviet Union and have made new lives for themselves as Jews in Israel or, somewhat ironically perhaps, in Germany. Many well-established congregations in Europe, the United States and elsewhere have developed links with emerging communities in eastern European countries such as Poland or Ukraine. Such links are intended to offer support and encouragement to these new congregations; they also provide a telling example of the connections and shared destiny of Jews all over the world.

The bond that joins the Jewish people together is one that transcends time as well as space. For not only are there Jews in the remotest corners of the world, so too have there been Jews in numerous locations throughout history. The historical, as well as the geographical, connections are also acknowledged in various ways in Jewish communities today.

During the Second World War, when the Nazis rounded up all the Jews in Bohemia and Moravia, the religious artefacts were taken from the synagogues and placed in a large warehouse, even as the Jews themselves were taken to Terezin[1] and then on

---

[1] A concentration camp 30 miles north of Prague. Here the Nazis sought to demonstrate a 'normal' way of life for the Jews, chiefly for the benefit of a

to Auschwitz. The origin of every item was carefully documented; the intention being to establish in Prague what Hitler apparently described as a 'Museum of an Extinct Culture'.

After the War, these items – Torah scrolls, the silver bells, breastplates and pointers and elaborately embroidered covers – remained in the warehouse under Soviet rule. But a Rabbi of Czech origin, Rabbi Harold Reinhardt, who was based at the Westminster Synagogue in London, knew of the existence of this warehouse and its contents. After lengthy negotiations with the Czech authorities, and the contribution of a generous benefactor, the scrolls were released and in 1964 were despatched to London. There were over 1,500 of them – some in good condition, many torn, burnt or otherwise damaged. Over the years, these scrolls have been repaired and many of them are in use in congregations all over the world. Because of the careful documentation and record keeping, the origin of each scroll is known and so a living link with communities that were wiped out during World War Two is maintained in thriving Jewish communities the world over.

This is living proof that there is an invisible yet undeniable global link between all Jews, regardless of their race or ethnic origin, appearance or national culture. Perhaps a final example of this link can be found in the following reality of Jewish life. Many synagogues are not large enough to contain the entire membership of their particular congregation. This is not usually a problem since even in a thriving congregation the average attendance at regular Sabbath services - and most festival services – may be only a minority of the total membership. But on the High Holydays – *Rosh ha-Shanah* and

---

visiting Red Cross delegation, while continuing to despatch inmates to the extermination camp at Auschwitz in neighbouring Poland.

Yom Kippur – larger venues need to be hired or marquees added to existing buildings in order to accommodate the vast turnout of Jews who, for the rest of the year, have little or no contact with their synagogue. There is something that calls to all Jews at key moments of the year – and of their lives – and reminds them of their undeniable association with the Jewish people, its history and its destiny. This connection is encapsulated in the rabbinic dictum *kol Yisra'el aravin zeh ba-zeh:* 'All of Israel are sureties for one another.'[1]

---

[1] Talmud *Shevu'ot* 39a

7

JEWISH HISTORY

We affirm our pride in Jewish history: a unique record of survival and creativity in many lands and diverse circumstances, including times of persecution and suffering, which reinforce our commitment to Judaism's survival.

Jewish History

There is some question as to when, precisely, Jewish history begins. The description of our ancestors as Jews probably came into being after the destruction of the biblical kingdom of Israel (722 BCE[1]), following which the kingdom of Judah was the sole centre of what would eventually become Judaism. The inhabitants of this small kingdom, known in Hebrew as *Y'hudah*, (Judah) were described as *Y'hudim*, which in time came to be translated as 'Jews'.

The first recorded event in 'history' as far as Jewish tradition is concerned, is the creation of the world. Calculations made in medieval times on the basis of biblical data, and with significantly less awareness about the history of the universe than is currently available to us, led to the conclusion that the world was created in the year 3760 BCE. So, for example, *Rosh ha-Shanah*, the new year, welcomed in September 2009, heralded the Jewish year 5770 (which continues until the following September).[2]

Adam and Eve, the mythical first human beings who are considered in Jewish understanding to be prototypes for all humanity, can hardly be described as the first Jews. This is a title that is usually bestowed upon Abraham and Sarah, who, twelve chapters into the book of Genesis, are told by God to leave their home in Mesopotamia and travel to the land of Canaan to become a great people. While early Progressive Judaism, influenced by scholarly criticism of the Bible, tended to doubt the existence of the biblical patriarchs and matriarchs, later twentieth century archaeology has uncovered sites that confirm the existence of nomadic peoples in the land of Canaan in the second millennium BCE, whose ranks very probably included the biblical ancestors of the Jews.

---

[1] See footnote, page 26
[2] The suggestion that the world is less than six thousand years old is not taken literally by most Jews.

Whether Abraham and Sarah regarded themselves as the founders of a new tradition is a moot point; their place in our earliest oral traditions that eventually became enshrined in the Hebrew Bible led to them being defined as such. Thus a line was drawn that connected Abraham via Isaac to Jacob and subsequently to the tribes of Israel, which name Jacob adopted after his overnight struggle with an angel in Genesis 32 and which is still applied as a title for all Jews, his children – *b'nei Yisra'el*. The second half of the Book of Genesis brings these Children of Israel to Egypt. This is unlikely to be an accurate portrayal of history but its purpose, to set the scene for the most critical moment in Jewish history, the Exodus from Egypt, is skilfully achieved.

It is perhaps at this point that Jewish history might truly be said to have started. As with the accounts in Genesis, early Progressive Judaism was somewhat sceptical about the biblical account of this event, finding the seeming cruelty of God in punishing the Egyptians improbable and unacceptable. Again, archaeology has stepped in and suggested that the 'miraculous' events described in the Book of Exodus may well have been the consequence of a volcanic eruption. As well as causing what the Bible calls the plagues, the effects of this would have included the destabilisation of the society in which a group of people was enslaved. History would call this group 'the Israelites'. They had the courage to use the opportunity, afforded them by the collapse of the society that enslaved them, to escape to freedom. Guided by a man called Moses, they would go on to establish the religion we now know as Judaism.

Their experiences, including a mystical encounter at a mountain in the wilderness to which they had escaped, would, in time, be written down and form the focal point of the religion and culture their descendants would develop. This would be many centuries in the making and would be condensed into an idealised form that saw all the people enter the land of Canaan (the land that had been promised to Abraham, Isaac and Jacob) and take it as a possession. During this period, occasional charismatic leaders, known as Judges, would emerge to see off the threat of various enemies. However, the arrival of one group – the Philistines – required a more unified organisation of defences. To this end, a monarchy was established, initially under the tragic figure of Saul and subsequently the beloved David, who captured Jerusalem and made it the centre of his kingdom. The Philistines were defeated, which allowed the Israelites to argue among themselves over who would succeed David. The eventual result was the division of the kingdoms – the larger Israel in the North and tiny Judah in the South. This occurred at the time of the death of David's son Solomon in 922 BCE. Two centuries later, the northern kingdom was swept away by the Assyrians, leaving Judah as the home of all the history, tradition and culture that had been developed by the descendants of Abraham and followers of Moses. This included the establishment of the Jerusalem Temple as the focal point of the cult as well as the development of rituals and celebrations that are still central to Judaism today.

The kingdom of Judah, ruled by a hereditary dynasty descended from King David, was itself destroyed by the Babylonians in the year 586 BCE and its leaders taken into exile. At this point, Jewish history should have ended, for the intention of the Babylonians was to transplant tribal leaders and have them assimilate into their new environment. This first experience of diaspora was vital for the exiles of Judah, some of whom refused to forget their origins and their traditions, and yearned for a return to Jerusalem.

This dream was granted when the Persians overthrew the Babylonian empire later in the sixth century BCE. Many exiles returned, though many more chose to remain in Babylon – a decision that was to prove crucial several centuries later. A second Temple was built and the Jews re-established themselves in their ancient city. The Kingdom of Judah did not enjoy autonomous Jewish rule for long – the Greeks and then the Romans swallowed up this tiny country in their vast empires – and the latter eventually wiped it out, first by destroying the Temple in the year 70 CE, then by forcing the Jewish leadership out of their land and effectively eradicating the possibility of – or the need for – Jewish self-rule in that country.

Again, the end of Jewish history seemed likely, as without the Temple and its associated worship, the survival of Judaism seemed impossible. But a group of scholars and teachers, had, for some time, been re-fashioning Judaism into a form that could survive without the Temple and the era of rabbinic Judaism began. These Rabbis faced continued persecution by the Romans and, following a further failed rebellion in 132-135 CE, the remaining Jews were expelled from the land of Judea, which was re-named Palestina by the Romans.

Thus began a period of enforced diaspora – a time when the Jews moved from one country to another, seeking a home in someone else's land. Some countries welcomed them and they stayed and flourished for many centuries. In other lands, their stay was only brief before they found themselves cruelly oppressed and summarily expelled.

At the time the Jews were expelled from their home by the Romans, the two main areas in which Jewish communities were established were Alexandria and Babylon, places where thriving diaspora communities had already been present for many centuries. It was in the latter that the basis of Jewish survival in exile was explored and developed. With the production of the Babylonian Talmud, this was a time of great achievement for Judaism. Eventually – inevitably perhaps, given the treatment meted out to the Jews in most of the lands of their dispersion – Babylonian Jewry declined and new centres were sought.

Spain proved to be particularly fertile ground for Judaism. Captured by North African Muslims in the early eighth century, Spain saw the Jews achieve extraordinary heights in a variety of areas: there were Jewish philosophers, astronomers, doctors and poets – in some cases they even ruled local states in place of the absentee Muslim landlords who preferred to remain in Africa. The Golden Age of Spain, as it is known, produced some of Judaism's most profound philosophy and beautiful poetry. The reconquest of Spain by the Christians after the twelfth century did not reduce the prominence of the Jews: they were uniquely able to translate and transmit Arabic cultural works to their new Christian rulers. But this too came to an end with the Spanish Inquisition of the 15th century and the expulsion of the Jews in 1492.

Meanwhile further north and east in Europe, Jews experienced mixed fortunes. Welcomed because of the financial opportunity they offered (a biblical prohibition against exacting interest from a brother was interpreted to mean that Christians could not lend to fellow Christians[1]), Jews became money-lenders. This profession – one of the very few that Jews were permitted to adopt – did not endear them to the local populace and they often found themselves vilified and persecuted. This pattern, of achievement and persecution, of acceptance and rejection, followed the Jews across the world as they sought to establish communities and develop their religion and their relationship with God.

The second half of the last millennium saw Jewish communities established in – and often uprooted from – locations as far apart as the Ottoman Empire and Holland. To both, the Jews brought the trading expertise and connections that had been cultivated

---

[1] E.g. Deuteronomy 23:19-20

in Spain. Other European rulers recognised the economic potential of the Jews, who were encouraged to settle in Poland in the sixteenth century to that country's benefit. Prosperity and security there was short-lived, and soon the Jews found themselves on the move again, fleeing economic ruin and persecution. This time, Prussia and other German states beckoned as some fortunate Jews found favoured status in intellectual and business circles, though the majority continued to live financially impoverished existences in *shtetls*[1] in central and eastern Europe. The tide of tolerance and acceptance ebbed and flowed, but Jews seemed gradually to find a measure of acceptance with the dawning of the Enlightenment in western Europe – an acceptance that grew in the wake of the French Revolution in 1789 – while suffering increasing persecution further east.

This pattern continued in the nineteenth century – and was extended further west as thousands of Jews escaped the harsh realities of Europe to seek new lives in America, while the following century heralded perhaps the most tragic and the most dramatic developments in this ongoing history of our people: persecution sank to new depths with the Nazi Holocaust while the establishment of the State of Israel and the return of the Jews to a homeland they could once again call their own added a new dimension to Judaism and to Jewish history.

That history is still unfolding, and Progressive Jews are as proud of it and as committed to its continuation as any branch of Judaism. Jewish history tells an extraordinary story of a group of people committed to an idea and to each other, a commitment that has withstood over two thousand years during which other peoples and kingdoms have come and

---

[1] *Shtetl* – Yiddish word meaning 'small town'- the section of a town or village in which the Jews were obliged to live.

gone. Jews are rightly proud of their people's history and their achievements. They inspire Jews to do their utmost to contribute to the future of Judaism, playing their part in the ongoing and unfolding drama that is Jewish history.

8
THE STATE OF ISRAEL

We affirm our commitment to the State of Israel, our duty to seek its security, aid its development, support its absorption of immigrants, and further the fulfilment of the high ideals of Justice and Equality for all its citizens set out in its Declaration of Independence. We also commend peace initiatives directed at both creating a State of Palestine alongside the State of Israel, and establishing the conditions for peaceful co-existence between the two peoples.

A key part of the history and the destiny of the Jewish people has been tied up with the land of Israel, the place where Jewish history began and unfolded, and the place to which Jews have, within the last century or so, returned to claim as their homeland. On May 14th 1948, David ben Gurion, the first prime minister of the State of Israel,[1] read the Declaration of Independence to an excited audience in Tel Aviv. This famous document includes the following noble intentions:

"The State of Israel
- will promote the development of the country for the benefit of all its inhabitants;
- will be based on the precepts of liberty, justice and peace as envisaged by the Prophets of Israel;
- will uphold the full social and political equality of all its citizens without distinction of race, creed or sex;
- will guarantee full freedom of conscience, worship, education and culture;
- will safeguard the sanctity and inviolability of the shrines and Holy Places of all religions and
- will dedicate itself to the principles of the Charter of the United Nations

We appeal in the very midst of the onslaught launched against us now for months – to the Arab inhabitants of the State of Israel to return to the ways of peace and play their part in the building up of the State, on the basis of full and equal citizenship and due representation in all its bodies and institutions.

---

[1] It might seem strange that the name chosen was 'Israel', that of the shorter-lived Northern Kingdom after Solomon, from which the population was dispersed (the 'Ten Lost Tribes'), rather than 'Judah', name of the Southern Kingdom from which the term 'Jew' is derived. However, the whole area settled by Israelites is referred to as 'Eretz Yisrael' (the Land of Israel), and indeed the Jewish people is called 'Yisrael' in Hebrew, as in 'Sh'ma Yisrael'.

> We extend our hand of peace to all the neighbouring states and their peoples, and invite them to establish bonds of co-operation and mutual help with the sovereign Jewish people settled in its own land. The State of Israel is prepared to do its share in a common effort for the advancement of the entire Middle East."

These are the ideals that Progressive Judaism believes should underpin the policies of the government of Israel to this day.

The establishment of the State of Israel in 1948 was the culmination of a process that had begun just over half a century earlier when Theodor Herzl had arrived at the conclusion that the Jews could never be safe from persecution in any country other than their own. The Zionist movement that he founded and the vigorous policies it pursued in order to achieve its aim of a homeland for the Jews were, however, strongly opposed by many Progressive and orthodox Jews in the early days (although there were notable exceptions such as Rabbi Abba Hillel Silver, and in the Australasian region, Rabbi Dr Herman Sanger who arrived in Melbourne in 1936).[1]

Progressive Judaism's belief that Judaism had a role to play in the establishment of social justice throughout the world meant that it had initially generally regarded the idea of a Jewish homeland as a retrograde step in the progress of Judaism towards this universal role. And other Jewish groups were similarly unenthusiastic about the idea of a Jewish state – Hermann Adler, who was Chief Rabbi of the United Synagogue at the time Herzl conceived his ideas, described Zionism as 'an egregious blunder'.[2]

Nevertheless, political events in Europe in the first half of the twentieth century convinced ever greater numbers of Jews the

---

[1] See page 175
[2] Quoted in 'Troubled Eden', Chaim Bermant, London 1969, p. 183

The State of Israel

world over that a Jewish state would offer a haven to persecuted Jews. This was all the more necessary once traditional refuges like America and Western European countries began to tighten restrictions on immigration.

By the end of the Second World War and as the effects of the Holocaust became clear, opinions regarding a Jewish state changed dramatically, both in the Jewish and the wider world, though there can be no way of gauging exactly to what extent the decision of the United Nations on November 29th 1947 to partition Palestine to allow the establishment of the State of Israel was influenced by the horrific suffering the Jews had experienced under Nazi rule.

Whatever may have moved the member countries of the United Nations in 1947, the result was the birth of a Jewish homeland. Since independence was formally declared on Friday afternoon May 14th 1948 (Hebrew date 5th *Iyar 5708*) Israel has made remarkable advances and achievements. There is insufficient space to list them all here, but the dramatic reclaiming of land that was deemed uninhabitable and unsuitable for agriculture (a process that had begun several decades before independence) has underpinned extraordinary progress in science, technology, education and culture in ways that may have seemed unimaginable to those listening to David ben Gurion that Friday in May 1948.

Sadly, these achievements have been accomplished against a difficult background. From the moment of her birth, Israel has found herself under threat from her Arab neighbours. Several wars – including the War of Independence in 1948, the extraordinary Six Day War of 1967 and the *Yom Kippur* War of 1973 – have claimed the lives of many Israelis as well as many Arab soldiers. In those early years of Israel's existence, when her very survival seemed often to hang by a mere thread, it is reasonable to say that Jews the world over, regardless of their affiliation, watched anxiously, wondering whether the fledgling Jewish state would indeed succumb to the Arab threat to 'push it into the Mediterranean'. That Israel survived that traumatic first quarter-century of life seemed to many to be a miracle, though the combination of Israeli determination to survive, along with substantial Western financial and military support, certainly helped enormously.

During the 1970s, however, a change occurred in what can best be described as Israel's collective psyche. Encouraged by apparently astonishing military success – particularly in 1967, when east Jerusalem, the West Bank, the Gaza Strip and the Golan Heights (sometimes collectively referred to as the Occupied Territories) and large areas of the Sinai desert all came under Israeli occupation – a new Israeli mindset seemed to develop. The roots of what some regarded as a form of messianism became apparent as settlement was encouraged on land captured from Jordan, Syria and Egypt, while Israel's behaviour towards the Palestinians, as an occupying power, sometimes appeared to be heavy-handed. The handing back of the Sinai desert, a peace treaty with Egypt in the late 1970s, and with Jordan some 15 years later, have not yet been followed by similar progress with the most vexing issue: the status of the Palestinians.

The voices of the Palestinians have grown louder and attracted more attention, and it has become clear that the Israeli account of the events of 1948 told only part of the story. It would seem that David ben Gurion's plea to the Arabs to remain in the Israeli parts of the newly partitioned Palestine in the late 1940s did not entirely reflect official Israeli government policy of the time. Since the late 1980s, when the first Palestinian *intifada* (uprising) occurred, efforts at a political solution to the Israeli/Palestinian problem have veered from being close to historic compromise (such as in 1994 when the late Yasser Arafat shook hands on the lawn of the White House with

Yitzchak Rabin – who was assassinated just over a year later) to violence and despair (as demonstrated in the seemingly endless cycle of suicide bombings and Israeli Army reprisals that were a feature of the early years of the 21st century). Rhetoric has become more bellicose, attitudes have become increasingly entrenched, and a peaceful political solution generally appears more remote than at any time in the last six decades.

That this situation has not been helped by the policies of the Palestinians or of some Israeli government decisions is a source of concern and pain to many Jews around the world, and nowhere more than in Israel itself. The principles of social justice, to which Progressive Judaism is unswervingly committed, sometimes seem to be conspicuously absent in the Palestinian Territories, from where accounts of human rights violations are too often reported. Progressive Jews feel a duty to join the voices of many like-minded citizens of Israel – to speak out against any such injustices, whoever the perpetrators.

To speak out in this way, however, may result in Progressive Judaism being branded as less supportive of Israel. Nothing could be further from the truth. Progressive Judaism recognises that Israel plays a vital part in world Jewry today and that her achievements give us much to be proud of and to celebrate. Progressive Judaism enthusiastically supports and encourages a wide variety of Israel's activities and institutions – particularly those established under the auspices of the Israel Movement for Progressive Judaism, a movement that has shown steady growth and great influence and potential. Progressive Judaism's staff team around the world includes Israeli emissaries *(shlichim)* to ensure that there is appropriate Israeli input into its congregations and youth activities, and it regularly sends groups (youth and adult) on Israel tours. The pre-college *shnat* year in Israel is particularly popular and successful. Progressive Judaism fully endorses the right of the State of Israel to exist within safe and secure mutually recognised international borders (unlike ultra-Orthodox Jewish groups, such as the *N'turei Karta*[1], who believe that the State of Israel can only be brought about by the Messiah and so expect and await Israel's destruction).

It is unfortunate that Progressive Judaism, whilst growing daily in influence, is not yet recognised in Israel as an equal stream of Judaism to the orthodox denominations. Our Rabbis are not authorised to conduct conversions, weddings or funerals, and our congregations do not get the financial support that other synagogues, and indeed other faiths, receive. However the Supreme Court regularly finds in our favour, and though this sometimes leads to changes being made to the laws, or the rulings being ignored or implemented very slowly, it is also clear that an increasing percentage of the population understands and identifies with the Progressive perspective.

The position in the Middle East remains precarious and an end to the conflict seems to be but a distant hope. Progressive Judaism is keen for a just political solution to the bitter dispute between Israelis and Palestinians to be found. Within its ranks, as within Judaism as a whole, ideas as to how to reach such a solution are varied, but the prophetic commitment to an end to all violence is one which applies as much to this situation as to any other. In the meantime, while supporting efforts for a just and peaceful settlement, Progressive Judaism demonstrates its commitment to Israel by annually acknowledging and celebrating Israel's Independence Day, *Yom ha-Atzma'ut*. On this occasion, Progressive Jews mark Israel's achievements but also remind themselves of Israel's responsibilities as laid out in its Declaration of Independence, and look forward to their full implementation.

---

[1] *N'turei Karta* – 'Guardians of the gate' – an ant-Zionist ultra-religious group (which nevertheless benefits from the protection of the Israeli armed services and the support of the Israeli government's welfare system).

9

JEWISH LITERATURE

We affirm our devotion to Jewish literature – Bible, Mishnah, Talmud, Midrash and all great literary expressions of the Jewish spirit – as an inexhaustible source of wisdom to which we constantly turn for guidance and inspiration.

Jewish literature is, in many ways, the written record of the history of the Jewish people and, in particular, of the development of the religion we now call Judaism. At the heart of the Jewish literary tradition are the Five Books of Moses, the Torah. Orthodox Jewish tradition regards these books as having been revealed at Mount Sinai where Moses received them in their entirety. The complete text either had divine authorship or was dictated by God to Moses. This 'event' is described in the Torah itself, in the Book of Exodus and re-told in Deuteronomy. This would mean, based on the most widely accepted dating of the Exodus from Egypt, that the text of the written Torah came into existence some time around the thirteenth century BCE.

This date presents a number of difficulties for various reasons. The origins of writing and the nature of the events being described, for example, would suggest a much later date for the production of the written text of what we now call the Five Books of Moses. It is now widely accepted in scholarly circles that many of the stories in the Pentateuch[1] – particularly those in Genesis and Exodus – were originally transmitted orally, perhaps over a period of many centuries, before they came to be written down.[2]

The same is probably true of many of the other books of the Hebrew Bible (referred to in Christian usage as the 'Old Testament'– though the order of the books differs significantly in Jewish and Christian traditions). The complete Hebrew Bible is made up of three sections:
- the Five Books of Moses (*Torah*),
- the 'historical' books (Joshua, Judges, Samuel I & II and Kings I & II) plus the prophetical books (Isaiah, Jeremiah, Ezekiel and the twelve minor Prophets) collectively referred to as 'Prophets' (*N'vi'im*)

---
[1] Greek for 'five books' – reference to the Five Books of Moses
[2] See page 186 for more details on the Documentary Hypothesis of the origins of the Torah.

- various writings (*K'tuvim*) that include Psalms, Proverbs, the five *m'gillot*[1] and other, later accounts. The entire collection, fixed by the Pharisees towards the end of the second century CE, is known as the *Tanach*, a mnemonic taking the first Hebrew letter of each of the three sections (*T'NaKh*).

Whatever the origins of the written texts that make up the *Tanach*, their effect on the development of Judaism cannot be overstated. They provided a solid base upon which was constructed the subsequent rabbinic interpretation, which regarded the words of the text as a divinely written source upon which to build their version of Judaism. It was the early proponents of this interpretation of Judaism who decreed that direct communication between God and human beings had ended with the prophecies of Haggai, Zechariah and Malachi[2]. Therefore any books known to have been written after that time, or otherwise lacking the marks of divine inspiration, were excluded from the canon of 'Holy Scripture'. It was forbidden to read them publicly, and they became known as 'extraneous' or 'hidden' books or 'Apocrypha'. These books include those of the Maccabees (whose militarism and political machinations the Rabbis greatly disliked) along with other Messianic and apocalyptic writings such as the Book of Jubilees.

The main contribution made by the Rabbis to Jewish literature came only when Judaism reached a time of crisis. Roman persecution and the dispersion of the Jews meant that what had for centuries been an oral tradition was in danger of being forgotten. Convinced as they were that the *Tanach*, and in particular the Torah, contained God's written word, the Rabbis refused to allow any of their opinions or rulings to be written

---

[1] *M'gillot* – literally scrolls; these 5 books – Song of Songs, Ruth, Lamentations, Ecclesiastes and Esther are read on *Pesach, Shavu'ot, Tisha b'Av, Sukkot* and *Purim*. See chapters 20 and 21.
[2] See, e.g., *Tosefta, Sotah* 13:12. See p. 54 for definition of *Tosefta*.

down, lest they come to be regarded as having the same authority as the divine word. Thus developed what came to be known as the oral Torah, an ever-growing body of verbally transmitted opinion and interpretation that was the basis for the development of Judaism – but never intended to be the final word on it. The Rabbis seemed to believe that every generation should be able to re-interpret the divine word for itself and should not be bound by the decisions or customs of one particular era. They feared that any written version of those interpretations would militate against that. So instead of writing their decisions down, a group of skilled people was charged with the task of memorising the various decisions made by the Rabbis.

But the decision was taken at the end of the second century CE, led by Rabbi Judah ha-Nasi, to record the oral Torah in written form, lest its contents be lost, and despite the tradition that it should remain an oral and flexible tradition. What could be recalled was written down and became known as the *Mishnah*, which literally means 'repetition'. Judah gathered together as many of those who had memorised the information as he could find, and they repeated and reported what had been handed down over a period of centuries. These recollections were recorded and organised into six Orders: *Zera'im, Mo'ed, Nashim, Nezikin, K'doshim and Taharot*. These translate, somewhat misleadingly, as 'Seeds, Seasons, Women, Damages, Holy Things and Purity' respectively, but contain just about every aspect of ritual life as experienced in Judea, built around and based upon the traditions and regulations recorded in the Hebrew Bible. These documents were studied and discussed – alongside a body of opinions and decisions that eluded Judah's collection, known as *Tosefta* (additions) – among the remaining Rabbis in Judea (which was by now renamed Philistia or Palestina by the Roman authorities, after the Philistine coastal cities), and particularly in the academies which had been established in Babylon.

The deliberations of the generations of rabbis who followed Judah ha-Nasi were recorded in their turn and were combined with the text of the *Mishnah* to produce the Talmud, which was completed at the end of the fifth century CE. In this extraordinary document, the opinions in the *Mishnah* quoted by the Rabbis (who were referred to in Aramaic – now the common language of the Jews – as *Tannaim*) were discussed and supplemented by the opinions of the *Amora'im* (the sages) in what came to be known as the *Gemara* (completion). The *Mishnah* and the *Gemara* together made up the Talmud. This process took place in Babylon and in Palestina and there are consequently two Talmuds – the Babylonian (*Bavli*) and the Palestinian (called *Y'rushalmi*). The former was completed a century later, is far more comprehensive, and is the one most widely used and quoted.

The *Gemara* in its turn was explained and augmented by generations of individual rabbis such as Rashi[1] (1040-1105), who was based in central Europe, and Abraham ibn Ezra (1089-1164), Maimonides[2] (1138-1204) and Nachmanides[3] (1194-1270), who were prolific Spanish commentators. These many Jewish scholars offered interpretations of Talmudic decisions as well as their opinions regarding the commentaries of others. In short, the concerns of Judah ha-Nasi's period, namely that by making the *Mishnah* a written text, they might not only record but also arrest the continued interpretation and development of Judaism, seemed to be unfounded. Jewish thought, discussion and wisdom expanded anew every time a decision was considered and debated. Only in our own times can we see that their concerns were indeed well-founded – that the millions of written words of the oral law have sometimes limited and stagnated the application of Torah in our lives, so that, for

---

[1] Rashi is an acronym made up of the initials of his name: **Rabbi SH***lomo ben* **I***tzchak*
[2] Also known by the acronym RambaM - **Rabbi Moshe ben Maimon**
[3] Also known by the acronym RambaN - **Rabbi Moshe ben Nachman**

example, an orthodox person cannot drive to attend *Shabbat* services, or, surprisingly, lettuce, broccoli and even figs are no longer considered kosher in some orthodox communities!

Another process developing parallel to the legal one was known as *Midrash,* an especially creative form of literature, always taking as its starting point a connection with the words of the Bible text. The title *Midrash*, which is an abstract description of a process as well as a generic title for a body of written material, is based upon the root of the Hebrew verb that means to search or explore. Generation after generation of rabbis and scholars looked at the text of the Bible and discovered new interpretations and nuances in every word and phrase, in every repetition and omission. Two brief examples must suffice here. The first is in the section of the Book of Deuteronomy that details the laws that the Israelites are commanded to observe. In these laws, words are often repeated – e.g. Deuteronomy 22:1, where the verb requiring the finder of someone's lost ox or sheep to return it to its owner is repeated twice. The original intention was doubtless to emphasise the obligation; the *midrashic* interpretation is that the initial use of the verb requires one to return the animal if one knows the identity of the owner while its repetition means that the obligation applies even if the owner is not known to the finder.

The second example takes us to the start of chapter 12 of the Book of Genesis, where Abraham (still known at the time as *Avram* or Abram) is commanded by God to leave his home. No introduction precedes this, nor is any explanation offered. So several stories have been created to explain why Abram had to leave so suddenly. Perhaps the best known is the one that suggested Abraham's father, Terach, was a maker of idols who one day left his son in charge of his products. Abraham, who, according to the Bible, was the first man to recognise the importance of worshipping the one God, proceeded to smash all the idols except one and explained to his horrified father that the remaining idol had destroyed all the others. Terach's response was that the idol could not possibly be responsible as it had no power. This offered the storyteller an opportunity to teach about the difference between Abraham's God and the gods of the Ancient Near East, to highlight the futility of idol worship as well as providing a plausible explanation for Abraham's departure from his home town: to escape his father's wrath. Some *midrashim* are as well known as the biblical events they seek to explain, even though they post-date the original stories by many hundreds of years.

There are many other aspects of Jewish literature the purpose of which has been to guide and inspire the Jewish people through the ages and to offer them new insights. There is a rich mystical tradition, which flourished with the production in the twelfth century of the *Zohar* ('Book of Splendour'), a book whose authorship was fancifully ascribed to Rabbi Shimon bar Yochai, who lived a thousand years earlier. Contrasting with this medieval mysticism, Jewish literature was also enriched by the development of Jewish 'codes' during the Middle Ages. This trend sought to provide a definitive set of rules to govern every aspect of Jewish life from personal hygiene to the conduct of synagogue worship, from rules about diet to customs relating to burial. This process culminated in the collection of extensive Jewish legal works of which the most authoritative has become Joseph Caro's *Shulchan Aruch*, ('Prepared Table'), published in 1517. This book was initially conceived as a précis of an extensive summary of the customs and regulations in Mediterranean Jewish communities (known as *Sephardi*, based on the Hebrew word for Spain – *Sepharad*). Many of these customs differed from those in Northern Europe (an area generally referred to at the time as *Ashkenaz* – the Hebrew word for Germany), and so Moses Isserles, a Polish Talmudist added *ha-Mappah* ('The Tablecloth'), annotations showing the *Ashkenazi* rulings for Caro's *Sephardi* 'Prepared Table'.

The authority that was bestowed upon this book seemed to stifle any possibility of continuing the discussion or debate that had permitted Judaism to develop and adapt. Had it been able to travel back 1,300 years, the *Shulchan Aruch* may well have dismayed Judah ha-Nasi. But it too evoked literary responses, as commentator after commentator added their wisdom even to this volume. In more modern times, the development of Jewish literature has continued, with contributions from each generation. These range from the poetry of Spanish writers such as Judah ha-Levi and Solomon ibn Gabirol, much of which is incorporated in modern liturgy,[1] to the philosophical writings of Moses Maimonides in the twelfth century, or those of Martin Buber eight centuries later. To this can also be added the emergence of modern Hebrew literature and the wealth of Progressive and other Jewish thought that has been produced in the past two centuries. This provides an ever deeper and broader sea of literature for the Jewish people as they draw on their tradition for guidance and inspiration.

---

[1] see, e.g. World Union Edition of *Mishkan T'filah* p. 5, p. 59, p. 71, p. 81.

10

TORAH ('TEACHING')

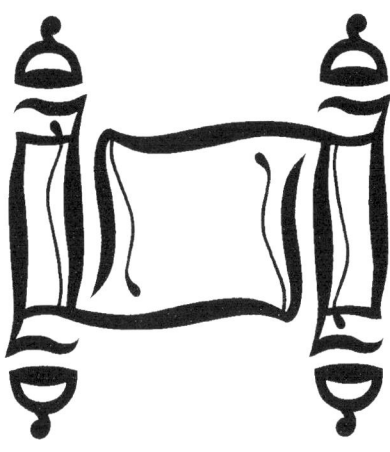

We affirm the Jewish conception of **Torah** *("Teaching"): that at Mount Sinai as well as subsequently, through revelation and inspiration, reflection and discussion, our people gained an ever growing understanding of God's will, and that this is a continuing process.*

Torah is at the heart of Jewish literature – and indeed the whole of the quest we call Judaism. There are one or two popular misconceptions about this word that need to be clarified. These relate to the meaning, use and translation of the word 'Torah'.

Firstly, it is important to understand what is being talked about when the word Torah is mentioned. In its narrowest sense, it refers to the written text of the Five Books of Moses, the first five books of the Bible. In Jewish tradition, these are contained in a scroll from which a section is read every week in synagogue. This scroll is referred to as '<u>the</u> Torah', often translated as 'the Law'; a definition that is not strictly accurate even with regard to the contents of the Five Books of Moses and that completely fails to convey the weight and significance of the word in Jewish tradition.

The word 'Torah' derives from a Hebrew root that means 'teaching'. In its broadest sense, then, Torah can be said to describe the development of human understanding of the divine will. More specifically, however, the Five Books of Moses are referred to in Judaism as the 'written Torah' – the text from which subsequent teaching and tradition derives. According to Orthodox Jewish tradition, the written Torah – that is, the five books of Genesis, Exodus, Leviticus, Numbers and Deuteronomy – were either written or dictated by God at the encounter at Mount Sinai[1] and represent immutable divine truth. Opinions of the source of these texts vary greatly[2] but one thing is clear: these five books contain much more than merely a list of rules and instructions as the partial translation 'the Law' suggests.

We cannot say for certain what occurred at Mount Sinai. In the end, what matters even more than what actually happened is the effect of this encounter between the human and the Divine

---

[1] Exodus 19 ff., see p.24
[2] See chapter 28

Torah ('Teaching')

and the ensuing tradition that every Jew was, in some mystical way, present at Mount Sinai.[1]

This serves to illustrate both the nature of the Jewish approach to Torah and to highlight a particular Progressive attitude to it. Since, from a traditional point of view, the Torah is regarded as having divine authorship, every verse, every word, every repetition or omission has a significance that allows for interpretation and elaboration. For most Orthodox biblical scholars, such interpretations were already intended by the divine author of the text as received by Moses; they were simply waiting for a future time when their significance would be understood.

Whereas an Orthodox approach would say that the Torah contains all possible interpretations and is indisputably true, a Progressive view would regard the Torah as a part of the process of the human endeavour to discover truth: a product of that search at a particular point of the journey rather than the final word.

Such a perspective on the written Torah is known as 'Progressive Revelation'. Put simply, this view of the relationship between humanity and the Creator is one in which humanity's appreciation develops gradually, according to our human ability to understand our world and our place in it. As we read in our prayerbook; 'Sinai was only the beginning. The Torah has never ceased to grow. In every age it has been refined and enlarged. It has a permanent core and an expanding periphery. It expands as the horizon of human vision grows.'[2]

---

[1] See p.29 This is even understood to extend to those who join the Jewish people: *Talmud* - Shavu'ot 39a
[2] World Union Edition of *Mishkan T'filah,* p.399

This is 'Torah' in its truest sense – a process of learning and understanding that is at the heart of Judaism.

The ancient Rabbis were aware of this; their concept of 'oral Torah'[1] acknowledged that certain aspects of human life – and the role of God within it – would only be perceived once human beings had achieved sufficient insight and knowledge. They recognised too that regulations and decisions based on the teachings of Torah should always reflect and be shaped by the environment in which its adherents found themselves. To this must be added, however, their belief that such adaptations were somehow built into the fabric of Torah itself by a divine author who anticipated the particular circumstances that would require these adaptations. Thus the Rabbis were able to sustain their belief in the divine authorship of the Torah and still make changes to it. Progressive Judaism sees itself as inheriting this mantle, understanding Torah using modern scholarship; but it has liberated itself from the restriction of believing in the divine authorship of the Five Books of Moses. It recognises instead that every step in this ongoing and holy process is, in fact, a human endeavour'; to try to determine for our own time 'What does God want of us?

We engage in that process through revelation and study, reflection and discussion, adding our own insights and those of our age to those of the generations of Jews who have come before us. We have an understanding of the world that is radically different to that of, say, the author of the creation story in the opening chapter of the Book of Genesis. While our scientific awareness of the origins of our planet and its place in the universe is very different from that of the biblical writer, the first chapter of Genesis still offers a view of the world that gives

---

[1] Oral Torah refers to the wealth of rabbinic opinion based on the Torah (and other biblical literature) which was distinct from the <u>written</u> Torah – the Five Books of Moses. The oral Torah could not be written down as it might be seen to challenge the supreme authority of the written Torah. See p.54

Torah ('Teaching')

humans a particular place in the scheme of things and puts forward the idea of a Creator, and the connection between the Creator and the creation. In short, then, it could be said that while our scientific knowledge gives us insight as to how life started, the questions addressed in the Genesis creation story are intended to help us understand the meaning and purpose of human existence.

Such an understanding, such a fusion of modern knowledge with the teachings and insights of previous scholars and sages, whose search for truth was no less valid or earnest than our own, describes and defines Progressive Revelation. It demonstrates the true nature of Torah: an ongoing process of learning and understanding, of teaching and awareness that in turn, if properly understood and applied, serves to bring us closer to an understanding of our Creator and the will of that Creator for the life of humankind.

11

MITZVAH ('COMMANDMENT')

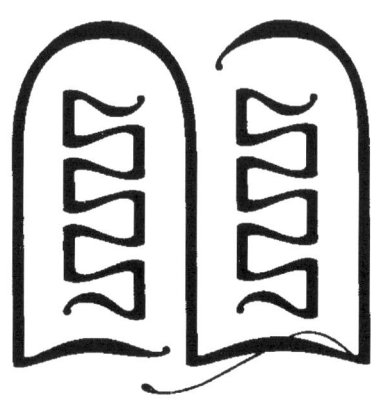

We affirm the Jewish conception of **Mitzvah** *('Commandment'): that as Jews we are obligated to lead a life of exemplary ethical quality, to work for the betterment of human society, and to practise a devotional discipline of study, prayer and observance.*

Mitzvah ('Commandment')

Like the word 'Torah', *mitzvah* (plural, *mitzvot*) is another of those words used regularly by Jews in ways and contexts that do not convey its full meaning. Most commonly, one might hear one Jew congratulating another on 'doing a *mitzvah*' when a kind or helpful deed has been carried out. Although this might constitute one interpretation of the Hebrew word *mitzvah*, its actual origin is far more complicated – and profound – than simply doing a good deed.

Mitzvah derives from the Hebrew root meaning 'commandment'. This implies two things: a 'commander': the source from which the command emanates; and the 'commanded': the person who is required to carry out the commandment. *Mitzvah* defines the nature of the relationship between the Jewish people and their God. The concept – and purpose – of *mitzvah* therefore now needs to be further defined.

Judaism recognises that there are two different types of *mitzvah*. There is the requirement to avoid carrying out an action that might contravene an ethical or religious code – these are known as negative commandments. Well-known examples of these, in a traditional Jewish context, might be the prohibition against eating non-*kosher* food for example, or of engaging in any kind of work on the Sabbath. Then there are the positive *mitzvot*; commandments that, through their observance, might enrich the life of an individual or the community. These might include the requirement to study or to donate charity.

Many activities in Judaism are preceded by a blessing that has a particular formulation, offering praise to God '...*asher kid'shanu b'mitzvotav v'tzivanu*...'; 'who hallows us with mitzvot, commanding us to...'[1] followed by whatever it is that has been 'commanded' (e.g. lighting *Shabbat* candles, affixing a *m'zuzah* to a doorpost or circumcising newborn sons.)

---

[1] The World Union Edition of *Mishkan T'filah* – see, e.g., p. 118

A Judaism for the Twenty-First Century

This formulation, introduced by the Rabbis of two thousand years ago, might be said to represent a certain hubris on their part. Believing that the Five Books of Moses contained the direct word of God and that therefore every instruction or commandment in it carried divine weight, they introduced the idea of certain actions (or refraining from certain actions) as being a response to divine commandment. They calculated that there were a total of 613 commandments – *mitzvot* – in the Torah. (Incidentally, it was never possible for any Jew to observe all 613 *mitzvot* since some relate to men, some to women, some to those living in the land and others to those outside it, and a number of the commandments in the Torah relate to the ways in which sacrifices should be offered in the Temple in Jerusalem, which of course no-one has been able to observe for almost two thousand years.)

Many of the actions that are preceded by the blessing beginning with the above formula, however, are not found in the Torah. Nowhere, for example, are the Israelites commanded to kindle lights to welcome the Sabbath. And the requirement to study, as evidenced by the blessing that states that it is by divine commandment that we are instructed 'to engage with words of Torah'[1], is not borne out by any explicit instruction in the Torah.

Yet these actions – and many others – are deemed to be *mitzvot*; that is, actions carried out by Jews in response to a divine commandment even when the source of the commandment is quite clearly a human interpretation or even invention. Although Orthodox Judaism is quite happy to ascribe divine roots to such clearly human regulations, based upon its belief in the authority of the oral Torah, Progressive Judaism cannot be so unquestioningly accepting. Add to that the fact that the Progressive view of the Torah is that, though perhaps divinely inspired in some way, it, too, is of human origin (a conclusion reached not least because many of the *mitzvot* in the Torah

---
[1] The World Union Edition of *Mishkan T'filah,* p.42

Mitzvah ('Commandment')

make demands that are entirely inappropriate in our modern age), and a situation is reached where Progressive Jews must reassess their attitude towards the concept of *mitzvah*. If we are not commanded by a divine source via instructions revealed in a written document, from where, then, do we derive guidelines for our behaviour?

One response might be that we are indeed commanded in some mystical way, in the words of this particular affirmation, to lead a life of exemplary ethical quality, to work for the betterment of human society, and to practise a devotional discipline of study, prayer and observance. The requirement to engage in such activity comes not necessarily from an external 'commander' but rather from an internal awareness and consciousness that we have a moral duty to behave in this way – and that when we do behave in such a way, we are carrying out the divine will.

When confronted by a choice between doing the right or the wrong thing, our instincts should guide us towards doing the right thing, towards making the correct ethical choice. When presented with an opportunity to make a contribution to society that will improve it in some way, our conscience should steer us towards making that contribution. There is nothing intrinsically Jewish about this; it is an aspect of universal human nature. Judaism, however, seeks to urge us in this direction: it suggests that a devotional discipline and a state of awareness recognising that this is our duty as human beings and as Jews can guide us towards this goal, this proactively ethical life. From a traditional perspective, there is no doubt that Jews are commanded by specific instructions to make those particular choices. The Progressive Jew may find the source of such requirements somewhat less obvious but, as a result of a broader approach to the nature of *mitzvah*, is able to distinguish between those ritual commandments that are clearly limited in time and place and those that are incumbent upon all Jews –

and, indeed, often, upon all human beings – at all times and regardless of where they lead their lives.

12

TALMUD TORAH
('STUDY OF TORAH')

We affirm our commitment to **Talmud Torah** *('study of Torah'): the formal and informal education of children and adults in Jewish history and literature, thought and practice, and the Hebrew language, as the foundation of Jewish life and the precondition of its perpetuation from age to age.*

A Judaism for the Twenty-First Century

Perhaps the most critical element of Judaism, and the one that, more than any other, has ensured its survival, is the emphasis that is placed on education. The duty to transmit knowledge of Jewish teachings is clearly stated in the *Sh'ma, the* central affirmation of Judaism, where Jews are instructed *v'shinantam l'vanecha* 'and you shall teach them (i.e. the teachings of Judaism) to your children.'[1] The requirement to study and teach is emphasised throughout Jewish literature. It is found in the *Sh'ma* and is clearly demonstrated in a well known rabbinic dictum, quoted in *Mishkan T'filah*,[2] which offers a list of some of the highest moral obligations. These include honouring one's parents, welcoming guests, visiting the sick and making peace between people. But the teaching then concludes with the phrase: *v'talmud torah k'neged kulam* – but the study of Torah is equal to (or leads to) them all.

Many and varied are the rabbinic debates regarding the emphasis that should be placed on study as distinct from ethical acts. There can be little doubt that study alone does not equate to a full Jewish life and that ethical action is equally, if not more, important. Conversely, a devotion to ethical actions without an understanding of their place in Judaism and the means by which the teachers of Judaism arrived at an appreciation of their importance as an element of living a full Jewish life also only represents half the story. *Talmud* Torah, the study of Torah in the widest sense of the word, is crucial to a full grasp of Judaism, making it more meaningful to Jews and, most especially, providing a conduit without which it would be impossible to transmit Judaism to future generations.

The most obvious way to ensure that an awareness and knowledge of Judaism is perpetuated from generation to generation is to establish formal educational structures. This is something Judaism has always endeavoured to do and it has

---

[1] Deuteronomy 6:7
[2] p.206, quoting *Mishnah Pe'ah* 1:1

Talmud Torah ('Study of Torah')

consistently excelled. The emphasis that Judaism has always placed on education has been one of the keys to its survival in times and in places when its demise seemed assured. This is as true of the establishment of academies at places such as Yavneh following the destruction of the Temple in 70 CE as of the learning that took place in Terezin[1] during the Nazi Holocaust.

Formal Jewish education was an integral part of life in any Jewish community, where the transmission of knowledge – particularly for boys – commenced at a very early age. Such education began with a thorough grounding in the 'holy tongue', Hebrew, which was the language of prayer and study, even though it ceased to be a conversational language many centuries ago until its re-emergence in modern Israel in the twentieth century. From there followed formal study of the classical Hebrew texts, beginning with the Torah, then extending to the rest of the Hebrew Bible, then *Mishnah, Gemara* and other rabbinic texts.

In our modern world, the situation has changed in two critical ways. In the Middle Ages, when education was a privilege reserved for just a small elite in wider society, every Jewish boy had the opportunity to learn and study his heritage in the institution that was at the heart of every Jewish community. Nowadays, when education is regarded as a right rather than a privilege, and is provided for children by the state in most societies, Jewish educational programmes in synagogues tend to be regarded as significantly less important than a child's secular education, and are often limited to one morning at the weekend.

Recent years have seen an increase in the numbers of Jewish day schools in many larger Jewish communities, most of them catering for Jewish children up to the age of eleven or twelve; some offering a Jewish environment for their pupils to the age

---

[1] See p.33

of eighteen. A number of these schools operate under strictly Orthodox auspices while others, with a pluralist ethos that welcomes all Jews, regardless of their synagogue adherence or personal level of observance, have also emerged. Attitudes to religious schools vary and their effect is currently being debated in wider society as well as in Jewish circles. This is a debate that attracts opinions ranging from unqualified support for the opportunity to expose children to religious education on a daily basis, to strong opposition on the grounds that such exposure creates elitism and an unrealistic view of the place of religion in a pluralist society.

But whether it be in a day school or at a weekly religion school (often called *cheder,* based on the Hebrew/Yiddish word meaning 'room', which used to refer specifically to the classroom), the transmission of Jewish knowledge and awareness remains a key element of Progressive Judaism. Here we see the teaching of the Hebrew language (the main purpose of which being to teach familiarity with the prayerbook rather than a desire to encourage pupils to be able to converse in modern Hebrew) and aspects of the Hebrew Bible and other elements of Jewish history and culture. The emphasis of the Progressive Jewish religion school is not just on the imparting of knowledge about Judaism. Such a school also seeks to emphasise and to encourage the Progressive view and approach to that Judaism, to foster a spirit of questioning and challenging Jewish tradition as well as inculcating a love and respect for it. Such an attitude seeks to guarantee the future not just of Progressive Judaism but of Judaism itself, for we believe that without such an approach, Judaism would be doomed to stagnate and lose its relevance to modern life.

Of course, all this cannot possibly be achieved in one morning a week. Progressive Judaism is particularly proud that, in addition to its formal religious education, it runs a series of informal educational programmes that complement the

Talmud Torah ('Study of Torah')

movement's efforts to make it a meaningful and relevant part of the lives of its young people. Progressive Judaism offers a range of youth events (mainly through our youth movement *Netzer*) that brings together Progressive Jewish young people from all over the region and encourages them to participate in educational, social and cultural activities that aim to increase both their Jewish knowledge and their commitment to Judaism. In particular, *Netzer*, in common with other Jewish movements, offers annual residential summer and winter camps that have, over the many years of their existence, produced several of the rabbis who now play a vital role in the movement and its future, both here and overseas.

Jewish education does not, of course, conclude with its children. We learn that 'If to neglect Jewish education altogether is the worst mistake, the second worst is to think of it as something we owe our children but not ourselves.'[1] If the purpose of Jewish education for our children is to ensure the perpetuation of our tradition, then the adults too have a responsibility to ensure that the quality of their own knowledge is sufficient to permit and inspire this.

At present, there seems to be a welcome renaissance of interest in adult Jewish learning. Progressive Judaism is associated with – and indeed at the forefront of – this development. Opportunities for teaching adults have always been at the heart of Progressive Judaism's educational enterprise and the majority of Progressive synagogues will offer some form of adult education in addition to that which is available to its children. We also encourage the development of family education programmes in synagogue congregations – just one of a number of ways of promoting the acquisition of knowledge and awareness of Judaism and its traditions, the development of love and respect for them and a desire to pass them on to future generations to ensure the survival of our heritage.

---

[1] *Siddur Lev Chadash* p.358.

13

ETHICAL VALUES

We affirm our commitment to Judaism's ethical values, which include reverence for life, respect for persons and property, love of neighbour, practical kindness (**g'milut chasadim**) *and charity* (**tz'dakah**), *social justice and peace, the conservation of nature and the humane treatment of animals.*

The previous chapter, which focused on Judaism's emphasis on study, began with a rabbinic dictum suggesting that study can lead to a whole range of ethically worthy and morally laudable actions. The teachers of Judaism have always recognised that no matter how much a Jew may study, no matter how much a Jew may observe religious practices, it is in action that a true commitment to the Jewish heritage manifests itself.

From the earliest sayings of the Prophets and the biblical instructions in the Book of Leviticus, the teachings of Judaism are filled with the divine requirement for ethical behaviour. Chapter 19 of Leviticus, which lies virtually at the heart of the Torah, contains a series of regulations demanding that the Israelites establish a society based upon justice and the ethical treatment of others. Although our modern ethical views differ significantly from those of our biblical ancestors (for example in their treatment of homosexuals as shown in Leviticus 20:19 or of troublesome children in Deuteronomy 21:18f), the idea that religion is about one's relationships with one's fellow human beings, the society one constructs, and respect for the world has its roots in the teachings of the Prophets and many biblical laws.

One often hears the observation that the God of the 'Old Testament' (the Christian description of the Hebrew Bible) is a vengeful and cruel God. The biblical verse often quoted to justify this opinion is Exodus 21:24, where we are told that God requires 'an eye for an eye, a tooth for a tooth'. But the intention of this verse was probably an early attempt to establish justice in a society where wholesale revenge seemed to be the order of the day (for example Lamech in Genesis 4:23 who states 'I have killed a man for bruising me, a young boy for striking me'.) 'An eye for an eye' was an early attempt to try to make punishment commensurate with whatever was the original offence, confirmed by subsequent rabbinic opinion, explicitly stating that the ruling referred to monetary compensation[1]. Nevertheless, it would seem that in biblical times[2], such laws were applied literally, making all the more laudable the emergence of rules such as those in Leviticus chapter 19 that require people not to hate each other in their hearts, and to love their neighbour as they love themselves.

The roots of Judaism lay in biblical times[3], so most of the laws upon which the ethical requirements of Judaism are based are built around the social and economic realities of that ancient world. The requirement to respect others' property, for example, which features in the book of Deuteronomy, begins by referring to a person's lost ox or sheep, where the finder is required to make every effort to return it to the owner. That this is a general principle is highlighted when the instruction continues 'this is how you shall treat your neighbour's donkey, or garment or anything that your neighbour has lost and that you find – you shall surely return a lost item; you may not ignore this.'[4]

For the Rabbis, such *mitzvot* in the Torah, were the basis of Jewish ethics. They recognised that the ethical requirements underpinning all these commandments could be easily summarised: 'There are 613 commandments in the Torah', we read in the Talmud:[5] 'The prophet Micah reduced these to three: "Do justly, love mercy and walk humbly with your God." Then came Isaiah and reduced them to two: "Thus says the Eternal One: Keep justice and act righteously." Amos reduced them to one: 'Seek Me and live."'

---

[1] eg *Mechilta d'Rabbi Ishmael* to Exodus 21:24, Babylonian Talmud *Bava Kamma*, 84a

[2] approximately 2000-500 years BCE – see Chapter 9

[3] see note 2 above

[4] Deuteronomy 22:1-3

[5] *Makkot* 24a The biblical quotes are Micah 6:8, Isaiah 56:1 and Amos 5:4

Ethical Values

If Judaism has a 'golden rule' that encapsulates the ethical emphasis of its teaching it is an anecdote involving *Hillel*, a Pharisaic teacher of the first century BCE. The Talmud[1] tells of a non-Jew who would convert to Judaism if the whole Torah could be explained to him by a teacher standing on one leg. He first asked *Hillel*'s rival, *Shammai*, who sent him away, but *Hillel* said, 'All that is hateful to you, do not do to your fellow,' then added, 'The rest is commentary – go and learn.'

The Rabbis certainly followed *Hillel*'s advice. Rabbinic writings, particularly *Pirkei Avot* (literally 'Chapters of the Fathers' but the first word is often translated as 'Ethics') contain many observations the intention of which was to encourage the Jewish people to think carefully about the effects of their behaviour on their fellow human beings and on their environment.

There is insufficient space here to detail the various aspects of human responsibility that Judaism emphasises. A brief summary will have to suffice.

The Rabbis emphasised the importance of acts of practical kindness (*g'milut chassadim*). Such acts should include (but by no means be limited to) visiting the sick, welcoming guests and consoling the bereaved[2]. They also stressed the requirement of *tz'dakah* – a word whose original meaning was righteous behaviour but which, with the passage of time, has come to mean the giving of charity. While it might be a mistake to assume that the Hebrew term *tz'dakah* refers exclusively to the giving of donations (and modern research is revealing that while giving money may make the donor feel better, its benefit to the needy may not prove lasting), it is fair to say that charity

---

[1] Shabbat 31a
[2] These actions are included in the dictum from *Mishnah Pe'ah* 1:1, quoted on page 70.

is the most generally accepted translation and use of the word today.

The biblical Prophets were at pains to remind the Israelites that the absence of social justice – or, more importantly, their failure to work to remedy its absence – was an abdication of their religious duty. These teachings were to provide the basis for Progressive Judaism in a later age.[1] In the meantime, this emphasis on the promotion of social justice was affirmed by the Rabbis, who themselves lived under Roman oppression, and they strove to imbue the Judaism they were creating with a sense of obligation to work for justice within their society and peace in the wider world.

Criticism has often been voiced against religions and their adherents involving themselves in causes that have been described as 'political' – an area into which, it is implied, religion is not expected to stray. A brief look at some of the prophecies of Amos, Isaiah or Jeremiah should make quite clear the fact that in the biblical environment from which such visionary teachings emerged, there was no distinction between religion and politics. A religious commitment to seeking to do and implement God's will necessarily requires an engagement with the political and social issues of the day. And, despite the separation between church and state, which has prevailed for several centuries in the western world, Judaism – and particularly Progressive Judaism – has always insisted that religious values must provide the ethical underpinning for political attitudes and decisions.

The primacy of ethical behaviour and attitudes in adhering to a religious way of life has always been integral to Judaism. Whether it be a concern for the future of the planet, in the role people play as stewards of creation, or the demand for the

---

[1] See chapter 38

Ethical Values

humane treatment of animals (demonstrated for example in the laws of *sh'chitah* – ritual slaughter, whose prime purpose was to endeavour to ensure that the slaughtered animal endured as little suffering as possible),[1] Jewish responsibility and duty have always been made clear. Judaism demands of its adherents that they commit themselves to raising awareness of and seeking to eradicate poverty and the persecution of minority groups as well as protecting human rights and encouraging fair trade.[2] The modern world, with its advances in science, technology and medicine, throws up new possibilities and challenges almost on a daily basis. Religion needs to confront difficult areas such as the prolonging of life through medical intervention and its converse, the voluntary termination of life, by revisiting the well-established ethical principles that Judaism has espoused and promoted throughout its long history. The Jewish tradition of reflection and discussion and of finding ways to apply its teachings to new and varied circumstances ensures that Progressive Judaism is well placed to respond to the ethical challenges of the modern world by employing an approach that balances the wisdom of our tradition with the knowledge and insight of our own age.

---

[1] See p. 249
[2] See p. 251

14

THE JEWISH HOME

We affirm our commitment to the Jewish home as a 'little sanctuary' (**mikdash m'at**), *filled with the beauty of holiness, in which the values and traditions of Judaism can be exemplified, taught and transmitted from generation to generation.*

The Jewish Home

In biblical times, the heathen soothsayer Balaam was ordered by the Moabite king, Balak, to curse the Israelites who threatened his borders. But as Balaam had warned, when he opened his mouth to speak, he was only able to speak words of praise and admiration: *'Ma tovu ohalecha Ya'akov, mishk'notecha Yisra'el;* how lovely are your tents, O Jacob, your dwelling places O Israel,'[1] words that are often used to this day to open our services.[2]

In times and places far removed from those biblical days, the notion of a Jewish home might conjure up an image of a mother and father sitting around a beautifully adorned table with their children and other relatives, enjoying a festival or Sabbath meal. Lit candles would shine from ornate candlesticks, food specific to the occasion would be on offer and wine would be served from special cups. Although such Jewish homes may indeed exist, for many Jews in the twenty-first century, such a scene would be familiar only from nostalgic picture books or films.

This is not to suggest that the homes in which modern Jews live are in some way failing to live up to a Jewish ideal. A Jewish home is defined by the individual or individuals living in it, the customs that they practise, and the values that they demonstrate. The potential for these customs and values to be present exists wherever a Jew makes his or her home, regardless of the family structure or the number of people in that home.

Nevertheless, there are a number of elements that might indicate that a home is Jewish, regardless of the practices of its residents. The most visually obvious of these can usually be seen from the street, close to the top of the doorpost of the main

---

[1] Numbers 24:5
[2] Eg. The World Union Edition of *Mishkan T'filah* p.192

entrance to the house. This small casing, made of metal, wood, ceramic or other material, known as a *m'zuzah* (which literally means 'doorpost'), is the rabbinic interpretation of the instruction to 'write them on the doorposts of your house'[1]. 'They' are the words of the *Sh'ma*, paragraphs that include that instruction regarding the doorpost, and inside a *m'zuzah* is a piece of parchment on which are written the first two paragraphs of this well known Jewish text.

This very literal rabbinic interpretation of a biblical verse is probably an adaptation of a Canaanite custom where amulets were attached to doorposts to protect a home from evil spirits (this itself was a development from a custom that saw the body of a sacrificed child buried beneath the doorposts of a house prior to its construction). Whatever the origins of this custom, its observance marks out a house as being a Jewish home. A brief ceremony can accompany the affixing of a *m'zuzah* (normally one on the main door will suffice, though some people have the custom of attaching one to the doorpost of every room in the house except the lavatory) – a ceremony known as *Chanukat haBayit* – the dedication of a home.[2]

It is more than a coincidence that the word *bayit* was also regularly used to refer to the Temple in Jerusalem. A Jewish home is referred to in rabbinic tradition as a *mikdash m'at* (little sanctuary); *mikdash* being an even more specific reference to the Temple of biblical times. So a ceremony dedicating a house does indeed carry a heavy weight of tradition and symbolism. It acknowledges that, since the destruction of the Temple, the home (in partnership with the synagogue) has been a bedrock of Jewish knowledge and values.

---

[1] e.g. Deuteronomy 6:9
[2] See The World Union Edition of *Mishkan T'filah* p. 617

The Jewish Home

The following chapters will give details of the Jewish festivals and life cycle events – many of these can be welcomed and celebrated in the home. Many Jewish homes contain a number of artefacts for use on these occasions. Such items might include candlesticks in which are placed the lights to welcome the Sabbath, and an ornate *kiddush* cup from which an entire family might drink wine to welcome this weekly day of rest[1]. Annual events such as the Passover meal or the celebration of *Chanukkah* have their own artefacts – a *seder* plate[2] and a *chanukkiyah*[3] respectively – and these are celebrations that are designed to take place in the home.

Alongside these ritual items, it is likely that there will be various Jewish books, relating to particular occasions. Prayerbooks to take to synagogue that also contain liturgy for home rituals, *haggadot*[4] for the Passover *seder*, books about Jewish history, culture or other aspects of Jewish knowledge may well be present. As Elie Wiesel once said, 'I do not recall a Jewish home without a book on the table.'[5] Jews are often referred to as 'the people of the book' and although the book in this case is probably the Bible, there are often many books on Jewish themes to be found on the shelves.

Some of these might be cookery books, for another of the realities of Judaism is its fondness for food. Although the 'traditional' family meal suggested in an earlier paragraph might belong mainly to the realms of nostalgic fantasy, eating remains a favourite Jewish pastime and the kitchen in a Jewish home is a major focal point. The actual layout of the kitchen

---

[1] See chapter 18
[2] See p. 127
[3] An 8-branched candelabra with a ninth branch for the servant candle, often referred to (incorrectly) as a *menorah*, which has 7 branches. See p. 136
[4] See p. 128
[5] Actual source unknown; found at http://www.whatquote.com/quotes/Elie-Wiesel/15250-I-do-not-recall-a-Je.htm

would depend on the residents' attitude towards the Jewish dietary laws *(kashrut)* – a strictly *kosher* kitchen would require two sets of crockery, cutlery and cooking utensils (and in some cases even two refrigerators) to comply with the rabbinic ruling to keep milk and meat separate. The laws of *kashrut* are dealt with in a later chapter[1] but the important place that eating occupies in the Jewish home and the opportunity to attach aspects of Jewish ritual and celebration to meals is a vital element of the Jewish home.

Moreover, Judaism is not just about ritual and celebration. It is, as the previous chapter indicated, about living an ethical life. These are values that can and should be demonstrated in the home as examples for those who live in it to follow so that they might be tolerant peace-loving individuals and make a valuable contribution to society. There is nothing exclusively Jewish about such values, but Judaism offers many possibilities for such values to be introduced into life in the home. Particularly in homes where children are growing up, these are opportunities that can and should be grasped. Those emerging from such a domestic environment to confront the world as adults will then have a solid sense of their identity and an awareness of their responsibility as well as a desire to maintain and practise Judaism in the Jewish home that they will one day establish for themselves.

---

[1] Chapter 39

15

THE SYNAGOGUE

We affirm our commitment to the Synagogue **(beit ha-knesset)** *as Judaism's democratically governed community centre, serving its traditional threefold function as a house of prayer, study and fellowship.*

Wherever there is a Jewish community, there will almost certainly be a synagogue – a building owned or hired by the local Jewish community as a centre for its activities. A synagogue building may be a grand, purpose-built edifice, with an imposing entrance hall, offices for administration and the rabbi(s), classrooms, library, a function hall and a kitchen. Such a synagogue would have as its centrepiece an imposing sanctuary, the focal point of which would be an elaborately designed ark containing the Torah scrolls. Or a synagogue might be, for instance, a disused church or school that has been purchased or rented by members of a small or new Jewish community, enthusiastically developed and decorated by volunteers as a place in which they might gather to pray, to study and to celebrate the opportunities that being part of a Jewish community offer to them.

The exact date of the establishment of the first synagogue is not easy to ascertain. The origin of the word is Greek, meaning a place of meeting, and it is certain that by the time the Greek Empire had reached the Jews (the accepted date for the arrival of Alexander the Great in Jerusalem is 333 BCE), the concept of a building that was a focal point for the local community was well established. The fact that its Greek designation refers exclusively to the synagogue's function as a meeting place suggests that its other roles, as a place of prayer and study, were subsequent developments.

Historically, this would certainly accord with the emergence of the synagogue and its different functions. The Temple stood proudly in Jerusalem for the duration of the Greek rule over Judea; it was only following its destruction by the Romans that the synagogue truly emerged as a place of worship (though the origins of the services we now associate with the synagogue were present in some form while Temple worship still took place). The gradual emergence of the Pharisees with their intense study of the Five Books of Moses and other biblical books has its roots in Greek times and it seems reasonable to assume that such study would use the synagogue as a base.

Whatever its origins, this development of the synagogue was such that it stood ready to embrace and nurture the future of Judaism when the Temple was destroyed. And once the Jews found themselves dispersed ever further afield from their geographical origins, the institution of the synagogue proved to be a versatile and adaptable means of ensuring that the Jewish community remained just that: a Jewish community. Once established, the community would give a name to itself and its synagogue. Sometimes that name would reflect its geographical location, in other cases a Hebrew title such as *Sha'arei Shalom* (Gates of Peace) or *Beit Tikvah* (House of Hope) might be selected. Whatever the chosen name, it would be prefixed by the two Hebrew words *k'hillah k'doshah* – 'holy congregation'.

A synagogue is and always has been a voluntary institution. The establishment and maintenance of a synagogue requires a group of committed Jewish individuals who recognise the importance of a centre for their community, a place for Jewish worship and religious education. The organisation is overseen by a group of volunteers (usually elected), often known as the Council or Board of the synagogue. This voluntary committee is responsible for ensuring that the necessary funding, personnel and facilities are provided for the synagogue to fulfil its various functions.

These functions are encapsulated in the three titles that are traditionally applied to the synagogue, known in Jewish tradition as house of meeting *(beit ha-knesset)*, house of study *(beit ha-midrash)* and house of prayer *(beit ha-t'fillah)*.

As a *beit ha-knesset*, the synagogue serves many functions. It is a place where members of the congregation may gather for social or cultural events that may range from a quiz or fund-raising dinner to a talk by a local celebrity or perhaps an inter-faith discussion. Social events that attach to certain Jewish festivals might also be regarded as part of the synagogue's role as a house of meeting: a *Chanukkah* party or a *Purim* carnival[1] for example or even a *chavurah*[2] supper following an *Erev Shabbat* service[3]. Clearly, the different roles of the synagogue can overlap, demonstrating the versatility of this age-old institution.

As a *beit ha-midrash*, a synagogue has a particularly important function. The ancient Rabbis emphasised the importance of education[4] and this has been enthusiastically embraced by the synagogue. No matter what facilities a synagogue may have, whether it be fortunate enough to possess a purpose-built block of classrooms with state of the art learning areas and equipment or is simply a second hand building with perhaps just one large hall, the teaching of children will always take place there. Some synagogue communities are sufficiently large to require several teachers, while in others a single teacher has the responsibility of providing an educational programme for half a dozen children whose age range might cover several years. Nor is the educational role of the synagogue limited to its children. Another key aspect of its role as a house of study is the opportunity it offers for adults to extend their level of Jewish knowledge.

It was as a *beit ha-'t'fillah* that the synagogue played its most important historical role in preserving and developing Judaism. Although its founders never intended that it should replace the Temple as the place of Jewish worship, the fact that the

---

[1] See chapter 21.
[2] *Chavurah* literally means fellowship or group of friends; in this context it refers to a communal meal.
[3] *Erev Shabbat* - the eve of the Sabbath – *Shabbat* begins on a Friday evening. See chapter 18.
[4] See chapter 12.

synagogue already existed as a focal point for the Jewish community in various towns and cities in Greek- and Roman-ruled Judea meant that it was ready to respond to this latest demand and quickly adapted itself to become a house of prayer alongside its other functions. Discussion of the origins, content and development of the liturgy in synagogues follows; it will suffice here to say that, as with its other responsibilities, the synagogue has refined its role as a house of prayer along with those of study and meeting to ensure that its place at the heart of Judaism is as vital at the beginning of the twenty-first century as when it first appeared more than two thousand years ago.

16

PRAYER AND WORSHIP

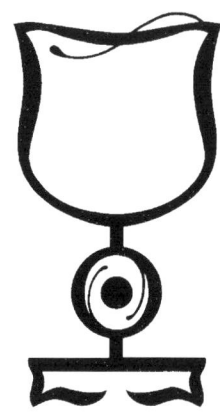

We affirm the importance of prayer and worship, through which individual and community seek ever anew to experience God's presence, to draw spiritual sustenance from their religious heritage and to dedicate themselves to their responsibilities.

Prayer and Worship

Notwithstanding its role as a place of study and meeting, the synagogue's function as a place of prayer and worship is, for Jews and non-Jews, the one with which it is most readily associated. The expression and demonstration of the relationship between human beings and whatever they perceive as being the power that controls and orders their world and their lives has always been a feature of human society. Whenever human beings confront the unknown or inexplicable, the tendency has always been to look to a superior power and to attempt to make some kind of communication with that power. That form of communication might generally be described as prayer.

Prayer can be divided into four different categories. There is petitionary prayer, in which a request – specific or general – is made of the divine power. There are prayers of thanksgiving, in which gratitude is expressed. Doxological prayers are prayers of praise that exalt and glorify the divine power to which the prayer is being offered. And finally there are penitential prayers, offerings or utterances that ask for forgiveness. In addition to these types of prayer, the Rabbis introduced the concept of *b'rachah*, of uttering a blessing on various occasions, to elevate everyday experiences to a spiritual level. Examples of such blessings can be found in the *World Union Edition of Mishkan T'filah*, p.124

Ancient Israelite worship, the attempt of our ancestors to communicate with the divine, features in the earliest episodes of the Five Books of Moses: its development is an ongoing theme in Judaism. Clearly the ancient Israelites were influenced by the customs and practices of the peoples among whom they dwelt – customs and practices that they copied, adapted or rejected as they developed their relationship with the One God who was the unique feature of their religious culture.

From the building of altars in various locations (Jacob, for example, establishing shrines in the places where, according to the stories in the Book of Genesis, he experienced a divine revelation[1]), to the establishment of the Temple in Jerusalem as the centre of the Israelite cult, to the development of the Jewish liturgy, Judaism has a long tradition of attempting to structure its communication with its God.

One of the earliest forms of worship in the Ancient Near East, from which ancient Israelite religion drew its roots, was that of sacrifice. Although the origins of this custom are not clear, the symbolic significance of giving back to God a portion of that which God has given to human beings is self-evident. Particular emphasis was placed upon the first born of every creature – including human beings. 'That which opened the womb'[2] was believed to belong exclusively to God. The existence of Canaanite gods to whom first born children should be sacrificed is well documented, both in the Bible[3] and archaeological findings. Indeed, it is likely that the story of Abraham binding his son Isaac on the altar for sacrifice[4] was penned with the intention of dissuading the Israelites from engaging in this practice (and the fact that this was necessary is attested to in the Book of Jeremiah[5]).

The sacrifice of human beings was clearly abhorred by the priests and lawmakers of ancient Israel, but the offering of other animals – and that of crops and other produce – was the centrepiece of the relationship between the ancient Israelite people and their God. The development of rituals to accompany the sacrifices and the emergence of a priestly class to oversee them was inevitable, though some of the accounts in the Book

---

[1] e.g. Genesis 28:19, 35:14 (both at the same location – Beth-El)
[2] (e.g Exodus 13:1)
[3] e.g. Leviticus 18:21; 20: 1-5
[4] Genesis 22
[5] Jeremiah 32:35

Prayer and Worship

of Numbers suggest that there may have been power struggles between different priestly groups at various points in ancient Israelite history[1].

A crucial factor in the development of Israel's relationship with its God was the centralisation of the cult in the city of Jerusalem. The focal point of worship – at least in the minds of the authors of the Bible – was the Ark of the Covenant: the gold-covered box which, according to tradition, contained the stone tablets on which were inscribed the Ten Commandments given to Moses at Mount Sinai. This precious box and its contents were carried through the wilderness before finding their first resting place in the 'Promised Land' at the shrine of Shiloh[2]. From there, via a rather circuitous route, it was eventually brought to Jerusalem where the Temple was constructed to house it.[3]

It was at this location that Israel's attempt to establish and develop its relationship with its God truly emerged. The details of the sacrifices, so precisely (and graphically) described in the Book of Leviticus, were refined here, as was the role of the Levites and the priests. The sophistication of the ritual was matched by the elaborate nature of the priestly dress and the ornate design of the ritual objects. The sense that human beings should set aside for the divine power the most precious materials at their disposal and ensure that their offering was of the highest quality found expression here, as ritual and practice developed ever greater levels of sophistication.

Although the Temple is long gone, elements of it, and the worship that took place in it, are still a feature of Jewish worship today. The ark, which is to be found in every

---

[1] e.g. Numbers 16
[2] Joshua 18:1
[3] The locations and journeys of the Ark of the Covenant in the 'Promised Land' are described in Judges 20, I Samuel chapters 4-7 and II Samuel 6-7.

synagogue, recalls the Ark of the Covenant that resided in the Holy of Holies at the centre of the Temple, the eternal light *(ner tamid)* that shines permanently above the ark recalls the lamp that burned continually outside it, and the breastplate on the Torah scroll is a reminder of that which was worn by the High Priest.

This emphasises both Judaism's connection with its past and also the importance of symbols in assisting human worship. Although the worship service that takes place in modern synagogues is far removed from the animal sacrifices of Jerusalem or the even older 'high places' that preceded the establishment of a central cult, its aim is nevertheless the same. It is to communicate with the divine power, to establish and develop a relationship with that power, to offer thanks and atonement to it and to seek guidance from it. This task, which has been the duty of Jews throughout the ages, takes place within an environment that can trace its roots back to the earliest days of human attempts to communicate with the divine, using rituals, symbols and language that remind us of our ancestors' search for God even as we engage upon our own.

One of the most significant features of Jewish prayer, emphasised by the Rabbis, is the importance of praying as part of a community. Many Progressive Jewish congregations do not observe a specific minimum number defining what constitutes a community, though there is clearly a 'critical mass' which distinguishes 'a few' from 'a congregation'. Orthodox Judaism insists that certain prayers can only be recited when a *minyan* - ten men (women do not count for them as part of a *minyan*) is present. And yet, in a traditional environment, community prayer often gives the impression of a group of individuals praying alone within a larger group. This is one of the intriguing features of traditional Jewish worship: the opportunity for individual prayer that is facilitated when one is surrounded by others engaging in the same activity.

Progressive worship tends to be more of a shared, communal experience.[1]

This communal environment is rich with symbolic objects, the purpose of which is to focus the worshipper's mental and spiritual endeavours. In addition to such focal points as the ark and the *ner tamid* shining above it, Judaism offers several personal ritual objects to assist the worshipper. The fact that such ritual objects have, in many cases, become the focus of worship itself (rather than just an aid to it) is one that Progressive Judaism regrets. In the early days of the movement, Progressive Jews were encouraged – or even required – to dispense with such objects. The return of many rituals and symbols as part of Progressive Jewish worship is based on a recognition that they can assist with prayer, though they should never become the focus, or take the place, of it.

Such symbols include the *tallit*, (prayer shawl), which is traditionally worn by men though there is nothing, except the force of tradition, to prevent women from wearing one also – and indeed some women congregants (and all women rabbis) in Progressive synagogues choose to do so. The origins of this garment are to be found in the third paragraph of the *Sh'ma*[2] where the Israelites are commanded to place fringes on the corners of their garments. Another aid to – or part of – daily prayer are *t'fillin*, often translated as phylacteries. These are two boxes to which are attached straps for binding around the arm and the head. Contained within the boxes are the verses of the *Sh'ma*, which include the words 'and you shall bind them as

---

[1] See chapter 31
[2] Numbers 15:37-41. Progressive Judaism's earlier ambivalence towards the *tallit* and, in particular, its everyday equivalent, the *tzitzit* (a vest-like undergarment with fringes worn by Orthodox Jewish men) is reflected in the fact that the section of the Sh'ma (eg see The World Union Edition of *Mishkan T'filah* p.68) referring to the fringes was often omitted from the Progressive liturgy.

a sign upon your hands and they shall be as frontlets between your eyes.'[1] As with the *m'zuzah*,[2] the Rabbis have applied a very literal interpretation to this biblical verse. *T'fillin* are not normally a feature of Progressive Jewish worship. One reason for this is that *t'fillin* are not usually worn on *Shabbat* or festivals, which is when Progressive Judaism holds most of its services, only rarely hosting communal daily worship. Some Progressive Jews also object to the Rabbis' literalism, preferring to interpret the instructions to carry God's commandments as signs on the hand and between the eyes in a metaphorical way. A mention must be made here of the Jewish custom of men covering their heads while at prayer. Although the *kippah,* (also known as *cappel* or *yarmulke*) is a well-established religious item for Jewish men, there is no reference to it in the Bible or any source of Jewish law. It is a convention that has emerged, probably as a means of showing respect, but nowhere is there any requirement for it in Jewish law, nor any suggestion that it should apply only to men.

Key questions about prayer still remain, of course. What is the purpose of prayer, what should be expected from it and how can one gauge if it has been successful? These are issues that cannot be very easily addressed, perhaps except by asserting what prayer is not and what it cannot achieve. Prayer cannot, for example, alter events that have already taken place or whose outcome cannot be changed. There are, of course, those who believe in the power of healing prayer; such prayer is not a feature of mainstream Judaism but its possibility at least cannot be denied. Many are encouraged by the knowledge that such prayers are being offered on their behalf. In terms of Jewish tradition, it seems sufficient to say that prayer is an attempt to reach a spiritual level on which one can gain a sense of encounter with the divine presence. The rituals and symbols of

---

[1] Deuteronomy 6:8, 11:18
[2] See p. 82

Judaism exist to assist individuals and communities in that attempt (but do not, in themselves, create or represent it). The 'success' of prayer – if, indeed, such a thing can be measured at all – should be based upon the behaviour that follows it, since an encounter with the Divine should encourage and inspire us to seek to carry out our responsibility: to endeavour to implement God's will through action in the world. Prayer should lead to such action and engagement, not serve as an alternative to it. As an American Reform rabbi, Emil G. Hirsch, wrote, 'True worship is not a petition to God: it is a sermon to our own selves'. [1]

To this must be added the opportunity that prayer offers for individuals to find moments of peace and tranquillity in this busy world. For some worshippers, the reciting of psalms and other readings from Jewish tradition, old and new, carries its own meaning and significance. For others, such words and songs provide a platform for efforts to engage in a spiritual encounter, which might best be achieved through moments of silent contemplation. The ways in which Progressive Judaism endeavours to assist with this are detailed in a later chapter.[2] In general, though, the words of nineteenth century English novelist George Meredith can best be used to sum up this aspect of worship: 'Who rises from prayer a better person, that person's prayer is answered.' The prayerbook can be considered a mirror in which we may measure ourselves and compare the current reality with the ideal it sets out for us.

---

[1] Quoted in 'Judaism for Today', p.113
[2] See chapter 31

17

JEWISH LITURGY

We affirm the importance of the Jewish liturgy, including the recitation of the **Sh'ma**, *the public reading of Torah and other biblical writings, and an abundance of blessings, prayers and hymns composed by Jewish sages, poets and mystics in many lands and ages.*

The emphasis on prayer as a communal activity meant that a form of liturgy had to be instituted and adhered to. Although it cannot be said with any certainty when the recitation of particular passages was introduced into worship, the use of psalms in and around the Temple is evidenced by the content of some of those very psalms (e.g. Psalm 150) and it is possible that one of the Levites' roles was the performance of music.

The origin of the use of the spoken – or chanted – word is more difficult to chart. It is thought that the recitation of the Ten Commandments may have been one of the earliest elements of verbal public liturgy as well as the sections of the Books of Deuteronomy and Numbers we refer to as the *Sh'ma* (Deuteronomy 6:4-9, 11:13-21 and Numbers 15:37-41). The Book of Kings contains a prayer purportedly uttered by King Solomon on the occasion of the completion of the first Temple – and if this were genuine, it would indeed be an early example of public liturgy. To this day, the phrase with which public worship begins is *Bar'chu et Adonai ha-m'vorach* ('Praise the One to whom our praise is due' – see, e.g., *World Union Edition of Mishkan T'filah,* p.146). This is the point in the traditional service beyond which a *minyan* is required, and it is thought that this was a formula used by the Levites to call the people to attention – and the people's response was *Baruch Adonai ha-m'vorach l'olam va-ed* (We praise the Eternal One to whom our praise is due for ever). The people in the Temple would prostrate themselves as they uttered this response: a tradition that is recalled, perhaps unwittingly, by some worshippers who bow towards the ark as these words are recited.

The emergence of the synagogue, initially as a house of meeting and study, then as a house of prayer, signified radical changes in the development and practice of Jewish liturgy. In keeping with the tradition of oral Torah, the blessings and prayers that developed in this institution were not written down for many centuries. Instead, various themes were assigned to particular sections of the central prayer, known as the *T'filah* (*The* prayer) or *Amidah* ('standing' as one traditionally stands throughout it). As long as the leader of the service *(shaliach tzibbur* – literally 'emissary of the congregation') opened and concluded a particular prayer with the assigned formula, he was at liberty to extemporise on that theme. For example, the opening paragraph of the *T'filah* is known as *Avot* (literally 'fathers') and it begins by praising the God of Abraham, Isaac and Jacob and concludes with the words 'We praise You, O God, shield of Abraham[1].' Before the content of the liturgy was formalised, what went between those two phrases was entirely up to whoever was leading the service, provided that it followed the general historical theme and emphasised God's protection.

The formalisation of the liturgy, built around certain key sections of the worship service that remain virtually unchanged to this day, began in the ninth century CE, when the *Seder Rav Amram* was produced by Amram ben Sheshna, head of the academy of Sura in Babylon. Subsequent books were produced, setting out the order and content of the prayers to be recited and, although there were some variations in wording, the structure of Jewish liturgy was established. This structure is retained in Judaism's various current traditions, though with some important differences. Over the centuries, Orthodox Judaism has added much to its liturgy, mostly in the form of *piyyutim* (religious poetry), the production of which began in Talmudic times and flourished especially in the Middle Ages. Jewish liturgy, being traditionally keen to accept new and reluctant to discard any older material, grew and grew. There was a practical purpose for these additional prayers, which fell into two categories: morning blessings *(bir'chot ha-shachar)* and Songs of Praise *(p'sukei d'zimrah)*. In Orthodox tradition, certain

---

[1] Progressive Judaism has added the matriarchs, Sarah, Rebecca, Rachel and Leah to their male partners – one of various changes to the traditional Jewish liturgy that are detailed more fully in chapter 31.

Jewish Liturgy

sections of liturgy require a *minyan*,[1] so the inclusion of prayers and introductory readings is to prepare the worshipper for these central prayers (and probably also to fill the time spent waiting for the tenth member of the *minyan* to arrive!). Consequently, an Orthodox service on a *Shabbat* morning may be as long as three hours. Progressive Judaism, from its inception, sought to trim what it regarded as an excess of religious poetry from Jewish liturgy and return to the essential core elements.

The first of these core elements is the *Sh'ma*, which is bracketed by other blessings. Once again, as with the *m'zuzah*[2] and *t'fillin*,[3] the Rabbis literally incorporated the instructions contained in this short section of Deuteronomy. The requirement to 'speak of them (i.e. these words)…when you lie down and when you rise up…'[4] translates into a recitation of those very words, every evening and morning. This liturgical unit is introduced with the *Bar'chu* (as described above) and is followed by prayers relating to creation and God's love for Israel. Then comes the *Sh'ma* itself, and this section concludes with references to the redemption from Egypt. There are some variations between the evening and morning versions of the prayers preceding and following the *Sh'ma* but the themes are identical. An additional element at an evening service at this point is a prayer asking for God's overnight protection.

The next unit is the *T'filah*, the prayer originally intended to serve as a temporary substitute for animal sacrifice. The opening three paragraphs deal with our biblical ancestors, God's power and God's holiness respectively and carry the Hebrew names *Avot, G'vurot and K'dushah*. This prayer concludes with three paragraphs on the theme of worship

---

[1] See p. 94
[2] See p. 82
[3] See p. 95
[4] Deuteronomy 6:7

(Avodah), thanksgiving *(Hoda'ah)* and peace *(Shalom)*. There are some variations between the evening and morning versions of these prayers, but their content reflects those themes. What comes between them depends upon the day: a regular weekday service contains a series of thirteen petitionary prayers, requesting a variety of blessings from God, ranging from health and freedom to redemption and the banishment of evil. The traditional formulation of these prayers reflects the rabbinic yearning for the rebuilding of the Temple and the ingathering of exiles. This theological view is entirely unacceptable to Progressive Judaism, and so Progressive liturgy has made radical adjustments to these sections.[1] On a Sabbath or festival, however, it is deemed inappropriate to disturb the Almighty with such a barrage of requests and so this middle section of the *T'filah* is replaced with shorter readings that make specific reference to the occasion being celebrated. This is known as *k'dushat ha-yom* – the sanctification of the day.

A service concludes with the prayer known as the *Aleinu* (so named, like the *Sh'ma* because of its opening word) – a prayer that traditionally acknowledges the sovereignty of Israel's God and looks forward to a future of universal harmony. This prayer, like some elements of the petitionary prayers in the *T'filah*, once contained obviously anti-Christian references; modern political sensitivities have led to such sentiments being toned down in all but a few prayerbooks.

The final prayer is the *Kaddish*, which glorifies God's power. This Aramaic prayer appears in various guises at different points of the service – in Orthodox liturgy, a shorter version of it (called the half *Kaddish*)[2] is recited between each of the sections of the service outlined above. It is perhaps best known as a prayer to be recited by mourners, not just at the time of

---

[1] See chapter 36
[2] Eg see World Union Edition of *Mishkan T'filah*, p.57

bereavement but, more obviously in an Orthodox context where they stand and say it alone, for the year following, and on the anniversary of,[1] the death of a close relative or loved one.[2,3] A service would then be completed with a final hymn.

As already mentioned, Progressive Judaism tends only to conduct communal worship ceremonies on *Shabbat* and festivals. Weekday prayers are a matter of personal preference and Progressive Jews are encouraged to engage in individual daily worship and reflection. Because of the traditional preference for a *minyan*, communal worship, services take place in some Orthodox communities three times daily (though this includes the *Sh'ma* only in the evening and the morning, as it includes the words 'when you lie down and when you rise up'). Moreover, in Orthodox tradition, an additional service is appended to the morning service on *Shabbat* and festivals as a parallel to the extra sacrifice offered on those occasions in Temple times – adding still more material and length to their services.

---

[1] Traditionally referred to as *Yahrzeit* (German/Yiddish for anniversary). See p. 151

[2] Recognising that everyone – not just mourners – should acknowledge God as the ultimate power of the Universe as embodied in these words, and also that, following the *Shoah*, there are many victims who have no-one left to say kaddish for them, it is usual today within Progressive synagogues for the entire congregation to join in its recitation, preceding this with a reading that offers consolation to the bereaved - See The World Union Edition of *Mishkan T'filah*, pp. 592-7. However, congregants who are not mourning for their own loved-ones may use an undertone, joining in full voice with the traditional responses which are indicated in bold print, see World Union Edition of *Mishkan T'filah*, p. 598.

[3] It is important to note that the Mourner's *Kaddish* is not said to assist the person who has died, but rather the mourner themselves. Therefore it is perfectly in order to say *Kaddish* even for a loved one who was not Jewish.

Despite the manner in which they are read or chanted, many 'prayers' in the *siddur* (prayerbook) are not prayers at all. They are opportunities or invitations to study – an activity the Rabbis believed to be an essential element of the act of prayer. The traditional liturgy includes several passages from the *Mishnah*, for example, which are clearly aimed at developing the knowledge and awareness of the worshipper rather than petitioning the Almighty. This is particularly evident in the public reading of Torah, the purpose of which is to instruct the congregation.

Regular public readings from the Torah were introduced in rabbinic times, though they are referred to in the Bible (e.g. Nehemiah 8:1-8). Historically, these took place on occasions when the people would gather together (Mondays and Thursdays which were traditionally market days) and on *Shabbat* (when, presumably, in the absence of commercial activity, public gatherings for the purpose of study and prayer were encouraged). The development of the vocalisation of the text of the Hebrew Bible was the work of a group known as the Masoretes, (from *m'sorah,* meaning 'tradition'). By the ninth century, this task had been completed and, in addition, the Five Books of Moses had been divided into sections to be read each week. One tradition suggests that there were over 150 such sections, and that the reading of the entire Torah was spread over three years. The current accepted practice is the division into 54 sections or *parshiyyot* (allowing for leap years, with an extra month[1]), with the entire Torah being completed and restarted every autumn, at the festival of *Simchat Torah.* Sometimes, when there are fewer Sabbaths in a Jewish year owing to fluctuations in the calendar[2] and the dates on which

---

[1] See p. 115
[2] For more detail about the Hebrew calendar, which is based on lunar months, see p. 115

particular festivals fall, certain portions can be combined and there are special readings assigned to particular festivals.

The Masoretic division of the biblical text means that each *Shabbat* in the Jewish calendar is defined by the portion that is assigned to it. Thus, the first *Shabbat* after *Simchat Torah* is *Shabbat B'reishit* (taking its name from the opening word of the portion that is to be read on that *Shabbat*) when Genesis 1:1 to 6:8 is read. The second is *No'ach* (Genesis 6:9 – 11:32), and so on. There is clear evidence that the reading of Torah was regarded as an educational process. In rabbinic times, the everyday language of the people was Aramaic and there are many accounts of the Torah being read aloud in Hebrew a verse at a time and then translated into Aramaic – and often elaborated upon by the translator. This principle, that the reading of Torah should be an educational exercise, comprehensible to the congregation, has been wholeheartedly adopted by Progressive Judaism. A short section of each weekly portion is read, translated and explained to the congregation and, in some congregations, a discussion might well ensue.

In an Orthodox synagogue, the entire week's portion is chanted solely in Hebrew. On Shabbat it is divided into seven sections, and the reading of each section is preceded and concluded with a blessing recited by a member of the congregation who has been called to the Torah. The first of these 'honours', known as an *aliyah*,[1] is given to a *kohen*,[2] the second to a Levite and the other five to those members of the congregation who are known

---

[1] *Aliyah* – Hebrew word meaning 'ascent' – when a person is 'called up' by name to recite blessings before and after the reading of the Torah.
[2] Based on tribal divisions outlined in the Bible, a *kohen* (priest, plural *kohanim*) is a descendant – via paternal descent – of Aaron the High Priest. Members of the tribe of Levi (Levites) were assigned the task of assisting the priests with Temple worship while the remaining 11 tribes, the Israelites, looked on.
These divisions, generally regarded as archaic and irrelevant by Progressive Judaism (see chapter 31), are still a feature of Orthodox Judaism.

as Israelites. The eighth and final reading is called the *maftir* ('concluding') and the person reading it also reads the *haftarah* – an Aramaic word from the same root, meaning 'conclusion.' This is an additional reading from the Prophets, usually based on a theme suggested in the Torah portion – referred to in traditional Ashkenazi pronunciation as '*haftorah*' and often assumed, wrongly, to derive from the same root as the word 'Torah'.

The reading of the Torah on a *Shabbat* morning follows the conclusion of the *T'filah*. The removal of the scroll from the ark for the public reading is an elaborate affair, accompanied by liturgical elements and, in most synagogues, a procession of the scroll before and/or after its reading. The person who is given the honour of carrying and elevating the scroll is called *hagba'ah* and the one who removes and replaces the mantle and other ornaments is referred to as *g'lilah*. A reading of the Torah usually sees a member of the congregation on hand with a fully pointed text (i.e. with vowels and cantillation marks; the handwritten text of the Torah has only consonants) to correct any misreading and ensure complete accuracy.

Because of the focus on the educational rather than the ritual purpose of reading from the Torah, in a Progressive synagogue fewer people are likely to be called up to recite the blessings, a much shorter selection from the week's portion is read or chanted, and generally translated, or preceded by an introduction, and the *haftarah* is usually read in English. Some Progressive synagogues would not process the scroll since the practice of bowing to it and touching it with the fringes of the *tallit* was frowned upon. This custom has however been reintroduced in many Progressive congregations, perhaps to emphasise that the Torah (and its message) should not be restricted to the *bimah* (the rostrum from which the service is conducted) but rather belongs to the entire congregation.

The Torah is also read at the major festivals[1] when there are specific readings allocated to particular days, reflecting the nature of the festival being celebrated. Again, the readings in Progressive synagogues tend to be shorter than those heard on such occasions only in Hebrew by Orthodox congregations: the purpose is to provide insight about the origins and purposes of the festival in question.

Jewish liturgy has always endeavoured to fulfil the Jewish yearning to establish and maintain communication between the Jewish people and their God. As such, it serves a dual function: a series of statements or requests directed towards the Almighty, acknowledging the role God plays in human life, mixed with reminders of our human responsibility and duty to conduct ourselves in such a way as to encourage and inspire us to carry out the divine will. This process has undergone many changes with the passage of time – and will doubtless continue to do so in the future. Its purpose remains the same and it is a major feature of Judaism past, present and future, however expressed.

---

[1] High Holydays and Pilgrim festivals; see chapters 19 and 20

18

THE SABBATH

We affirm the importance of **Shabbat** *('Sabbath'): the sanctification of the seventh day as a day of rest and joy, study and worship, which may be observed by cessation from work and positive acts of celebration, such as the kindling of lights,* **Kiddush** *('Sanctification') and* **Havdalah** *('Separation').*

The Sabbath

Although Jewish tradition dictates that Jews should pray three times a day, the reality is that worship on the Sabbath features far more prominently in Judaism than regular daily worship. 'More than Israel has kept the Sabbath, the Sabbath has kept Israel.' This oft-quoted observation by the Ukrainian (later Israeli) Jewish writer Achad Ha-am, is an ideal starting point for a consideration of the vital place of *Shabbat* in Judaism.

The historical origins of a day of rest to be taken every seventh day are difficult to identify, as is the reason that the seventh day was selected. Orthodox tradition might point to the creation story in the opening chapter of the Book of Genesis, where God creates the world in six days and rests on the seventh, as being the reason for resting every seventh day while a Progressive view would suggest that the Genesis story was written to explain the custom rather than being a basis for it.

Whatever the origins of *Shabbat*, its importance in Jewish tradition cannot be overestimated. There are frequent references to it in the Torah, including the Ten Commandments. There are two reasons underpinning the commandment relating to *Shabbat*: it should remind those who observe it of the Israelites' escape from slavery in Egypt and it should cause us to remember the creation of the world and our place in it. These are specified in the fourth commandment in Deuteronomy and Exodus respectively,[1] along with the instruction that people should refrain from working on the Sabbath day.

Shabbat is referred to on several other occasions in the Torah, each reference emphasising the requirement to refrain from work and, sometimes, adding further restrictions. For example, Exodus 35:3 adds a prohibition against lighting fires on *Shabbat* in addition to the instruction not to work, while Exodus 16:29

---
[1] Deuteronomy 5:12-15; Exodus 20:8-11

states that no-one may leave their abode on *Shabbat*. Moreover, the punishments for breaking *Shabbat* laws are severe indeed. Exodus 31:15 demands that anyone working on *Shabbat* should be put to death. In an incident in the Book of Numbers, when an Israelite is found gathering wood on *Shabbat*, this is precisely what occurs.[1]

Modern-day observance of *Shabbat* is a long way from this brutally enforced biblical prohibition against working. The basic premise of a Progressive Jewish observance of *Shabbat* is a recognition that its purpose is to allow human beings to take a break from their weekly routine to recuperate spiritually and physically from the rigours of the working week. Progressive Judaism does not believe that this can necessarily be achieved by imposing a series of restrictions on human activity. It prefers to seek out the spirit of Jewish law rather than abide by its precise letter. Thus, Progressive Jews are encouraged to find a level of observance that is meaningful to them as individuals and families. A starting point for this might be a sense that *Shabbat* activity should be qualitatively different from regular weekday activities. In a Progressive Jewish context, any activity that encourages relaxation, reflection and an opportunity to share time with family could be considered a suitable for *Shabbat*, even though it might fall foul of strict rabbinic interpretation of biblical law. Moreover, Progressive Judaism prefers to focus on the celebration of *Shabbat,* reflecting Isaiah's statement that, 'you shall call the Sabbath a delight.'[2], rather than on the upholding of biblical prohibitions. As such, it encourages rituals and practices that will inspire and uplift rather than restrict and prohibit, in the hope that Progressive Jews might – in the words of American Reform Rabbi Gunther Plaut '...understand that doing nothing, being silent and open to the world, letting things happen inside, can be as important

---

[1] Numbers 15:32-36.
[2] Isaiah 58:13

as, and sometimes more important than, what we commonly call useful.'[1]

There are many such opportunities offered by *Shabbat*. The ordering of time suggested at the end of each day of creation in the opening chapter of Genesis ('and there was evening, and there was morning'[2]), means that each day in the Jewish calendar begins at sunset. So it is that *Shabbat* is welcomed by lighting candles on a Friday evening. Progressive Jews are encouraged to kindle *Shabbat* candles at a time that denotes the conclusion of their working week rather than at a specific time (in Orthodox tradition this should be no less than twenty-three minutes before sunset). The blessing for the candles for *Shabbat* can be found on page 118 of the World Union Edition of *Mishkan T'filah*, and concludes '*asher kid'shanu b'mitzvotav, v'tzivanu l'hadlik ner shel* **Shabbat** (*v'shel Yom Tov*). Although traditional Judaism regards this kindling as the woman's role (the housewife and mother), this moving ritual to mark the end of the working week and the start of *Shabbat* can be carried out by anyone – with or without the presence of other Jews.

This Progressive approach to Jewish tradition should be borne in mind as rituals and customs relating to *Shabbat* are outlined (similarly the approach to other festivals and occasions in subsequent chapters). The fact that Progressive Judaism does not require its members to adhere rigidly to the Orthodox practices relating to the observance of festivals and life cycle events should neither be regarded as a rejection of them nor as an expression of weakness or laziness (an accusation that is often levelled against Progressive Judaism by Orthodox opponents). Rather it is an attempt to incorporate those elements of tradition that best emphasise the spirit of Judaism the ritual is intended to encourage. This is more fully examined

---

[1] *A Shabbat Manual*, Rabbi Gunther Plaut, CCAR, 1972, p.79
[2] e.g. Genesis 1:5

in a later chapter that focuses specifically on this Progressive principle of informed choice.[1] What follows will outline the traditions that have developed over centuries and that are the basis of the choices about which Progressive Jews should seek to inform themselves.

Attending synagogue is one way to foster the spirit of *Shabbat*. Services take place on Friday evenings and Saturday mornings. Progressive synagogues tend to hold their *Erev Shabbat* (Sabbath Eve) services at the same time every Friday evening; like the candle lighting, their timing is not tied to the setting of the sun. Such services may incorporate a communal supper, providing an opportunity for many congregants to share *Shabbat* customs that might traditionally be conducted in the home. These customs would include *kiddush* - a blessing over wine to welcome *Shabbat* – and *ha-motzi,* the blessing for bread recited over two special *Shabbat* loaves, called *challot*, (two loaves to represent the double portion of *mannah* the Israelites gathered on the sixth day in the wilderness[2] - a single loaf is called a *challah*). Following the *Shabbat* meal, *birkat ha-mazon* (Grace after Meals) might be recited and the singing of *z'mirot* (*Shabbat* songs) would conclude the evening. Whether these customs are observed in the synagogue or in the home, they are conducted in a festive atmosphere designed to emphasise the distinction between *Shabbat* and the other days of the week.

A service is also held on Saturday morning. The emphasis on the combination of learning and celebration that is a feature of Jewish worship is evident here. As described elsewhere,[3] the reading and explanation of a portion of the Torah is a major element of this service, as is the *kiddush* – a celebration with wine, bread and various snacks – that follows it.

---

[1] See chapter 39
[2] Exodus 16:5
[3] See previous chapter.

As *Shabbat* draws to a close and the ordinary weekdays beckon, there are symbols and rituals with which to conclude this special day. This ceremony is known as *Havdalah* (separation) and it separates the holiness of *Shabbat* from the six ordinary days of the week. Three ceremonial items are used for the *havdalah* service: a glass of wine, a special multi-wicked candle and a spice box. A blessing is recited over each and then the wine is used to extinguish the candle, symbolising the conclusion of *Shabbat* after which members of the family greet one another with the words *Shavu'a Tov* – a good week![1]

As already explained, the purpose of *Shabbat* in Progressive Judaism is to relax, reflect and benefit from its spirit – a sense of appreciation of the world and an opportunity for spiritual and physical rest and renewal – rather than strict adherence to *Shabbat* regulations. But the place and the importance of *Shabbat* in the life of all Jews is indisputable: an awareness of this weekly day of rest resides in the heart of every Jew, regardless of how it is acknowledged or observed.

---

[1] The short service for *Havdalah* can be found on pages 610-616 of the World Union Edition of *Mishkan T'filah*

19

THE CALENDAR AND THE DAYS OF AWE

We affirm the importance of the Days of Awe **(Yamim Nora'im)**, *comprising* **Rosh ha-Shanah** *("New Year") and* **Yom Kippur** *("Day of Atonement"), devoted to deep reflection, repentance and spiritual renewal.*

The Calendar and the Days of Awe

The Jewish year is punctuated by a series of festivals, the most ancient of which relate to the agricultural origins of Judaism and are closely linked to the seasons. The calendar is, however, based on the lunar cycle. A lunar month lasts twenty-nine or thirty days, and in ancient times a new month was deemed to have begun with the sighting of the new moon in Jerusalem.[1]

Twelve lunar months total only 354 days whereas the solar year (the time for the earth to revolve around the sun) is 365¼ days. This means that, if no adjustments were made, within a decade *Pesach* – the 'spring' festival – would find itself 90 days earlier (so in the Northern hemisphere winter) while the 'autumn' harvest festival of *Sukkot* would be in their summer. In order to regulate this, a thirteenth month is added seven times every nineteen years between *Adar* and *Nisan*, known as *Adar Sheni* (second *Adar*), to ensure the festivals, based on lunar dates, remain in conjunction with the solar cycle and its seasons.

The order of the months and the festivals that fall in them is shown in the table below – note that the biblical calendar (possibly based on the Babylonian reckoning) regards the year as beginning in the spring of the Northern hemisphere.

HEBREW MONTH	Approximate civil equivalent	FESTIVAL(S) IN THAT MONTH (the **'Major Festivals'** – those referred to in the Five books of Torah – are shown in bold).
1. Nisan	March/April	15th *Pesach* **(first and last days** of 7) 27th *Yom ha-Sho'ah* – Holocaust Memorial Day
2. Iyar	April/May	5th *Yom ha-Atzma'ut* – Israel's Independence Day

---

[1] The need for the sighting of the new moon in Jerusalem to be reported by two independent witnesses became redundant once the establishment of a calendar in the 4th century CE by Hillel II enabled the timing of the new moon to be calculated mathematically.

HEBREW MONTH	Approximate civil equivalent	FESTIVAL(S) IN THAT MONTH* (Festivals referred to in the Torah are shown in bold.)
		18th – *Lag b'Omer* – 33rd day of *Omer*
3. Sivan	May/June	**6th *Shavu'ot***
4. Tamuz	June/July	
5. Av	July/August	9th *Tisha b'Av* – Fast of the 9th of *Av*
6. Elul	August/September	
7. Tishri	September/October	**1st *Rosh ha-Shanah*** **10th *Yom Kippur*** **15th *Sukkot* (first day** of 7days) **22nd *Sh'mini Atzeret*/*Simchat Torah***
8. Cheshvan	October/November	
9. Kislev	November/December	25th *Chanukkah* (8 days) – a 'Minor' festival
10. Tevet	December/January	
11. Sh'vat	January/February	15th *Tu biShvat* – New Year for Trees – a 'Minor' festival
12. Adar - or Adar Sheni in a leap year	February/March	14th *Purim* – a 'Minor' festival

* Minor fast days are not included here.

ROSH HA-SHANAH

Rosh ha-Shanah (literally 'head of the year') is, in fact, the only festival that begins on the first day of the lunar month (*Pesach* and *Sukkot* commence when the moon is full while *Shavu'ot* is a prescribed number of days after *Pesach*). In ancient times, every new moon (*Rosh Chodesh* - literally 'head of the month') was an

The Calendar and the Days of Awe

occasion for celebration in the Temple but the new moon of the seventh month was one of particular importance because it heralded the month in which the most important biblical festival[1] – *Sukkot* – occurred. According to the instructions in the Torah, the *shofar*[2] is sounded on the new moon of the seventh month – most probably to alert the people that final preparations for the harvest should be completed by the full moon.[3]

The sounding of the *shofar* remains a key feature of *Rosh ha-Shanah* celebrations today, though the emphasis of the festival has shifted from an agricultural to a spiritual alert. According to rabbinic tradition, the Book of Life is opened on *Rosh ha-Shanah* and between that day and *Yom Kippur*, God considers who will still be alive the following *Rosh ha-Shanah*. The Rabbis, through the liturgy, assure us that the divine decree can be averted through repentance, prayer and good deeds.[4] So *Rosh ha-Shanah* and the days leading to *Yom Kippur* (known as the Ten Days of Repentance – *aseret y'mei t'shuvah*) are a time for personal reflection and self-judgment. Progressive Judaism rejects the idea of God writing names in a divine book – a concept that troubles many Jews today when, on the occasion of the death of a loved one, they find themselves asking what they, or that individual, failed to do during the most recent period of repentance that led to their name being omitted from the Book of Life.

The act of repentance, in which all Jews are encouraged to engage at this time of year, is known as *t'shuvah*. This word

---

[1] The prominence of *Sukkot* is explained in the next chapter. See p. 131
[2] A horn, usually of a ram, that is hollowed out and used to call the people to attention or as a battle cry (see, e.g. Joshua 6, Psalm 81)
[3] Leviticus 23:24. It is interesting to note that Deuteronomy's description of the festivals, which parallels chapter 23 of Leviticus, makes no reference to *Rosh ha-Shanah* or *Yom Kippur*, emphasising the later emergence of these days.
[4] eg **Gates of Repentance p.109**, *Machzor Ru'ach Chadashah* p. 142.

literally means 'returning' and the implication is that sinning is equivalent to turning away from the correct path and the possibility of returning to that path is always present and should be sought. That this is an ancient concept is attested to by references in Amos, where the people's failure to return to God is bemoaned[1] and in the words of Malachi, 'Return to me that I may return to you.'[2] Thus the idea of the High Holydays being an opportunity to turn one's life around has much popular appeal.

Perhaps because of this, the notion of being inscribed in the Book of Life still prevails and one of the traditional greetings offered at this season is *l'shanah tovah tikkateivu v-t'chateimu* ('May you be inscribed and sealed for a good year'). Despite this most solemn element of this time of year, *Rosh ha-Shanah* is a joyous festival and is welcomed by the exchange of greeting cards. In the home, festival candles are lit and *kiddush* is made to usher in the festival and a feature of this is the dipping of a piece of apple in honey to symbolise the wish for a sweet new year.

In the synagogue, the scrolls and the ark have special white coverings to symbolise the search for purity during this period; a custom that, in some communities, even extends to the Rabbi and some members of the congregation, who may wear a white gown known as a *kittel*. White is also a symbol of death in Judaism, reminding visitors to the synagogue of the challenge, posed in Deuteronomy 30:19, to 'choose life.'

The services are longer than usual and contain additional readings encouraging the reflection and self-examination that are a feature of this solemn time. Special Torah and *haftarah* readings are incorporated in the *Rosh ha-Shanah* service: Progressive Jews usually choose between the story of the

---

[1] Amos 4:6-11
[2] Malachi 3:7, also Zechariah 1:3.

The Calendar and the Days of Awe

Binding of Isaac (Genesis 22) or the previous chapter, which talks about the banishment of Hagar and Ishmael. In Orthodox synagogues, where two days of *Rosh ha-Shanah* are observed, one of these chapters is read on each day.[1] An invitation to 'Seek the Eternal One while God can be found...'[2] is the call from the Prophet Isaiah that features in the *haftarah*.

The blowing of the *shofar*, from which *Rosh ha-Shanah* derives another of its names – *Yom T'ru'ah* ('the day of blowing the horn'), – occurs towards the end of the service, when the service leader calls out the notes for the *shofar* blower to play. There are three distinct notes: *t'ki'yah* (blowing) is a long single blast, *sh'varim* (broken) is three shorter blasts while *t'ru'ah* (alarm) is seven staccato blasts. Each sequence of blasts on the *shofar* is preceded by a series of readings emphasising God's sovereignty (*malchuyyot*), God's remembrance of our ancestors (*zichronot*) and the anticipation of the messianic age that will be heralded by the blowing of the *shofar* (*shofarot*). An extended single blast, *t'ki'yah g'dolah* (*g'dolah* = great), concludes each of these sequences.

Orthodox tradition prohibits the blowing of the *shofar* on *Shabbat* since it was decreed that this could only happen in Jerusalem while the Temple stood. According to a legend, when *Rosh ha-Shanah* fell on a *Shabbat* for the first time after the destruction of the Second Temple, the Rabbis – whose new centre was in Yavneh – were debating whether or not to blow the *shofar*. Rabbi Yochanan ben Zakkai, who believed it should be blown, announced that as the time for blowing the *shofar* was approaching, the *shofar* blowing should take place and the discussion should continue afterwards. When the debate resumed, he pointed out that the precedent had now been

---

[1] The reason for the Orthodox practice of observing an extra day for some festivals – including *Rosh ha-Shanah* – can be found in chapter 41, on p. 261.
[2] Isaiah 55:1

119

established and so henceforth the *shofar* could be blown on *Shabbat*. His colleagues overruled him, however, so the prohibition remains in Orthodox synagogues. As most Progressive Jews celebrate only one day of *Rosh ha-Shanah*, and so might not hear the *shofar* at all were this prohibition to remain in place, it is usually blown in Progressive Synagogues.

YOM KIPPUR

Ten days after *Rosh ha-Shanah* comes the Day of Atonement – *Yom Kippur*. This is the most solemn day in the Jewish calendar. The instructions relating to it in the Torah tell the people that they should 'afflict their souls'. [1] This is interpreted as meaning that we should refrain from eating or drinking for the whole day in order to demonstrate a level of sacrifice and self-discipline and to help us to concentrate on the self-examination that is the focus of this most awesome of days.

The biblical significance of *Yom Kippur* is described in detail in chapter 16 of the Book of Leviticus. As the concept of divine reward and punishment became a feature of the developing relationship between Israel and its God, a sense emerged that the autumn rains – requests for which were a feature of *Sukkot* celebrations – could be withheld by the divine power if the people had sinned in some way. In order to protect against this potential catastrophe, a day of repentance was introduced into the calendar shortly before the full moon of the seventh month. This was effectively a national apology to God, asking that any sins be forgiven ahead of the annual request for rain. The 'apology' was offered by the High Priest on behalf of himself and his family, the priesthood and the whole Israelite people. The sins of all these were symbolically placed upon the head of a goat (the scapegoat) that was despatched into the wilderness, to carry those sins away, allowing the Israelites to look forward

---

[1] Leviticus 23:27

to the *Sukkot* celebrations with – they hoped – a clear conscience.

This ancient priestly ritual is referred to at the very heart of the day of *Yom Kippur*. In traditional services, it is related – to some extent even re-enacted – during the *Musaf* (additional) service, where the words of the High Priest are recited and many congregants respond as did their ancient ancestors – by prostrating themselves before the open ark, which symbolises the Holy of Holies, the heart of the Temple to which only the High Priest had access. The Progressive version of the service makes reference to this ancient rite but only as part of the development of Judaism, acknowledging that it belongs firmly to Judaism's ancient past and is not something that Progressive Jews wish to see reintroduced.[1]

The other worship services that surround the *Musaf* contain many features that are unique to *Yom Kippur*. The service that ushers in *Yom Kippur* is best known for the *Kol Nidrei* prayer (the name by which the eve of *Yom Kippur* is better known). The traditional version of this prayer asks that vows from the past year that cannot be fulfilled be annulled. This ancient Aramaic version has been replaced by a modern Hebrew version in the Progressive *machzor*[2], but the haunting melody has been retained. The evening service tends to be quite long and is the only occasion during the year when it is customary for worshippers to don a *tallit* for evening prayers.[3]

Services for the day of *Yom Kippur* are designed to carry worshippers through the day until the conclusion of the fast after sunset. Beginning with the morning service (*Shacharit*),

---

[1] See chapter 30
[2] *Machzor* – a prayerbook for use at festivals; particularly the High Holydays.
[3] A *tallit* is only worn at daytime services unless one is leading or taking an active part in the service; perhaps the implication is that everyone is taking an active part in this most important of evening services.

there may be a *Musaf* service, mentioned above, after which come the afternoon (*Minchah*), Memorial (*Yizkor*) and concluding (*Ne'ilah*) services[1]. Each of these services includes a version of the *T'filah*, which contains insertions specifically relating to the nature of *Yom Kippur*, asking for forgiveness and to be inscribed in the Book of Life (metaphorically, of course). Again there are special scriptural readings in the morning and afternoon services: from the Torah come powerful excerpts from Deuteronomy relating to the covenant and from the Holiness Code in Leviticus 19 while the *haftarah* readings come from Isaiah in the morning (a section reminding us that the fast God requires is one where 'the chains of injustice are loosened…')[2] and the story of Jonah is a highlight of the afternoon service. The Memorial service is a particularly solemn moment, when congregants have the opportunity to recall loved ones with whom they have observed previous High Holydays but who are no longer alive. It is worth mentioning that a 'custom' that says that children whose parents are still alive should not attend this service is little more than a superstition and is not observed in Progressive Jewish communities.

The *Ne'ilah* service brings the Day of Atonement and the ten day period of the Days of Awe (*Yamim Nora'im*) to a close with a final blast on the *shofar* – a resounding conclusion to the most significant and dramatic period in the Jewish year. It is no coincidence that many Jews who tend to ignore or neglect their Judaism for most of the year make an annual appearance at services on *Rosh ha-Shanah* or *Yom Kippur*. These days, perhaps more than any other in the Jewish calendar, mysteriously call out to all Jews from their ancient past to remind them of their heritage and their responsibility and attachment to it.

---

[1] In Orthodox tradition, the *Yizkor* (Memorial) service precedes the *Minchah* afternoon service
[2] Isaiah 58

20

THE THREE PILGRIMAGE FESTIVALS

We affirm the importance of the 'Three Pilgrimage Festivals', comprising **Pesach** *('Passover'),* **Shavu'ot** *('Pentecost') and* **Sukkot** *('Tabernacles') followed by* **Simchat Torah** *('Rejoicing in the Torah'), celebrating Freedom, Revelation and Joy*

The three pilgrimage festivals are so named because these were the three occasions in the year when the ancient Israelites were expected to make the journey to Jerusalem to take their offerings to the Temple. The festivals of *Pesach, Shavu'ot* and *Sukkot* were primarily harvest festivals and had enormous significance for the people of the Ancient Near East who were so dependent upon the land and its climate for their survival and well-being.

The Temple in Jerusalem was the focal point for the ancient Israelites to celebrate these special agricultural festivals. The occasions when the people came from far and wide to make their festival offerings were times of great joy, reflected in Psalms 113-118, known as *Hallel* (praise), which we recite or sing in our synagogue services on such occasions. Modern day renditions of the *Hallel* can feel like a rather pale reflection of the way the ancient Israelites would have uttered them as they climbed the hills to Jerusalem (it is for this reason several psalms are referred to as *'Shir Ha'ma'alot* - Songs of Ascent') with joyful exuberance and excitement. That much of this exuberance seems to be lacking from the modern celebration of these festivals is lamentable; increased awareness of the joy experienced by Judaism's ancestors at these special occasions might help to recapture some of it in our services.

PESACH

Pesach is a spring festival in the Land of Israel (although of course it is autumn in the Southern Hemisphere). As with the other pilgrim festivals, its significance is primarily agricultural; any connection with an historical event in the life of the ancient Israelites was subsequently added to a celebration that already existed. In time, *Pesach* came to have the Exodus from Egypt associated with it and, as a result, the theme of freedom implicit in and inspired by that ancient event is the focus of the festival. Progressive Judaism will always seek to emphasise this

The Three Pilgrimage Festivals

message, and Progressive observance of this – and all – festivals, seeks to encourage an understanding that rituals and ceremonies are meant to remind us of our human duty towards God and our fellow human beings rather than to be regarded as ends in themselves.

The agricultural significance of *Pesach* is that it celebrates the arrival of spring in the land of Israel, and the end of winter. For Ancient Near Eastern shepherds, it was a time to celebrate the birth of new lambs (by sacrificing some of them); for farmers in that region, it was the beginning of the barley harvest. *Pesach* is also known as *Chag ha-Matzot* (Festival of unleavened bread) perhaps a reference to the ancient practice of removing yeast and leavened material that may have gone bad during the winter months. So the festival was a type of 'spring cleaning', where leaven was effectively banished for seven days, after which fresh foodstuff was available for bread-making and other preparations.

In modern times, this is reflected in the traditional practice of clearing one's house of any leaven on the day before *Pesach* starts; there is a custom of searching for crumbs and of burning any leavened material prior to the start of the festival. The biblical instructions regarding the prohibition of leaven[1] have led to a host of regulations and restrictions on what foods may be used or kept in Jewish homes during *Pesach*. Progressive Jews are encouraged to decide their own level of *Pesach* observance – at minimum replacing ordinary bread with *matzah* (unleavened bread) for the duration of the festival as a symbolic reminder of its significance as 'the bread of affliction'[2], calling to mind the continued presence of suffering and oppression in the world. Orthodox Jewry, however, has elaborate procedures for defining leavened material, seeking it out, disposing of it and replacing it with food deemed to be free of it. A rabbinic

---

[1] Exodus 13:7
[2] This description of unleavened bread is found in the *haggadah*.

invention, presumably intended to avoid the wastage involved in burning leavened foods, is to provide a document that transfers the ownership of any such items in one's house to a non-Jew for the duration of the festival. Such legal fictions, designed to adhere to the letter of biblical law while paying scant regard to its purpose, are not a feature of Progressive Judaism. Once all leavened food is removed from the house, it may be replaced with items that are specifically marked '*Kosher for Passover*'. Supermarket shelves are filled with – and emptied of – such products during this time as this culinary aspect of *Pesach* carries great significance for many Jews.

The ancient agricultural customs associated with the spring that led to these practices were subsequently combined with the story of the Israelite Exodus from Egypt. Thus the custom of eating unleavened bread is explained by the suggestion that the fleeing Israelites did not have time to wait for their dough to rise before setting out on their journey.[1] The sacrifice of one of the enduring symbols of spring-time – a lamb – was also incorporated into the story of events immediately preceding the Exodus,[2] to give this historical experience a place in the Israelites' annual calendar; an egg is similarly included.

There are various explanations offered regarding the events commemorated at this festival: a literal reading of the story in the biblical Book of Exodus is difficult to support, and other theories, suggesting that the plagues were extreme and exceptional natural phenomena of which the Israelites were able to take advantage, may also be considered. In the end, however, the exact nature of what took place in Egypt over three thousand years ago is not as important as its effect: as the Talmud itself states, 'our story begins in degradation and ends in glory'.[3] In other words, the festival of *Pesach* is a celebration

---

[1] Exodus 12:34
[2] Exodus 12:3 ff.
[3] *Mishnah Pesachim* 10:4

The Three Pilgrimage Festivals

of the transition from slavery to freedom, however it may have occurred.

This transition – and the Jewish duty to work for freedom wherever there is oppression – is the focus of the *seder* meal. Traditional Judaism observes two *seder* nights[1]; Progressive Judaism observes the first night of *seder* to fulfil the commandment, but the second night is often used as an opportunity for a communal *seder* meal to be held in synagogues. The *seder* is a response to the biblical verse 'You shall tell your child on that day what the Eternal One did for me when I was brought out of Egypt'.[2] The entire purpose of the *seder* is for the transition from slavery to freedom to be explained to the next generation; all the symbols and rituals are designed to remind the *seder* participants of the content of the story to be transmitted. The fact that so many of the symbols are unique and unusual is a deliberate attempt to awaken the curiosity of the children so that they might ask the four questions of the reading known as *'Mah nishtanah'*, beginning with the words: 'Why is this night different from all other nights?'.

The night is different for many reasons. In the middle of the table is a *seder* plate that contains the following items: a roasted shank-bone *(zero'a)*, symbolic of the Paschal lamb, a roasted egg *(beitzah)*, symbolic of the festival offering or of fertility, bitter herbs *(maror)*, such as horseradish, symbolic of the bitter life endured by the Israelite slaves, green herbs *(karpas)* such as parsley, symbolic of the springtime, a paste made from nuts, apple, cinnamon and wine *(charoset)*, symbolic of the mortar that the Israelite slaves used to build the store cities, and a bowl of salt water, symbolic of the tears shed by the slaves. There is also a plate with three pieces of unleavened bread *(matzah)*.

---

[1] The reason for the Orthodox practice of observing an extra day for some festivals – including *Rosh ha-Shanah* – can be found in chapter 41, on p. 261.
[2] Exodus 13:8

Part of the middle *matzah* will be used as the *afikoman*, for which children will later search. The origins of this custom are uncertain, as is the meaning of the Greek word *afikoman,* but its main purpose may well be to keep the attention of the children.

The meal is meant to be a type of freedom banquet (hence the custom of leaning – an imitation of the Roman practice). At the time the structure of the *seder* was being formalised by the Rabbis, the Romans ruled Judea with brutal oppression, and to imitate the Romans was to imply freedom from their domination. The focal point is the reading of the *haggadah* (literally 'telling'), the book that explains the symbols, tells the story, and contains prayers and songs that are all elements of the *seder.* During the *seder*, four cups of wine are drunk – a number that invites various interpretations of the significance of the number four. The Rabbis of old had a disagreement as to whether or not a fifth cup should be drunk and this led to the custom of pouring, but not drinking, a further cup and leaving it for the prophet Elijah who, according to Talmudic tradition, would resolve all such unanswered questions. The fact that Elijah's arrival also heralds the coming of the Messiah in Orthodox tradition permits the fifth cup of wine to be regarded as a symbol of the Messianic Age when all will enjoy freedom. New customs and symbols are sometimes incorporated into Progressive *seder* ritual: a 'cup of Miriam' may note the role of Moses' and Aaron's sister Miriam as a source of sustenance for the Israelites on their journey from slavery, through the wilderness to the Promised Land, and an orange has become a reminder of women's equality. The purpose of all these symbols is to draw attention to the historical message of *Pesach* and the duty to seek to implement it in the modern world.

THE OMER AND SHAVU'OT

The festival of *Shavu'ot,* which literally means 'weeks', falls seven weeks after Passover. Beginning on the second day of Passover, the ancient Israelites counted forty-nine days and celebrated a festival on the fiftieth day. The instruction to count, by weeks and days, is still observed by some Jews every evening through this period.[1] The seven weeks, referred to as the *Omer*, was a time when a hot dry wind might blow in and blight the young crops (this wind is known today as the *hamsin*, which is Arabic for 'fifty') so the end of this weather and the newly grown harvest was an occasion for celebration. On this fiftieth day, the 6th of *Sivan*, the ancient Israelites would once again journey to Jerusalem to offer the first fruits (another name for *Shavu'ot* is *chag ha-bikkurim* – festival of the first fruits).

Once the Temple had been destroyed, the tradition of taking first fruits to Jerusalem inevitably came to an end. The Rabbis looked for a new significance for the festival of *Shavu'ot*. According to the Torah, the Israelites arrived in the wilderness of Sinai '....on the third new moon after the Israelites had gone forth from Egypt.'[2] It was at this point that the Israelites received the Ten Commandments at Mount Sinai. Since *Pesach* is celebrated in the middle of the first month and seven weeks from that date falls at the start of the third month, the Rabbis concluded that the revelation at Sinai must have taken place at *Shavu'ot*. Thus, once again, historical significance was attached to what had previously been an exclusively agricultural festival.

The consequence of this is that *Shavu'ot* is now regarded as *z'man matan torateinu* – the occasion of the giving of Torah. This theme of revelation has given rise to a custom of studying sections of the Torah all through the night – an event known as *Tikkun leyl Shavu'ot*. Another *Shavu'ot* tradition is that only dairy foods are consumed. Explanations for this are that Jews without Torah are like babies without milk, or that prior to the giving of Torah, the Israelites were not aware of the dietary laws relating to milk and meat, so we consume only milky

---

[1] Leviticus 23:15, and see *Mishkan T'filah*, page 570. The procedure is known as *S'firat Ha'Omer,* Counting the *Omer*.
[2] Exodus 19:1

foods. Anyway, it's a perfect opportunity to eat cheesecake! Other *Shavu'ot* traditions include the decoration of the synagogue with flowers (perhaps to remind us of the festival's origins in nature) and the reading of the Book of Ruth. This story, although set in the time of the Judges, was probably written following the exile in Babylon. This was a time when foreign wives were banned[1] and Ruth's commitment to the God of her mother-in-law Naomi[2] was intended to emphasise that belonging to the religion practised in the time of Ezra (which would eventually become Judaism) was dependent on one's sincerity, not lineage. This commitment is emphasised at *Shavu'ot* with the reading from the Torah of the revelation at Sinai, including the Ten Commandments.

SUKKOT

The earth's bounty, which grew in the Ancient Near East throughout the long hot summer, was ripe for harvest in their early autumn. For a society almost entirely dependent upon what the earth produced, this was a crucial time of the year. The need to gather in the harvest quickly and efficiently was paramount and the religious impulse to offer gratitude for God's gifts found expression once this had been carried out. But the festival of *Sukkot* was more than just a celebration of the ingathered harvest; the minds of those celebrating its festivities were also focused on the following year's harvest, for which rain was urgently required. If this did not happen, there was a danger of famine in the following year. The festival of *Sukkot* addresses all these aspects and concerns of a biblical autumn.

One of the best-known features of *Sukkot* is the tradition that derives from its name. The word means 'booths' (a single booth is a *sukkah*) and refers to the temporary shelters that the Israelites were required to build according to the instructions in

---

[1] See chapter 36, p. 229
[2] Ruth 1:16

Leviticus chapter 23.[1] Once again, it was the Rabbis who attached to this custom the historical connection of the journey through the wilderness; a more likely explanation for it relates to the gathering of the harvest and the need to protect it. Even in our day, native farmers in the area may construct crude huts made of branches and leaves in the midst of their fields at harvest time. They sleep in these for two reasons: firstly to be able to maximise the amount of time available to gather the harvest (rather than wasting time journeying to and from their homes) and secondly to guard the crops that have been gathered. The custom of building these temporary shelters, from branches and leaves, and decorating them with fruit, has remained until this day, even though the original agricultural purpose may have long since been subsumed by the 'historical' meaning. In Israel, the early autumn climate is entirely suited to the requirement to eat and even sleep in these *sukkot*; in many other parts of the world, their function is more symbolic.

The joyful celebration of the harvest is also a feature of this festival. It was without doubt the most popular of the three annual occasions for our ancient ancestors to make their pilgrimage to Jerusalem: it is often referred simply as *'the festival'* in rabbinic and other sources. We can be fairly sure that it was a week-long party, during which the fruits of the harvest were eaten and drunk in great quantity. An additional and unique element of the celebration is the use of the 'four species'. Based on instructions in Leviticus that required the Israelites to 'take the fruit of goodly trees, palm branches, branches of green trees and the willow of the brook and celebrate for seven days before the Eternal One'[2], the Rabbis developed the custom of the *lulav* and *etrog*. Branches from palm, willow and myrtle trees are combined with a citron and are ritually shaken during the recitation of the *Hallel* psalms.[3]

---

[1] Leviticus 23:42
[2] Leviticus 23:40
[3] Psalms 113-118, known collectively as *'Hallel'* (praise). See p. 124.

This custom may well have a connection with an older ritual that relates to another vital aspect of biblical *Sukkot* observance. As mentioned above, the need for rain at this time of the year was paramount in an agricultural society. When it behaved normally, the local climate offered our ancient Israelite ancestors the ideal autumn conditions: the early rain to prepare the ground for sowing and the later rain to water the planted seeds, as suggested in Deuteronomy 11:15 for example, which refers to the early and the late rains. The waving of the *lulav* may well be derived from an ancient rainmaking ritual; if so, it still has relevance in the modern Middle East that regularly suffers from severe drought. The need to request rain in some parts of the world in autumn is, perhaps, less obvious, but the festival of *Sukkot* offers an opportunity to celebrate nature's bounty while the *Sukkah* can serve to remind us of human frailty in the face of nature. The temporary nature of the *Sukkah* that is little protection from the elements can also be used as an opportunity to become involved in projects for the homeless.

SIMCHAT TORAH

Attached to the festival of *Sukkot* is *Sh'mini Atzeret* (the eighth day of conclusion),[1] a biblical festival in its own right. Many centuries later, it was given an additional meaning and name with the rabbinically ordained annual rejoicing of the Torah, *Simchat Torah*. As mentioned earlier, the Torah is divided into 54 sections: that means it is read from start to finish in a year.[2] *Simchat Torah* celebrates the conclusion of the cycle of readings and its immediate recommencement from the beginning.

As its name suggests, this is a day of great joy. The main feature of the celebration is the reading of the concluding verses

---

[1] In Orthodox Judaism, this takes place a day later because two days are observed at the start of *Sukkot* instead of the biblically prescribed one day. See chapter 41, p. 261.
[2] See p. 103

of the Book of Deuteronomy and the opening verses of the first chapter of the Book of Genesis. Two members of the community are given the honour of being called to recite the blessings before and after the reading of these two sections. *Simchat Torah* celebrates the symbolic 'marriage' between the Jewish people and the Torah, and the service is filled with references to a wedding. Those called to the Torah are regarded as being its bride or groom (in Orthodox Judaism, of course, there can only be grooms, as women are not permitted to approach the Torah). The Hebrew word for a bridegroom is *chatan* and that for a bride is *kallah* so those given the honour of reciting the blessings for the end of Deuteronomy and the start of Genesis are called *chatan/kallat Torah* and *chatan/kallat B'reishit* respectively. Before they are read, the scrolls are paraded around the synagogue seven times (the circuits are known as *hakkafot*), carried by members of the congregation to the accompaniment of singing and dancing. Children are encouraged to wave flags and have the opportunity to consume the goodies that are handed out. As well as being a joyful way of concluding the celebration of *Sukkot*, *Simchat* Torah also brings to an end the sequence of festivals that began with *Rosh ha-Shanah* at the start of the Hebrew month of *Tishri*.

This concludes the listing of the seven 'Major Festivals' (those which are listed in the Five Books of the Torah – although sometimes by different names).

The blessing for the candles for the major festivals[1] are found on page 384 of *Mishkan T'filah*, and concludes *'asher kid'shanu b'mitzvotav, v'tzivanu l'hadlik ner shel (Shabbat v'shel)* **Yom Tov**'

The next chapter continues with the more 'Minor Festivals' (which date to later events, but which, because of their festivities, are sometimes confused, especially by children, as the most important festivals!).

---

[1] Except *Rosh Hashanah* and *Yom Kippur*.

21

CHANUKKAH AND OTHER DAYS OF CELEBRATION AND MOURNING

We affirm the importance of the festival of **Chanukkah** *('Rededication') and we encourage the observance of other days of celebration, such as* **Purim** *('Lots') and* **Yom ha-Atzma'ut** *(Israel's 'Independence Day'), and days of mourning such as* **Tish'a b'Av** *('Ninth of Av') and* **Yom ha-Sho'ah** *('Holocaust Day').*

Chanukkah and other days of Celebration and Mourning

The major Jewish festivals, which have already been described, have their roots in the Torah, the Five Books of Moses (with the exception of *Simchat* Torah)[1]. In addition to these, there are a number of minor festivals and fast days the place of which in the Jewish calendar is more related to the history of the Jewish people than the agricultural society in which ancient Israelite religion developed.

CHANUKKAH (Rededication)

One of the best known of these is the eight-day festival of *Chanukkah* that falls on the 25th day of Kislev. The word means 'rededication' and refers to the cleansing of the Temple in Jerusalem after it had been desecrated by the Greeks during the reign of Antiochus in the second century BCE. This ruler, whose power extended over the land of Judea and the city of Jerusalem, wished to impose Greek culture upon the Jewish people (who, it has to be said, had quite enthusiastically accepted that culture) and eradicate Judaism completely (a less acceptable prospect). A group of zealots known as the Maccabees (meaning 'hammer') staged a rebellion against the Greeks who had gone so far as to ban many Jewish practices and establish their own sacrificial worship in the Jerusalem Temple.

The Maccabees and their small group of followers were successful in their attempt to defeat the might of the Greeks and in the winter of the year 165 BCE, drove them out of Jerusalem. They found the Temple in a desecrated state. They cleansed it and then held a festival of rededication. This lasted for eight days, probably in honour of the most recent festivals, the autumn festivals of *Sukkot/Sh'mini Atzeret,* which those involved in fighting the oppressors had missed. Some six hundred years

---

[1] See p. 132

later, an account in the Talmud[1] suggested that the reason for the eight day festival was related to a day's worth of oil lasting for eight days, but this was probably a metaphor for the determination of the Maccabees and their followers to keep the flame of Judaism alive against enormous odds. There is certainly no mention of such a miracle in contemporary sources[2].

Nevertheless, the story of the oil dominates many of the customs relating to the festival of *Chanukkah*, where, as a consequence, fried foods such as doughnuts and *latkes* (fried potato pancakes) are enthusiastically eaten. A special candelabra known as a *chanukkiyah* is used (it is often referred to as a *menorah* though this is less accurate since the original *menorah* was the seven branched candelabra that was constructed for the desert Tabernacle and later adorned the ancient Temple). The *channukiyah* has eight branches plus one holder for the servant candle (known as the *shamash*) that is used to light the other eight; one candle being added for each successive day of the festival, concluding on the eighth day when all the candles are lit. *Chanukkah* has become a time for the exchange of gifts, though this, along with the recent growth in popularity of this festival, may owe more to its proximity to other winter festivals (especially Christmas) than any Jewish custom. As with other festivals of light at this time of the year, its purpose was especially to brighten the dark days and nights of the winter in the northern hemisphere, where it originated.[3]

TU BISHVAT (New Year for Trees)

This minor festival is observed on 15th *Sh'vat* (*'Tu'* = 15), coinciding with the January - February period, and is first

---

[1] *Shabbat* 21b
[2] i.e. The Books of Maccabees
[3] The short home service for *Chanukkah* can be found on page 572 of the World Union Edition of *Mishkan T'filah*

Chanukkah and other days of Celebration and Mourning

mentioned in the *Mishnah*[1]. In Israel at this time, the winter is passing and the sap is beginning to fill the trees, bringing the spring blossom. Children are particularly encouraged to go out and plant saplings. In other countries it provides an opportunity to publicise the work of the Jewish National Fund with regard to land reclamation and afforestation. More recently, it has become an occasion to consider human responsibility for protecting the environment. Many congregations also use this theme as the basis for a *Tu biShvat seder* – a festive meal similar in style to the Passover *seder*, that celebrates the fruits of Israel and nature's gifts to humankind.

PURIM ('Lots')

The biblical book of Esther is the source of this carnival festival with its fancy dress and riotous behaviour. This book tells the story – certainly fictional – of events that befell the Jews in Persia during the reign of King Ahasuerus (believed by some, probably erroneously, to be the 4th century BCE Persian ruler Ataxerxes). An evil prime minister called *Haman*, allegedly a descendant of the biblical Amalek, decided to wipe out the Jews. He cast lots to decide the date (*pur* means 'lot' in Hebrew, plural *purim*) on which the execution should take place. The king's wife was a Jewess, Esther, and her uncle, Mordechai, found out about the plot and advised his niece to confront *Haman* and the King. She did so and the outcome was that *Haman* and his ten sons were hanged. This improbable account ends with brutal revenge being exacted on the Persians by the Jews in which more than 75,000 people were killed. An annual day of celebration of these events is established, falling on 14th *Adar*, in February or March (or *Adar Sheni* in a leap year[2]).

The fact that the story is fictitious (and has an extremely violent ending), along with the unruly and often alcohol-enhanced

---
[1] *Mishnah Rosh Hashanah 1:1*
[2] See p. 115

behaviour that is associated with the festival (it is traditional to make as much noise as possible, often using rattles known as *greggars*, to blot out the name of the evil perpetrator *Haman*), meant that for many years some Progressive congregations chose not to observe it.

More recently, however, *Purim* has re-established its place in the calendar of events celebrated in Progressive synagogues. Its serious message is that sadly, in every generation, some individuals seem to develop a baseless hatred against the Jewish people. Indeed our tradition teaches that the cowardly *Amalek* attacked the Israelites in the desert from behind,[1] and that in every generation we find the descendants of *Amalek*. *Haman* is apparently supposed to fit into this mould.[2]

Rather than dwell on this dark message, we celebrate life, and congregants are encouraged to dress up, excerpts from or variations of the Book of Esther are read and a jolly time is had by all. Festivities traditionally include the eating of *hamentaschen*, triangular pastries that are alleged to resemble *Haman's* ears, hat or pockets. Traditionally, *Purim* is the time for giving gifts (called *sh'lach manot*) to friends and to those less well off than ourselves (*matanot l'evyonim* – gifts to the needy).

YOM HA-ATZMA'UT (Israel's Independence Day)

The anniversary of the declaration of Israel's Independence in 1948 falls on the Hebrew date of *Iyar* 5th, at the end of April or early in May. It is an event that is marked in many communities with a ceremony and perhaps a presentation relating to Israel's achievements, and often accompanied by traditional Israeli food! The day preceding Israel's Independence Day is *Yom ha-Zikaron*, a day of memorial for

---

[1] In Deuteronomy 25:18, though there is no mention of this in Exodus 17:8.
[2] Haman is described in Esther 3:1 as an Agagite, and Agag was the king of Amalek whose life King Saul initially saved, contrary to his instructions; see 1st Samuel 15:3, 15:8

Chanukkah and other days of Celebration and Mourning

those who lost their lives establishing and defending the State of Israel, and this is also marked in some of our communities.

TISH'A B'AV (The ninth of Av)

Known as the saddest day in the Jewish year, this falls in July or August. It is the anniversary of the destruction of both the First and Second Temples in Jerusalem (by the Babylonians and Romans respectively) as well as the date on which other tragic events are said to have befallen the Jewish people. Either by coincidence or by design, for example, the decrees expelling the Jews from England (1290) and Spain (1492) were issued or implemented on *Tish'a b'Av*.

Because of its primary association with the Temple, *Tish'a b'Av* is not always observed in Progressive synagogues since we have no wish to see a return to Temple times, with a renewed priesthood, animal sacrifices and centralized Judaism,[1] though its more general reflection on the tragedies that have befallen Judaism over the generations is valuable. Traditionally, Jews fast from dusk to the following sunset and sit on the floor or low stools, and the Book of Lamentations is read. The *Shabbat* immediately preceding *Tish'a b'Av* is known as *Shabbat Chazon* (Vision), the name taken from the traditional *haftarah*, Isaiah's vision (Isaiah 1:1-17) warning of Israel's punishment for failing to do God's will. The *Shabbat* following *Tish'a b'Av* is called *Shabbat Nachamu* (Consolation), again named after the *haftarah* reading on this day which contains the words of consolation (*nachamu, nachamu ami*) offered to the exiled people of Judah by the 'second Isaiah' (Isaiah 40).

YOM HA-SHO'AH (Holocaust Day)

This day of memorial for victims of the Nazi Holocaust up to and during World War Two is marked on the 27th *Nisan*, a date

---

[1] See chapter 30, page 193

that falls during the uprising in the Warsaw ghetto in 1943.[1] The Hebrew word *Sho'ah* means 'catastrophe', and *Yom ha-Sho'ah* is an occasion that attempts to recall some of the horrors of persecution suffered by millions of Europe's Jews at the hands of the Nazis. It is a time for which liturgy and ritual are still developing, usually involving readings, reflections and traditional prayers of mourning.

The question of how one can possibly do justice to the memory of so many victims of barbarity is one that has to be asked. The choice of this particular date actually compounds the difficulty: the event it commemorates was a poorly armed rebellion by the tiny, desperate community of Warsaw's Jews against their Nazi oppressors, an event which, though greatly heroic, does not reflect the experience of the countless numbers of Jews who were led passively to their deaths. Some communities in the Diaspora considered either *Tish'a b'Av* or the anniversary of *Kristallnacht* – 'The Night of Broken Glass' more suitable dates to recall the atrocities of the Holocaust. *Kristallnacht*, the night of November 9th 1938 (16th *Cheshvan*), saw hundreds of Jewish buildings – homes, shops and synagogues – attacked and burned to the ground and countless Jews arrested in the first nationwide act of co-ordinated anti-Semitic violence by the Nazis. The decision to observe *Yom ha-Sho'ah* on the anniversary of the uprising in the Warsaw ghetto, made in 1950 by the Parliament of the then two-year-old Israeli State, may understandably have had as much to do with that fledgling country's self-image as a besieged, vulnerable but determined nation, as with the suffering of the victims of the Holocaust.

Recalling such atrocity, and learning the lessons of it, is a challenge that humankind as a whole has not managed to meet. The introduction of an annual International Holocaust Memorial Day, held on January 27th (the anniversary of the

---

[1] The uprising started on April 19th but this was during Pesach so a date two weeks later was chosen by the Israeli **Knesset** to mark ***Yom Ha'Sho'ah***

Chanukkah and other days of Celebration and Mourning

liberation of Auschwitz by the Russian army in 1945) has produced mixed feelings (particularly in Australia where January 27th is the day after Australia Day). Such a memorial can – and indeed should – serve as an opportunity to remind us of the barbarity of which humanity is capable and educate future generations about the potential consequences of stereotyping groups and harbouring prejudice against them. Nevertheless, there are those who feel excluded from, or a least wary of, such a memorial day because it seems to focus on a specifically Jewish event as distinct from focusing on all victims of genocide (a concern that sometimes leads to inappropriate and unhelpful comparisons between the systematic extermination that took place during the Holocaust and subsequent manifestations of inhumanity). Humankind, it would seem, is either unwilling or unable to recognise and learn from its many failings – of which the Holocaust is one of the most terrifying examples.

Within Judaism, there are several occasions in the year when the Holocaust is considered within the context of a longer history of Jewish suffering: *Tisha'a b'Av*, as already mentioned, is an occasion when other tragedies in Jewish history are recalled and these tragedies are revisited during *Yom Kippur*, in the section known as martyrology *(Eileh ez-k'ra)*.[1]

Such reflections offer an opportunity to consider the origins and manifestations of anti-Semitism, which, sadly, cannot be avoided or ignored. The persecution of Jews has been a feature of the human landscape for some two thousand years, beginning with the Romans and continued by successive generations. The details are too lengthy and the incidents too many to be contained in such a work as this. The Jews kept themselves separate from the communities within whose midst they found themselves dispersed. This was to a large extent imposed upon the Jews by their non-Jewish hosts, though it

---
[1] **Gates of Repentance p: 429 ff**, *Machzor Ru'ach Chadashah* p.314 ff

also suited the Jews to keep themselves apart in order to maintain and practise their customs and traditions – and it is interesting to note, in passing, that 'separate' is one translation of the word *kadosh*, usually translated as 'holy'.

The persecution of the Jews manifested itself in many different ways: the wholesale expulsion of Jewish communities, the frequent accusations of ritual murder[1] (namely the suggestion, both vile and incredible, that Jews would routinely kidnap a Christian child and use its blood in the preparation of unleavened bread for the festival of *Pesach*), and the murderous violence visited upon Europe's Jewish communities during the Crusades. All of these, it must be admitted, had their roots in England: events like that at Clifford's Tower in York in 1190, where the Jews of the city were surrounded by a Christian mob and ended their own lives, or the first-ever recorded case of an accusation of ritual murder, in Norwich in 1144. These are the fore-runners of the violent persecution suffered by Jews all over Europe in the Middle Ages, new justifications for which were the suggestion that Jews interfered with the wafers used in churches for Holy Communion ('desecrating the host') and poisoned Europe's wells to cause the Black Death in 1347. In addition, resentment towards the financial activities of the Jews led to brutal pogroms, particularly in Eastern Europe, that in their turn laid the foundations of the Holocaust.

It is unfortunate, but perhaps inevitable, that this chapter on minor Jewish festivals should end with reflections on anti-Semitism. Most of the events that are commemorated are the consequence of one group of people or another seeking to

---

[1] Also known as 'blood libel'. One case of this, in living memory, was in Kielce, Poland on July 4th 1946, after the end of the Holocaust, where, shockingly, 39 more Jews were killed. Many people in Arab countries seem to regard the blood libel as though it is fact (e.g. an anti-Semitic soap opera called *Ash-Shatat* ('The Diaspora'), made in Syria in 2003, presents Jews as people who murder Christian children, drain their blood, and use this blood to bake *matzah)*, and the regular stream of cartoons is shocking.

defeat or annihilate the Jewish people. That Judaism has survived this two thousand year long assault is a testimony to its durability and its ability to adapt. Perhaps there is no greater witness to the underlying unity of Judaism and the common heritage of all its adherents than the history of anti-Semitism through the ages: a prejudice that pays scant regard to the distinctions that identify particular groups of Jews.

22

JEWISH RITES OF PASSAGE

We affirm the importance of many of the traditional Jewish rites of passage, including appropriate acts of ritual relating to birth, circumcision, baby-naming, coming-of-age, marriage and the consecration of a new home, as well as death and mourning.

Jewish Rites of Passage

Just as the founders of the ancient Israelite religion marked the cycle of the year and the arrival of particular seasons with particular observances, so too they introduced – as did the founders of most major religions – ceremonies and rituals to mark key stages in the life cycle of human beings. No matter what culture, no matter what environment or location, every human society throughout the ages has noted that there are certain stages in life when crucial changes occur. Such stages evoke an awareness of something mystical that cannot easily be explained away, even in our scientific age. Although there are several points in the human life cycle when key developments are marked, it is birth and death that bring us closest to that mystery, and Jewish rituals relating to these stages will be considered in this chapter.[1]

The birth of a child is one of those occasions that bring us into contact with unanswerable mysteries about life. No matter how thoroughly science is able to describe to us the process of reproduction, assist us with it and show us extraordinary images of the development of the foetus, it cannot answer questions about the origins of an individual soul or the purpose of existence. Such matters are – and always have been – the province of religion, and Judaism, in common with other faiths, offers a series of rituals and traditions, the purpose of which is to offer thanks for a new life as well as to bestow a specific identity upon the newborn child.

It is this issue of identity that is first addressed in Judaism. One of the best known life-cycle rituals in Judaism is circumcision. This is a simple operation by which the foreskin of the penis is removed. Traditionally this is done by a *mohel* – someone who is specifically trained to carry out the procedure of circumcision. It usually takes place in the home, traditionally eight days after the birth of the boy (even if that day is a *Shabbat*

---

[1] For customs relating to consecration of the home, see chapter 14, for coming of age rituals see chapter 33 and for marriage see chapter 34.

or festival), though it can also be carried out in hospital. In a traditional ceremony, the baby boy is brought into the room and welcomed. He is then held by a male relative (referred to as the *sandek* – origin unknown but often erroneously translated as Godfather) while the *mohel* carries out the procedure. This is preceded by the reading of some scriptural verses and a declaration by the father of the child of his willingness to carry out the obligation of having his son circumcised. At the conclusion of the procedure, a celebratory cup of wine is drunk and the boy is blessed and given his name.

Circumcision is a widespread practice. Apart from Jews, it is also practised by Muslims and other groups. Nowadays it is often justified on medical grounds[1] - there is evidence that it reduces the risks of certain diseases such as cervical cancer. But it is also a very ancient custom that may have been a puberty rite in many different societies. Whatever its origin and original purpose, in Judaism it was interpreted as a sign of the Covenant. Hence it is known in Hebrew as *b'rit milah*, 'the covenant of circumcision' – a lifelong reminder to the Jew that he is a member of the Jewish people, with all the responsibilities that entails. The Bible traces this custom back to Abraham who circumcised his son Isaac in Genesis chapter 17 (after having circumcised himself at the age of ninety-nine!). Of course, at the time of a birth, there are many other emotions – as well as common sense – that cause modern Jews to question the value of carrying out what some might regard as a barbaric act on a tiny child. Progressive Jews observe the practice as a matter of conforming to a particularly ancient Jewish practice, deeply embedded in the Jewish psyche, for which intellectual justification cannot, and perhaps need not, be given.[2]

---

[1] Unfortunately it is increasingly also being contested on medical grounds – although there are some demonstrable health benefits, there are also some very slight risks associated with any 'unnecessary' operation.

[2] Trained and medically qualified *mohalim* who serve the Progressive Jewish community (though sometimes with certain reservations regarding status) can be contacted through your local synagogue.

Jewish Rites of Passage

In our modern age, however, the lack of ritual to similarly welcome a baby girl is not acceptable to Progressive Judaism. Accordingly, a covenant ceremony to welcome a newborn baby girl has been introduced in which the religious content of the *b'rit* is expressed[1] – though naturally without an equivalent surgical procedure. One further rite is worthy of brief mention. According to biblical tradition, every first-born son was to be 'given to God'[2] – interpreted as meaning that the boy should be given to serve in the Temple. Later tradition gave the role of Temple service to the tribe of Levi, so all first-born boys were 'redeemed' from this service by means of a donation of five silver shekels to the Levites, generally today repaced by a charitable donation. This ceremony, known as *pidyon ha-ben* ('redemption of the son') traditionally takes place on the thirty-first day of a boy's life. It is not considered meaningful by most Progressive Jews, who do not believe in any distinction between *kohanim* and other Jews, and therefore is rarely practised or observed.

As well as bestowing upon a child its religious identity and welcoming it to the covenant, Progressive Judaism also gives parents an opportunity to offer thanks for the birth of a child. A service of thanksgiving for the birth of a child is a popular ceremony in Progressive synagogues. Usually taking place when a child is around six months old, this ceremony provides an opportunity for the family to share its joy with the community. At this ceremony, the child's name is proclaimed as the parents and siblings join the rabbi before the open ark on the *bimah*. A newborn child is given a Hebrew as well as an English name. In *Ashkenazi* tradition, the child might be named after a deceased relative while *Sephardim* often name their children after relatives who are still living. A Hebrew name refers to the individual as son (*ben*) or daughter (*bat*) of their father (and Progressive Judaism includes the mother's name.)

---

[1] Eg see *Siddur Lev Chadash* p. 585
[2] Numbers 18:15-16

At this point it is worth mentioning the supreme value that Judaism places on life. It is well documented that, for example, any Jewish law may be broken if a person's life can be saved as a consequence. In this respect, traditional Judaism finds itself ill-equipped to deal with many modern ethical issues relating to the termination of life, either voluntarily by the individual or by the family of someone in a persistent vegetative state. Traditional Jewish principle will brook no interference with the 'natural' course of events. This is not the place to engage in such a debate; suffice it to say that Progressive Judaism is willing to debate such issues and to make decisions that are not anchored solely in Jewish tradition but that also take modern wisdom and individual circumstances into account.

When a person knows in advance that the end of life is approaching, it is possible and often helpful to offer prayers with or for that person. This is not in any way regarded as being essential as is, say, the Catholic sacrament of 'Anointing the Sick' (formerly known as 'The Last Rites') even though it offers the dying person an opportunity to ask forgiveness. Prayers can be as comforting for the family of the dying person; their anxious wait for the inevitable end to the life of a loved one can be eased by such rituals. In cases of sudden death, such opportunity is not always afforded to the bereaved family. Judaism can only offer consolation to those left behind. The traditional words with which the news of death is greeted are *baruch dayan ha-emet* – 'Praised be the True Judge', affirming that God's judgment must be acknowledged in death as in life, though most Progressive Jews would reject the idea that God actively causes death.

The death of a loved one is clearly a time of shock and bewilderment. It raises a number of questions – spiritual and practical – that have given rise to a variety of religious customs and practices. In older times, many of these traditions were rooted in fear of the unknown and in superstitions associated

Jewish Rites of Passage

with death. That Judaism has many such customs for death and burial is a testimony to humanity's lack of knowledge of what happens when life ends as well as the comfort offered by familiar practices at times of distress.

Progressive Judaism recognises the important role that such rituals can play in the lives of the bereaved but is keen to emphasise that their intention is to support the individual through a difficult time. None of the traditional customs described below is obligatory; they are only included in Progressive Jewish practice if they can ease the suffering of grief. Judaism's tradition of valuing life is reflected in this emphasis that Progressive Judaism places on the living and in its aim to be sympathetic to mourners by adapting burial practices to their individual preferences where possible. A Progressive Jewish funeral and mourning process is more concerned with helping the bereaved to come to terms with their loss than preparing the deceased for whatever awaits.

The Orthodox view is very different. Many traditional practices relating to death are based upon age-old fears and superstitions. These include the requirement not to leave a dead body unattended, to insist that only Jews (usually from the Jewish Burial Society – known as the *chevrah kadishah*) are allowed to handle or move the body as well as carrying out the process of ritual cleansing, *taharah*. Progressive Judaism believes that those who have cared for a person in life can equally be trusted to care for that person after death and encourages hospital staff to carry out their normal procedures. Some Progressive congregations do not have Burial Societies, leaving the preparation of a body for burial (which in the case of a man may include being wrapped in his *tallit*) to the appointed funeral directors.

For orthodox Jews, the custom of burial as soon after death as possible means that anything that delays the funeral – such as an autopsy – is greatly regretted. In fact, the traditional Jewish belief in physical resurrection means that any interference with the body is to be resisted, and the donation of organs has been similarly discouraged in Orthodox Judaism. This belief also means that, for Orthodox Jews, the idea of cremation is unacceptable. Progressive Judaism, however, rejecting the idea of any physical resurrection, therefore permits cremation, recognising that it is a form of funeral preferred by some today, though for others it has echoes of the *Sho'ah* (Holocaust). Progressive Judaism also encourages the donation of organs for the survival of others, a modern example of the traditional importance Judaism places on the value of saving life.

At the funeral, the emphasis is on simplicity, demonstrating the principle that all are equal in life as in death, so the coffin is a simple wooden one without ornamentation. The service is a short series of readings – mostly psalms – and usually includes a eulogy for the deceased. Following the interment, we encourage both male and female mourners to shovel the traditional three spadefuls of earth on to the coffin as a final farewell gesture, and some soil from Israel may also be added. *Kaddish*[1] is recited. The absence of flowers at a Jewish funeral is often remarked upon: Jewish tradition is to place a stone on a grave to represent the eternity of the soul. The ceremony at a cremation has the same liturgical content.

The mourning process can continue at home. The World Union Edition of *Mishkan T'filah* has introduced a prayer to be said when returning home and lighting the memorial candle (page 619). Progressive Judaism has adapted the Orthodox custom of holding prayers in the home during the week following the funeral. *Shiv'ah* (the name comes from the Hebrew word for seven) or *Minyan* prayers are usually held either in the deceased's home (or that of a near relative), or at their synagogue, the evening after the funeral. Occasionally

---

[1] See p. 102

Progressive Jews will hold prayers on two or three nights; but very rarely is the Orthodox six-night *shiv'ah* observed. In the house, the mourners may choose to sit on low chairs and may cover the mirrors – the origins of these customs are unknown, though modern interpretations (for example, the fact that one should not be concerned with how one looks at a time of mourning) are sometimes offered. The family should decide whether these traditions are helpful to them in their grief.

Towards the end of the first year following the death, a memorial is erected and may be consecrated with a short ceremony, with the family coming together to remember their loved one (usually called the Stone Setting or Consecration).

Finally, a year after the death, the formal period of mourning is deemed to be over and the mourner then observes the *yahrzeit* (anniversary) of the death of the loved one every year by lighting a memorial candle and reciting *kaddish*. Again, the World Union Edition of *Mishkan T'filah* includes a prayer to be said when lighting the *Yahrzeit* candle (page 619).

Progressive Jews may observe all, some or none of the above customs when bidding farewell to a loved one. As with other aspects of its approach to Jewish customs and traditions, Progressive Judaism offers educated choices to its members, explaining the likely origin and significance of these customs and seeking to take into account the feelings of individuals who may find comfort in more traditional rites.

That this section of the book concludes with customs relating to death is perhaps appropriate: it emphasises the common fate that awaits every one of us, regardless of religious persuasion. Nevertheless, there are choices that every individual can make within the parameters of his or her own religion. The nature and consequences of such choices will be considered more fully in the second section.

Part 2: Distinctive Approach

23

THE DYNAMIC, DEVELOPING CHARACTER OF JUDAISM

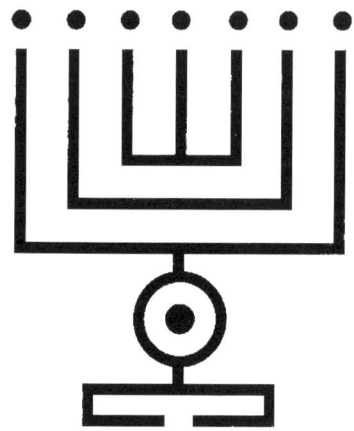

Judaism has never stood still. It has always moved forward, sometimes slowly, sometimes faster. Its history is a history of continuity and change. We affirm the dynamic, developing character of our Jewish religious tradition.

The Dynamic, Developing Character of Judaism

It is self-evident that Judaism must have changed and developed in order for it still to have a place in the twenty-first century – perhaps four thousand years after its ancestors Abraham and Sarah first walked the earth. A reading of the Bible makes it clear that our biblical ancestors shared their lives with several other tribal groups, many of them more mighty and numerous than the small number of Judahites who, in the fifth century BCE, returned from Babylonian exile to rebuild and re-establish the city of Jerusalem. Yet it would appear that such groups as the Amorites, Moabites, Hittites and others who had been Judah's neighbours simply disappeared without trace. A similar fate befell the Israelite tribes of the Northern Kingdom as a consequence of the Assyrian invasion of 722 BCE, leaving the people of Judah to contemplate the fate of their neighbours and cousins as well as the prospects of their own survival.

The effect of the destruction of the kingdom of Israel cannot be overstated. In the Ancient Near East, the prevailing belief was that defeat by a rival tribe or nation was an indication that the god of the vanquished was inferior to that of the victors. Consequently, the defeated were obliged to acknowledge the failure of their god and accept that their rivals' beliefs and practices were superior. Although there had been rivalry between the kingdoms of Israel and Judah for many centuries, the eradication of the kingdom that bore the name of Israel and worshipped the same God was truly shocking. An explanation for God's apparent abandonment of the northern kingdom – and the sparing of its southern cousin – was required. The theological justification that was established to underpin this was the fact that the first of the northern kings, Jeroboam, had established a rival cult in Dan and Beth-el, where the focus of worship was a golden calf. The fate of the kingdom of Israel, which seceded from the rule of Jerusalem under the House of David in 922 BCE, was sealed from the moment Jeroboam built his shrine, even though it took two centuries for the 'inevitable' to happen.

This explanation was one of several theological gymnastics that the sages and seers of what would become Judaism were required to perform through the ages. Less than a century and a half after the destruction of Israel, the same fate befell the Kingdom of Judah in 586 BCE. Again, an explanation was needed: what had Judah done to allow it to suffer a similar fate to that of its golden calf worshipping northern cousin? According to most biblical scholars, it was around this time that the Book of Deuteronomy was written, using Moses as a mouthpiece for God's instructions as to how the Children of Israel should behave once they entered the 'Promised Land' on the borders of which they received Moses' instructions. The authors of Deuteronomy (who are generally believed to have written the 'historical' books covering the period of history from the preparations at the borders of the 'Promised Land' to the destruction of Solomon's Temple[1]) made it clear that ownership of the land would be conditional upon the observance of certain regulations. This covenant[2] meant that all would go well if those conditions were met but disaster would ensue if the people failed to keep their side of the agreement. The description of this disaster, which includes graphic descriptions of invasion, siege and exile,[3] would have sounded alarmingly familiar to the exiled people of Judah who listened to them by Babylon's waters.

Here is a crucial example of Judaism's ability effectively to re-invent itself. By all that was normal in the Ancient Near East, the defeated people of Judah should have adopted the beliefs and customs of their conquerors. But the leaders and teachers

---

[1] Joshua, Judges, Samuel and Kings. See chapter 28 for a more detailed study of the origins of the Bible.
[2] See chapter 5
[3] Deuteronomy chapter 28:15-68

of the people refused to relinquish the traditions and beliefs that had been cultivated and developed over so many centuries. Instead of conceding that God had failed the people and so was no longer worthy of their loyalty, the Prophets made a daring and crucial shift (already hinted at in the words of earlier northern Prophets like Hosea and Amos) suggesting that it was the people who had failed God. Recognition of this, claimed Prophets such as Jeremiah, would enable the people to return from exile to their land[1] and Isaiah, who was in exile with the people of Judah, offered them comfort and hope of such a return.[2] At this point, history intervened: the Persians overthrew the Babylonians and those people of Judah who wished to do so were given permission to return to Jerusalem, some 70 years after its destruction.

Here is one of the first – and perhaps one of the most significant – examples of Judaism's adaptability when faced with a new set of circumstances when failure to adapt would result in its extinction. This characteristic was and is intrinsic to Judaism's development and underpins the dynamism that is integral to it. There have been other moments in Jewish history when such adaptations were needed to ensure continuity and when failure to make such changes would spell the end of Judaism. Six and a half centuries after the Babylonian destruction of the Temple, its successor, the Second Temple, was also under threat. This time it was the Romans who would destroy it in the year 70 CE and spend the following decades slowly trying to remove all traces of Jews and their religion from the land whose name they changed from Judea to Palestina. The Rabbis of the time realised that in order for Judaism to survive this cataclysmic

---

[1] e.g. Jeremiah 29:10-14
[2] The Book of Isaiah contains the writings of more than one author. The first Isaiah, who lived at the time of the destruction of Israel, was the author of chapters 1-39. The writings of the second (and perhaps also third) Isaiah, who lived at the time of the exile in Babylon, begin with chapter 40.

development, it must make changes that would allow it to continue without a Temple and, as time progressed, without a homeland. The earlier experience of exile was crucial here: it stood as an example of how this ancient religion could adapt itself to new circumstances as well as offering new geographical centres in which this development could take place.

The emergence of an oral tradition and the development of institutions that could serve as a home for many of the evolving practices ensured that Judaism would be continued. Wherever Jewish communities were established, the dynamic nature of their religion allowed them to shape a Judaism that responded to local conditions. It was Judaism's encounter with the developing outside world, together with its determination to maintain its identity within that world, that fed its constant change. It is no coincidence that Judaism's most productive and dynamic periods came in times and places when the Jewish community was exposed to and interacted with the wider community – as in Spain until the expulsion of 1492 or Germany until the rise of Adolf Hitler. And Judaism grew far more slowly, or at least in a more insular and even self-indulgent fashion, when it was closed off from the outside world, in ghetto-like conditions such as those that prevailed in eastern Europe in the seventeenth to nineteenth centuries.

It was the collapse of those ghetto walls at the beginning of the nineteenth century that posed the greatest challenge to Judaism since the destruction of the Temple by the Romans over 1700 years earlier. The responses to this dramatic change in Jewish life have been many and varied, following a tradition that reflects Judaism's propensity both for internal debate and disagreement as well as its dynamic developing tradition that has enabled it to survive for so long.

24

THE DIVERSITY OF JEWISH TRADITION

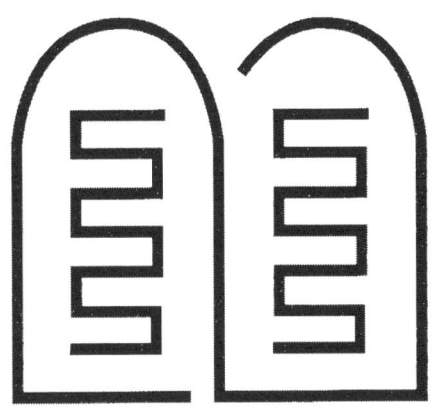

Judaism has never been monolithic. There have always been varieties of Judaism. The more conservative Sadducees and the more progressive Pharisees represent only one of many past differences. We affirm the diversity of our tradition.

One of the inevitable consequences of Judaism's developing character has been disagreement among Jews regarding the way in which their religion should grow. The internal debate within Judaism has been reflected in the number of variations in its expression, many of which have shown a keen rivalry that occasionally developed into outright hostility. There is a well-known observation that wherever there are two Jews, there will be three opinions. This implies – correctly – that there have always been varieties of Judaism and, invariably, rivalries between groups that existed contemporaneously.

The political division in biblical times between the kingdoms of Israel and Judah was an early forerunner of the rivalry between the Pharisees and the Sadducees at the time when the Second Temple stood. These rivals were divided along quite clear political and religious lines. The Sadducees were the priestly party, responsible for overseeing sacrifices in the Temple. They formed an elite, almost aristocratic, ruling group in the first century before and after the Common Era, until, of course, the Temple was destroyed, and with it their purpose, role and responsibilities. The Pharisees were more representative of the ordinary people of Judea among whom they lived and worked. But even they did not command the full loyalty of the Jewish people at the time of Roman oppression. Other political groups – militaristic and messianic (or both!) – vied for the loyalty of the Jews and the emergence of the Pharisees as the most influential group was as much due to the Romans eradicating other opposition (such as the Zealots who perished at Masada in 73 CE) as it was to their particular philosophy.

Even within the ranks of the Pharisees, there were divisions. As the Pharisaic tradition developed and its scholars and teachers, the Rabbis, began to interpret the instructions in the Torah, differences of opinion emerged. In the first century BCE, there were two schools of learning: the school of *Hillel* and the school of *Shammai*. The schools of these two teachers seemed to

The Diversity of Jewish Tradition

offer variant opinions on just about every aspect of Jewish tradition In general, the opinions of the school of *Hillel* tended to be the more liberal and lenient and *Hillel's* opinions are almost always the ones adopted by subsequent rabbinic tradition.

Although rabbinic tradition became the dominant feature in Judaism, with the emergence of the Talmud as the focal point of its development, there was some significant opposition. During the ninth century CE, different groups arose that denied the authenticity of oral Torah. These sects came to be known as Karaites (literally, 'people of the scripture'), and they were distinguished from the followers of Rabbinical Judaism.

The Karaites believed in strict adherence to the literal text of the scripture, without rabbinical interpretation. They did not accept that rabbinical law was part of an oral tradition that had been handed down from God, or even inspired by God; they believed it was newly created by the sages. The Karaites therefore believed that rabbinic teachings were subject to the flaws of any document written by mere mortals.

The difference between Rabbinic Judaism and Karaism that is most commonly noted is in regard to *Shabbat*: the Karaites recognised that the Bible specifically prohibits lighting a flame on *Shabbat*, so they kept their houses dark on *Shabbat*. Rabbinic Judaism, on the other hand, relied upon rabbinical interpretation that allowed people to leave burning a flame that was lit before *Shabbat*. Karaites also prohibited sexual intercourse on *Shabbat*, while the Rabbis considered *Shabbat* to be the most favourable time for it. The Karaites also followed a slightly different calendar from that established by the Rabbis. According to the Karaites themselves, this movement at one time attracted as much as forty per cent of the Jewish people.

A Judaism for the Twenty-First Century

Today, Karaites are a very small minority, and most Jews do not even know that they exist.

Another tiny remnant today are the Samaritans, living in Israel in Kiryat Luza on Mount Gerizim and in the city of Holon, just outside Tel Aviv and numbering less than a thousand. They trace their descent back to the Israelite tribes of Ephraim and Menasseh and the priestly tribe of Levi, having survived the Assyrian destruction of Israel in 722 BCE, and they were already a distinct group at the start of the Rabbinic period. It is their tradition that the original Holy Place was on Mount Gerizim and, refusing to accept the Rabbinic traditions, they continue to offer their annual Pesach sacrifice there to this day.

Many of the divisions within Judaism were on ideological or theological lines but there were also geographical issues. As Judaism spread into numerous countries, its adherents began to adopt and absorb various elements of the cultures in which they found themselves. As the centuries passed, marked differences arose between those Jews whose base was central and later eastern Europe, and those whose Judaism developed in communities on the Mediterranean coast, particularly in Spain and North Africa. These two groups, *Ashkenazim* and *Sephardim*,[1] developed distinctive customs and practices, as well as linguistic variations. In addition to developing their own everyday language – Yiddish (a mixture of Hebrew and German) for the *Ashkenazim* and Ladino (a mixture of Hebrew and Spanish) for the *Sephardim* – the two groups also developed two variant pronunciations of Hebrew. Differences can be noted in the word for the Sabbath bread, for example, the *Sephardi* pronunciation of which is *challah* (the first 'a' sounding like the 'a' in f<u>a</u>ther) whereas the *Ashkenazi* usage gives us *chollah* (the 'o' as in h<u>o</u>t). Indeed, the word for Sabbath itself demonstrates another key difference: generally known as *Shabbat*, in *Ashkenazi* tradition it is pronounced *Shobbes*. Today

---

[1] For the origins and definitions of these titles, see bottom of p. 57

The Diversity of Jewish Tradition

the *Sephardi* pronunciation of Hebrew has come to be accepted as the standard and is used by all speakers of modern Hebrew (*Ivrit*) and is used in Progressive synagogues. Nevertheless, the *Ashkenazi* pronunciation still prevails in those circles whose institutions trace their roots to the central and eastern European areas from which this variation emerged.[1]

Another distinct group of Jews that emerged from this location is known by the collective term of *Chasidim*. This branch of Judaism was, surprisingly, the reforming movement of its time when, in seventeenth century Poland, its founder, the *Ba'al Shem Tov*,[2] sought to reclaim Judaism from what he regarded as the ivory tower of scholarship to which learned Talmudists had taken it and give it back to the people as an expression of hope and joy. Those who opposed this novel movement were called, somewhat unoriginally, *Mitnagdim* (which means 'opponents') but they were unable to stop this novel form of Judaism spreading rapidly through the impoverished peasant communities of Polish Jews. Needless to say, variations of *Chasidism* then emerged, based largely upon the teachings of individual *Chasidic Rebbes*[3] whose followers often believed them to be endowed with mystical powers and therefore superior to other neighbouring *Chasidic Rebbes*. A number of these different *Chasidic* sects still exist today in major Jewish centres such as New York, Jerusalem and Tel Aviv, as well as in areas of London, Manchester and Gateshead in the UK. With their insistence on wearing seventeenth century Polish costume, they are now generally regarded as the 'ultra-Orthodox'

---

[1] Another distinction between *Ashkenazim* and *Sephardim* is a dietary one regarding foods permitted at *Pesach*. Orthodox *Askenazi* Jews do not eat legumes (*kitniyyot*) such as rice or peas at this festival though they may be included in the meals of *Sephardi* Jews during Passover.

[2] The name given to Rabbi Israel ben Eliezer, meaning 'Master of the Good Name'.

[3] *Rebbe* is a distorted *Ashkenazi* pronunciation of Rabbi, a title applied to *Chasidic* teachers

representatives of Jewish tradition. The fact that many of these different sects show distinct hostility towards each other should not come as a great surprise, given the history of divisions in Judaism covered thus far.

This brief exploration of some of the numerous occasions in Jewish history when there have been different groupings within Judaism should make clear the fact that this is not a monolithic tradition. One might wonder how, with so much internal dispute, Judaism has managed to survive for so many thousands of years. The answer is that it is precisely these differences in belief and practice, interpretation and application that have ensured that survival. The creativity and dynamism that is generated by this diversity within Judaism has been a driving force in ensuring that this religion has never become so fixed that it was unable to progress. It is the long-standing tradition within Judaism of discussion and debate – and, inevitably, disagreement and dispute – which has allowed it to flourish in so many ways and to ensure that it remains relevant and meaningful in the lives of its adherents, whichever part of it they may adhere to.

25

RESPECT FOR CONSCIENTIOUS OPTIONS

The Emancipation wrought far-reaching changes in Jewish life. It raised fundamental questions about Jewish belief and practice, and about the perpetuation of Judaism, and the resultant debate produced a multiplicity of options. We affirm the respect due to all conscientious options.

For the Jewish people in the Diaspora following the destruction of the Temple, history, for the most part, recorded a troubling and troubled experience. The suspicion and hostility with which one group of human beings tends to regard a group with differing origins or practices was frequently and often violently directed at the Jews of Europe. The roots and expression of European anti-Semitism have been detailed elsewhere.[1] Sadly, hostility to Jews appears still to be part of the European landscape. Nevertheless, the conditions in which the Jews live at the beginning of the twenty-first century are radically different from the ghettoised existence that prevailed for the majority of them little more than two centuries ago. This transformation stems from far-reaching intellectual, social and political changes in the late eighteenth and nineteenth centuries – beginning with the period that historians term the Age of Enlightenment. For the Jews, the main practical consequence of this development was the removal of many restrictions that had for so long kept them behind ghetto walls and so is referred to in Jewish history as the Emancipation.

Broadly, this period saw the development of an intellectual culture in Western Europe (particularly France, Britain and Germany) where many of the beliefs that had underpinned the old order for centuries were increasingly subjected to the critical scrutiny of reason. This new, enlightened approach had a profound impact on the Jews. At the heart of the *Haskalah* (as the Enlightenment was called in Hebrew), was Moses Mendelssohn (1729-86), a German Jew who, having found work with a silk merchant in Berlin, became one of the greatest figures of the German enlightenment. Mendelssohn was prominent in Berlin's intellectual circles and is widely believed to be the inspiration behind Gotthold Lessing's play *Nathan der Weise* ('Nathan the Wise,' 1779), the hero of which is a Jewish intellectual. Mendelssohn's contribution to the *Haskalah* was to

---

[1] See page 140

Respect for Conscientious Options

provide a bridge between German and Jewish culture in one of the centres of Western European civilisation, most notably with his translation (1780-83) of the Pentateuch into German[1].

The effects of the Enlightenment on the Jewish communities of Europe varied. With the emergence of international banking, Jews found themselves in places of prominence in the Netherlands and many German states, for example. As an emerging middle class with valuable financial skills, Jews were once again seen as useful to their hosts, but they were also regarded with some suspicion because of their religion. For many Jews, the solution was simple: the best way fully to assimilate was to convert to Christianity and be rid of the limitations placed upon Jews. A well-known view, usually attributed to Moses Mendelssohn, was that it was possible to be 'fully German on the street, fully Jewish at home'. Nevertheless, the extent to which Jews were accepted varied from one European country to another, and from one period to another. Despite Mendelssohn's assertion, the pressure on the Jews to abandon their heritage in such an environment was one of the major issues that confronted the Jewish community at the start of the nineteenth century.

For the vast majority of Jews, however, there was no positive interaction between their community and the wider Christian society among whom – and yet apart from whom – they made their homes. This was particularly true in central and eastern Europe. The culture within the ghetto was exclusively Jewish. Family and communal life was rigidly structured. Girls were trained by their mothers to keep a Jewish home and were prepared to be married off to suitable husbands while boys were trained in studies that were exclusively Jewish before

---

[1] The German text was written, in accordance with the custom that prevailed among German Jews, in Hebrew characters, and the commentary, *Biur*, in Hebrew.

either going on to higher education to study Talmud at a *yeshivah*[1] or taking up their father's trade and waiting for their marriage to be arranged. The language of prayer was Hebrew; the language of everyday was Yiddish. This insular, self-contained society was the norm for generations of Jews up until the turn of the nineteenth century. This is not to say, of course, that the outside world did not impinge upon the Jews in the ghetto; many were the instances of anti-Semitic pogroms, and their murderous consequences for the Jews gave little indication of a change in the way the world regarded them. So Judaism for the most part continued to tread a familiar path within its ghetto environment, the certainty of its beliefs and practices unimpeded and unchallenged by the outside world.

In the enlightened lands of Western Europe, the Emancipation swept this certainty away with such force that the shock waves are still being felt two centuries later as Judaism tries to come to terms with the changes it made possible. So swift were those changes, so manifold those possibilities, that grandparents living in the Jewish section of a village in Germany in the early nineteenth century whose daily language was Yiddish, whose education had been exclusively on matters Jewish and who had lived all their lives without ever leaving that village could have grandchildren who lived in large German cities like Hamburg or Berlin, spoke German, studied a range of subjects at university and enjoyed the bourgeois lifestyle of nineteenth century western Europe.

The effects of the Enlightenment continued to be felt in the nineteenth century. With the coming of the industrial and scientific revolutions, economic changes provided entrepreneurial or professional Jews with the opportunity to benefit. Intellectual upheavals played their part in bringing about a major change in the way that Judaism and other

---

[1] Academy for Jewish study.

religions viewed themselves and their traditions. The divine authorship of sacred scriptures was called into question and their very credibility was challenged by scientific exploration and discovery – most notably the publication in 1859 of Darwin's 'Theory of Evolution' and by novel textual criticism of the Bible by German Christian scholars Karl Heinrich Graf (1815-1869) and Julius Wellhausen (1844-1918).[1]

These changes presented so many challenges to Judaism that it is hardly surprising that a variety of responses to them emerged, each seeking in its own way to preserve the heritage of Judaism in a new and strange environment. This change in circumstances was no less profound – and no less threatening – to the survival of Judaism than the one it had faced when the Romans had destroyed the Temple. Judaism's ability to adapt to its environment, its tradition of discussion and debate that had, on so many occasions in the past, allowed it to develop, and its ability to contain a diversity of opinion – all these ensured that it would survive this latest encounter with the wider world.

Some elements within Judaism would seek to maintain as much of its original form as was possible or practical in this new cultural, social and economic order. Others would eventually find their solution in working towards the establishment of a national homeland in an era where the nation state emerged as the dominant political structure in Europe. Many Jews would abandon their Judaism altogether, preferring to divest themselves of what they saw as an archaic and irrelevant burden in their desire to assimilate into the new society that seemed so keen to welcome them to its ranks. Those who followed this route often converted to Christianity to assist their progress. Others would struggle, as Jews had done in so many previous times and places, to find a synthesis between the

---

[1] See chapter 28

demands of Judaism and the wider culture in which they were educated, lived and worked, seeking to meet the challenges of the modern world.

Each of these options represented and represents still a valid attempt to keep Judaism alive in an age where rapid change often threatened to sweep it away. One such option, Progressive Judaism, recognises that the challenges arising with the Emancipation made many choices possible. This tradition of diversity within Judaism is, as has already been suggested, part of what allows Judaism to respond constructively and creatively to changes in its environment.

One of the values encouraged by the Emancipation was that of tolerance of individuals and groups holding different opinions. It is a sad fact that the most bitter arguments seem to take place among different groups professing to represent the same faith or creed. By definition, the more progressive branches of Judaism respect this divergence of opinion within our ancient heritage, a respect that is not always reciprocated. It is to the emergence of this Progressive Judaism, and the balance it tried to establish and maintain, that our attention now turns.

26

PROGRESSIVE JUDAISM

We affirm our commitment to the movement known as Progressive Judaism, united in the World Union for Progressive Judaism, and especially note those pioneers who have included Abraham Geiger, David Einhorn, Kaufmann Kohler, Isaac Mayer Wise, Stephen Wise, Abba Hillel Silver, Claude Montefiore, Lily Montagu, Israel Mattuck, and, in Australia, Herman Sanger

A Judaism for the Twenty-First Century

The differing interpretations of Judaism through the ages and, in particular, since the Emancipation, have resulted in the word Judaism acquiring a variety of adjectives. One such adjective is 'Progressive', denoting and defining the approach that has sought to adapt Judaism to the dramatic, ongoing changes of the last two centuries. 'Progressive Judaism' is an umbrella term for Jewish individuals, groups and institutions that regard themselves as part of this dynamic movement (and includes 'Reform' and 'Reconstructionist' movements and Jews). Inevitably, there are several options as to where different groups position themselves beneath that umbrella. In general, what unites Progressive Jews is a recognition that the Five Books of Moses were not divinely revealed (the Hebrew phrase for divine revelation is Torah *min ha-shamayim* – literally Torah from heaven). Consequently, biblical and subsequent Jewish law can and should be scrutinised to establish its relevance (or otherwise) to modern life. The global body that has come to be the meeting point for all Progressive Jewish groups is the World Union for Progressive Judaism (WUPJ), which is the largest Jewish religious movement in the world.

Before we explore more closely its role and the different elements that comprise this global Jewish movement, some attention – and tribute – must be paid to key individuals whose insight and effort first brought Progressive Judaism to prominence. As is suggested in the title of this chapter, Progressive Judaism owes its existence and inspiration to those founders and pioneers who developed the progressive perspective of this branch of Judaism.

The first Jewish responses to the Emancipation[1] appeared in Germany, where Rabbis and lay people struggled to find a

---

[1] the process of freeing the Jewish people of Europe, following the 'Enlightenment,' including recognition of their rights as equal citizens, and

balance between the traditional world of the ghetto, whose walls were now shattered, and the modern world, whose opportunities enticed many Jews to abandon their Jewish roots in order to best take advantage of what was on offer.

One of the earliest of these Rabbis was Abraham Geiger. Born in 1810 in Frankfurt-am-Main, his experience of the conflict between the old and new worlds was manifested in his traditional Jewish education that was followed by a study of Greek and oriental languages in Bonn. Geiger developed what came to be known as a 'scientific' approach to Judaism, initially justifying his proposed reforms with reference to rabbinic law (*halachah*[1]) but subsequently seeking to remove from Judaism any element that might render it unacceptable to modern nineteenth century Jews. His actions, including the rejection of the dietary laws and ritual garb such as *tallit, kippah* and *t'fillin* and the removal of references to Temple sacrifice and the ingathering of the exiles, still strike a chord with some modern Progressive Jews,[2] even if they may feel that completely discarding rituals might have been too extreme.

One of Geiger's contemporaries was David Einhorn. His education in rabbinics and philosophy placed him firmly in the reform camp where he was greatly influenced by Abraham Geiger. Although he was appointed Rabbi to serve congregations in Bavaria, his religious and philosophical opinions were considered so extreme that the local authorities refused to grant the required permission for him to take up these posts. Although he did eventually procure a rabbinic pulpit, he realised – as did many Germans in the mid-19th

---

the formal granting of citizenship as individuals; it occurred gradually between the late eighteenth century and the early twentieth century.

[1] *halachah*: the Hebrew word for Jewish law that has developed over the centuries – literally 'the way to walk'.

[2] See p. 199-200

century, Jewish or otherwise – that America offered more opportunity for radical thinkers than did any European environment, and decided to emigrate. Once there, Einhorn proceeded to clash with the founders of American Reform Judaism, notably Isaac Mayer Wise and particularly Rabbi Stephen Wise, both of whom were concerned to make compromises to unify the trends of Judaism in America that Einhorn rejected. As was the case in Germany,[1] it was in the writing of prayerbooks that these differences were expressed. Isaac Mayer Wise produced *Minhag America* that shortened but did not significantly alter the traditional service, while David Einhorn's *Olat Tamid* (written mostly in German) offered a far more radical universal view of the messianic future of humanity that Reform Judaism saw as its task to promote.

A younger German-born Rabbi who found America a more welcoming home for his radical views on Judaism was Kaufmann Kohler. Born in 1843, Kohler received a doctorate from the University of Berlin before moving to Chicago. One of those who played a key role in his new life in America was David Einhorn – Kohler was influenced by his ideas, married his daughter, and succeeded him as Rabbi at Temple Beth-El in New York. Kohler later became president of the Hebrew Union College[2] and made a crucial contribution to the development of Progressive Jewish thought and practice in the late nineteenth and early twentieth century. He continued the trend of removing from Judaism all those aspects of practice and belief that were regarded as outdated – a position eloquently expressed in the 1885 Pittsburgh Platform.[3] His theological views sought to find a balance between religious belief and rationalism.

---

[1] where a succession of prayerbooks adapted or completely dispensed with many of the traditional elements: See p. 241-2
[2] The institution, founded in 1875, that trains Reform Rabbis in America.
[3] A statement of Reform Jewish principles that emerged from a rabbinic conference held in that city.

Across the Atlantic, in Britain, Progressive Judaism arrived somewhat later than had been the case in Germany or America. One of its prime philosophical movers was Claude Montefiore. Although he studied theology in Berlin, one of the centres of Reform Judaism, he found himself unable to identify fully with it and devoted himself instead to other studies and activities. These included the writing and editing of a number of works offering a scholarly perspective on Judaism, including the 'Jewish Quarterly Review' (established 1889 with Israel Abrahams and still published today) and a biblical commentary entitled 'The Bible for Home Reading.'

Claude Montefiore was also very involved in the field of education and particularly (and in the eyes of some of his Jewish contemporaries, notoriously) with the relationship between Judaism and Christianity. In this latter regard, he can certainly be viewed as one of the pioneers of Jewish-Christian dialogue.

As far as Progressive Judaism is concerned, he was involved in establishing the Jewish Religious Union in Britain in the early twentieth century, the group that was the forerunner of the movement now known as Liberal Judaism. He was one of a trio of founding figures, all of whose surnames began with the letter 'M'. The second, who might well be regarded as Progressive Judaism's prime mover at least in Britain, was Lily Montagu. Born into a well-established orthodox Anglo-Jewish family in 1873, at an early age Lily took an active role in caring for the needs of newly arrived and impoverished Jewish immigrants from Eastern Europe. This grounded her commitment to social justice, to which a religious dimension was added when she encountered the failure of Orthodox Judaism to address issues raised by the working conditions of these Jews. In particular, she recognised that there seemed to be no place for young women in Orthodox Judaism. These concerns – and the potentially disastrous consequences for the future of Anglo-Jewry – found expression in an article she published in 'The Jewish Quarterly' in 1899 entitled 'The Spiritual Possibilities of Judaism Today.'

Alongside these two founding figures of Liberal Judaism in Great Britain is the third of the so-called 'Three M's', preacher and author of prayerbooks, Rabbi Israel Mattuck. Originally from the United States, in 1911 Mattuck was invited to give rabbinic leadership to the first synagogue established by the Jewish Religious Union, the Liberal Jewish Synagogue. Although he shared Claude Montefiore's enthusiasm for Jewish-Christian dialogue (in 1927 he founded, with the Dean of St Paul's, the London Society for Jews and Christians), Mattuck was particularly noted for his contribution to Liberal Jewish liturgy. In contrast with the liturgical changes and developments taking place in America and, in particular, Germany, British Jewish liturgy had remained static. The Liberal Jewish Prayerbook of 1926 changed this. It was a collection of services for all occasions made up of readings, poetry and songs – mostly in English – whose intention was to inspire and uplift the congregation and, in seeking to achieve this, bade farewell to the traditional structure of Jewish liturgy with what seemed to Orthodox critics to be rather reckless abandon. Israel Mattuck also contributed significantly to the development of Liberal Jewish thought, including a book entitled The Essentials of Liberal Judaism, published in 1947 and dedicated to the memory of Claude Montefiore.

Once the Jewish Religious Union was established and developing (and had taken the name 'Liberal'), Lily Montagu saw the importance of an organisation to assist the spread of this modern approach to Judaism around the world, and was central to the establishment of the World Union for Progressive Judaism in 1926 in London. She worked in conjunction with the three Reform congregations in Britain, the first of which, the West London Synagogue of British Jews, had been established in 1840. Indeed the term 'Progressive' was chosen as an umbrella term that could include both Reform and Liberal with their slight differences of approach, as well as the variations found in Europe, America and increasingly elsewhere. From the late 1920s, Lily Montagu was instrumental in supporting the establishment of a Progressive Jewish community in Melbourne, an endeavour which finally took off with the appointment of Rabbi Dr Herman Sanger in 1936.

Lily Montagu had first met Herman Sanger when he was just nineteen and had accompanied his father, a Rabbi, to the first conference of the World Union for Progressive Judaism, in Berlin; and he had experienced her as the first woman ever to have given a sermon in a German synagogue.[1] After graduating, he studied at Cambridge and often celebrated *Shabbat* at Lily Montagu's home, the 'Red Lodge', in London. He returned to Germany in 1932 to study Rabbinics at the Theological Seminary in Breslau and at the Hochshule fur die Wissenschaft des Judentums in Berlin as well as working in the communities there, and, despite the Nazi regime, he was ordained in 1936. However his work had not gone unnoticed, and, having been twice arrested, and then receiving an anonymous warning to get out immediately, Rabbi Dr Sanger took the next train to London, from where Lily Montagu was able to help him get to Australia to serve the tiny and struggling Melbourne congregation.

Rabbi Dr Sanger was not only able to rapidly develop the congregation for those already in Melbourne, but also to welcome those European Jews who found their way there. Over the subsequent years he was a regular writer and broadcaster across Australia, and was able to assist in the

---

[1] Oranienburger Strasse Synagogue, August 1928

formation of new congregations in Melbourne, across Australia and in New Zealand.

To the list of names in the heading of this chapter must be added the name of the man who was British Liberal Judaism's chief liturgist and thinker in the latter half of the twentieth century. Responsible for writing the Affirmations that provide the basis for this work, Rabbi John D Rayner was, for forty years, the guiding light of Liberal Judaism in Britain and, for much of that time, an influential teacher of Progressive Judaism at the Leo Baeck College.

Like Reform and Liberal Judaism themselves, John Rayner was born in Germany, but into a very different environment from that which had fostered these new branches of Judaism. Born fifteen years after Herman Sanger as Hans Sigismund Rahmer into a secular Berlin family, in 1924, it was, ironically, the anti-semitic Nuremberg Laws introduced by the Nazis in 1935 that awakened the ten year-old's interest in Judaism. He arrived in England in August 1939 at the age of fifteen on one of the very last opportunities for escape afforded by the *Kindertransport*[1].

Ordained as a Rabbi in 1953, John Rayner served at the South London Liberal Synagogue and at the Liberal Jewish Synagogue, where he became senior minister in 1961. His sermons, articles and books clearly set out the principles of Liberal Judaism with its emphasis on ethics over ritual and the need to balance tradition with modern knowledge. Along with his dedication to teaching, particularly at the Leo Baeck College, it is John Rayner's contribution to Jewish liturgy that will best be remembered, as he co-edited the 1967 prayerbook '*Service of the Heart*' (on which '*Gates of Prayer*' was based), together with

---

[1] In 1938 and 1939, hundreds of German and Austrian Jewish children were brought to the United Kingdom by boat and train to escape the persecution to which their families, who remained behind, were subjected.

its High Holyday companion, '*Gates of Repentance*', and led the drive towards the production of a new UK prayerbook, '*Siddur Lev Chadash*', in 1995, which has itself been most influential in subsequent prayerbooks including the production of the World Union Edition of '*Mishkan T'filah*', developed in the Southern Hemisphere and published in 2010.

The Leo Baeck College/Centre for Jewish Education in London is perhaps the most significant of the many organisations on which the Reform and Liberal Movements in Britain work together; there Rabbis and Educators are trained for both movements, and also serve congregations around the world, and many of them have served the Australian and New Zealand communities.

In a sermon in October 2002 commemorating the centenary of Liberal Judaism in the UK, John Rayner re-emphasised the task of Progressive Judaism: 'Integrity was perhaps the outstanding quality of our founders. They imprinted it deeply on our Movement and we have tried… to maintain it ever since. As Rabbi Israel Mattuck said… "To sacrifice principle to conformity would jeopardise our cause." The temptation to do so is ever present: to follow fashion, to court popularity, to play to the gallery, to swallow scruples for political gain. All these temptations we must resist, fully knowing and accepting the cost. For integrity is not cheap… It may entail accepting a lower rate of numerical growth than we should have wished. It may mean remaining a minority for a long time to come, or even for ever. That too is a price we must be willing to pay, for it is better to be few and right than to be many and wrong.'

27

A SYNTHESIS OF JUDAISM AND MODERNITY

Orthodox Judaism carries on Judaism virtually as it was before the Emancipation. Conservative Judaism modifies it minimally. Jewish Secularism expresses Jewish identity in non-religious terms. We affirm Progressive Judaism because it alone seeks a synthesis of Judaism and modernity.

A Synthesis of Judaism and Modernity

The survival of Judaism has never been dependent on numerical size. It is unlikely that Judaism would have lasted beyond the destruction of Solomon's Temple and the exile in Babylon had it not been for its seemingly innate propensity for survival. Darwin may have challenged many of the certainties that had underpinned established religion with his theory of evolution, but his assertions of the requirement for a species to adapt in order to survive could be applied as readily to Judaism as to the plants and creatures he studied. Judaism had perfected the concept of adapting to its environment over a period of more than three and a half thousand years; nothing the nineteenth century could throw at it would alter that.

If the history of humanity can be seen as one of progress – however halting that progress may have been – then the history of Judaism itself must reflect that progress. The continuity of Judaism has been achieved precisely because it always sought a synthesis of its beliefs and practices with the conditions prevailing at any given time. It is no coincidence that the most fruitful periods of Judaism's development occurred in times and places where Judaism was most conspicuously in contact with the wider world around it. The history of the Jews in Spain or in the open society of Holland provides good examples of this. Conversely, the occasions when the Jews found themselves cut off from the outside world were, generally, times in which Judaism became increasingly insular and even self-indulgent – such as the increasingly sophisticated (and some would say irrelevant) dissection of the Talmud in seventeenth century Poland.

Sometimes Judaism generated its own internal dynamism by reacting to negative trends within itself to move itself forward. The emergence of *Chasidism*[1] was, in part, a reaction to the over-

---

[1] a branch of Orthodox that promotes spirituality and joy through the popularisation and internalisation of Jewish mysticism; see page 161

elaborate study of Talmud described above, though it also emerged against a background of poverty and persecution. The Enlightenment and the Emancipation[1] were major external pressures that demanded of Judaism that it once again respond and progress in order to survive. But, as at every stage of Jewish development, there were internal dynamics that encouraged the emergence of different responses, bringing with them the inevitable rivalries between differing interpretations over how best to carry Judaism forward.

The application of adjectives to describe these different interpretations of Judaism has already been noted. Two more were added at the start of the nineteenth century. German Jewish leaders feeling that the changes being introduced were too radical applied the prefix 'Reform', intending it as a criticism of them and those who were introducing them. One of the chief German critics was Isaac Bernays (1782-1849), who, in 1821, became Rabbi of Hamburg. Hamburg was the home of the first Reform temple,[2] the liturgy and practices of which he condemned for their radicalism. Those who, like Bernays, objected to these reforms, gave themselves and their version of Judaism another new prefix: Orthodox.[3]

The intention of Orthodoxy was to bring Judaism from the ghetto into the modern western world as untouched by modernity as possible. The idea of a sermon being given in the vernacular, for example, was unthinkable to eighteenth century German Jews, as was the suggestion that some of the traditional

---

[1] See note 1, page 170
[2] German Reform synagogues were called temples; see p. 196. This term was sometimes also used in America and elsewhere (eg Temple Beth Israel, Melbourne, and North Shore Temple Emanuel, Sydney).
[3] The prefix 'Reform' travelled to the United States of America where today the largest national synagogue movement in the world is the Union for Reform Judaism, as well as to Britain, where it is slightly more conservative than its sister Liberal movement; both are affiliates of 'The World Union'.

A Synthesis of Judaism and Modernity

prayers might also be recited in the mother tongue (even though many of the ancient Rabbis and subsequent commentators were in favour of this). Orthodox Judaism has based itself on the principle that Jewish practice and tradition can be added to but nothing can be taken away. The fact that nowadays sermons in Orthodox synagogues are routinely delivered in the mother tongue, as are one or two prayers, suggests an acknowledgement, however reluctant, of the need to adapt to the reality that the majority of emancipated Jews living in the western world are less familiar with Hebrew than were their ancestors. Recent developments within the world of Orthodox Judaism suggest that the role of women is changing, though this is not universally accepted – providing grounds for further divisions.[1]

In true Jewish tradition, Conservative Judaism emerged following a difference of opinion with another Jewish group. According to what may be folk-lore, the celebratory dinner to accompany the graduation of the first home-trained American Reform rabbis from the newly established Hebrew Union College in Cincinnati in 1883 included shellfish. This flagrant disregard for the Jewish dietary laws so incensed one of the Jewish guests that he formed a breakaway movement, which came to be known as Conservative Judaism. In fact, Conservative Judaism had been developing, both in Germany and the United States, since the mid-nineteenth century, and it was events in the 1880s (the publication of the Pittsburgh

---

[1] The orthodox 'United Synagogue' is the largest single synagogue movement in Britain, with around 65% of affiliated British Jews as members. At its head is the orthodox 'Chief Rabbi of Great Britain and the Commonwealth', an office which, despite its name, actually represents only members of the United Synagogue, not those other groups in Britain that are positioned to the left – and to the right – of that movement. Surprisingly, though, as his full title suggests, his authority even extends, at least theoretically, to some orthodox synagogues on our side of the world in Australia and South Africa.

Platform in 1885[1] in addition to the event described above) that led to a formal split with the Reform movement.

As its name – and origins – suggest, Conservative Judaism regarded some of the reforms that were taking place in Progressive Judaism as too extreme and so occupied a position on the traditional edge of that general movement, though it too rejects the idea that Torah was entirely given by God. Thus this movement would come under the umbrella that covers any non-Orthodox element of Judaism even though it regards itself as being a modern version of Orthodoxy. This is reflected in its practice, which, apart from its attitude towards women (about which it is also somewhat ambivalent) has more in common with that which is to be found in mainstream Orthodox synagogues than Progressive Judaism. In Israel and some other countries, Conservative Jews call themselves *Masorti* (traditional).

There are many Jews whose Judaism lacks any religious content but who, nevertheless, remain committed to their heritage. The description of such Jews as secular is a term that one hears most frequently in relation to Israel, where the title religious (*dati*) applies exclusively to the ultra-Orthodox Jewish sects with their black costumes and strict levels of observance and practice. Secular Jews may celebrate Jewish festivals and observe some Jewish customs but, particularly within Israel, these are a part of their national culture rather than a statement of religious conviction. From a Progressive Jewish perspective, the absence of a religious element in Judaism would seem to represent if not a betrayal, then at least a neglect of the very heart and purpose of Judaism's ancient heritage.

The responses to the Emancipation[1] described thus far can be characterised as being either an attempt to hold the influences

---

[1] See p.241

A Synthesis of Judaism and Modernity

of the modern world at bay by taking refuge in ancient religious customs or by abandoning those customs in order more fully to embrace modernity. In conceptual and practical terms, Progressive Judaism is the response to the modern world that most accurately reflects and continues the process that has allowed the development of Judaism through the centuries. The knowledge and insight gained at a particular point in humanity's development is measured against Jewish laws and practices. Those for which no justification can be found in the light of modern understanding are re-assessed and, where appropriate, adapted or set aside. This synthesis between the influence of a particular environment in which Jews found themselves at any time and Judaism's ancient customs has been the essence of Judaism's survival. Judaism has always been progressive; Progressive Judaism[2] affirms and seeks to continue this process.

---

[1] See note 1, page 170
[2] Progressive Judaism worldwide includes the American Reform and Reconstructionist movements, the British Reform and Liberal Movements, the Israel Progressive Movement and the Australian, New Zealand and Asia as well as the South African Progressive movements, those across the Former Soviet Union, and various other Reform, Liberal and Progressive Jewish communities worldwide. Though it does not include the Conservative movements, it generally works closely with them on various matters of common concern, particularly in Israel where both are under permanent pressure from the ultra-orthodox authorities who hold the balance of power.

28

BIBLE SCHOLARSHIP

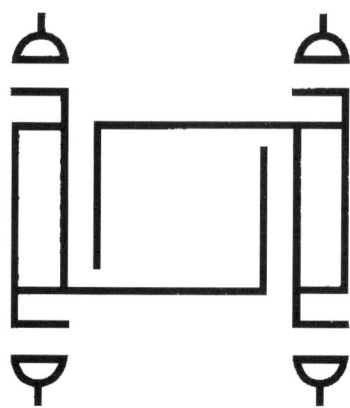

In the Middle Ages, Jews (like Christians and Muslims) held their sacred writings to be divinely revealed and free of error. Modernity rejects such fundamentalism and maintains that truth must be sought open-mindedly from all sources. We affirm the spirit of free inquiry. Among other things, we accept modern Bible scholarship, which has shown that the biblical writers, however divinely inspired, were fallible human beings and children of the Ancient Near East in which they lived.

Bible Scholarship

The distinction between the different responses to the Emancipation[1] is most clearly demonstrated by the attitude of the various groups to the origins of the Five Books of Moses, Judaism's 'holy book'. Orthodox Judaism sought to maintain the version of Judaism that had been established by the Rabbis seventeen hundred years earlier. This necessarily required an acceptance of the divine origin of the Torah, which meant that every repetition, omission or other inconsistency had a specific purpose that awaited the correct rabbinic interpretation. There had been occasional hints from biblical commentators that some inconsistencies could not easily be explained away. For example, in his commentary to Exodus chapter 20 (the revelation at Mount Sinai), twelfth century Spanish philosopher Abraham ibn Ezra could not conceal his puzzlement at the discrepancies between the two versions of the fourth commandment in Exodus and Deuteronomy, nor his contempt for those whose explanation resided in the possibility of God being able to utter two words simultaneously.[2] And the threat of excommunication from the Jewish community did not deter seventeenth century Dutch philosopher Baruch Spinoza from challenging the traditional view of the origin of the Bible.[3]

But it was Christian scholarship in the mid-nineteenth century that completely changed thinking about the authorship of the Bible and particularly the Five Books of Moses. Biblical scholars identified that variations and discrepancies in the text suggested that what had for so long been assumed to be a

---

[1] Note 1, page 170
[2] In his commentary to Exodus 20, Abraham ibn Ezra asks how the opening words of the fourth commandment in Exodus 20:8 (*zachor* – remember) and Deuteronomy 5:12 (*shamor* – observe) can have been heard simultaneously by humans even if it were possible for those words to have been so uttered by a divine power. The traditional response is found in the *Shabbat* song '*L'cha dodi*': '*shamor v'zachor b'dibur echad*'- observe and remember in one utterance!
[3] For example, in his work, *Tractatus Theologico-Politicus*, chapters 8-10, where Spinoza analyses the Bible in an attempt to ascertain its authorship.

single, unified document came, in fact, from a number of different sources.

The first method by which different sources were identified was the recognition that the divine name differed in some sections of the text. One of the clearest examples can be found in the creation stories at the beginning of the Book of Genesis. The first chapter, which tells the well known story of the creation of the world in six days, names the Creator as *Elohim* whereas in the second chapter, which offers a very different version of the creation of the world and the place of humankind in it, the Creator is described as *YHVH Elohim* – the Hebrew letters *Yud, Heh, Vav and Heh* forming the first part of this divine name. The source of the first chapter was defined as the 'E' source (as the first letter of *Elohim*) while that of chapter two was referred to as 'J' (because the first proponents of what came to be known as 'The Documentary Hypothesis' were German scholars who transliterated the Hebrew letter *yud* as a 'J'). Thus the existence of inconsistencies between the two stories was reconciled because instead of struggling to explain them, the recognition was that they had been written by two different authors in two different places with a different perspective and a different name for the Creator.

Later studies suggested that these two sources had specific geographical origins: the 'E' source from the northern kingdom of Israel and the 'J' source from Jerusalem. By this time, the existence of a priestly source, 'P', responsible for the laws outlined in the Book of Leviticus and other insertions that brought a priestly perspective to an earlier source, had been identified as had an editor or group of editors who had sought to impose a degree of unity on the history of Israel as described in the Five Books of Moses (and particularly in the 'historical' books, Deuteronomy – II Kings) a source known as 'D'.

There is much more that can be added, but this brief history of Bible scholarship must suffice to illustrate the progress that has been made in the past century and a half in understanding the origins of our sacred texts. This growth in understanding is important for a number of reasons. There are those who regard the biblical texts with the same eyes as did their medieval ancestors and who would claim that to question, criticise and challenge their divine authorship undermines Judaism.

But the critical examination of ancient texts does not in any way undermine them or diminish their value. On the contrary, it releases us from having to accept as divine truth episodes that are brutal (such as the command to annihilate the Canaanites in Deuteronomy 9:3) or seemingly impossible natural phenomena (such as the plagues having happened as described in the early chapters of the Book of Exodus). These can be regarded as our ancestors' own versions of their historical experience that have been orally transmitted (and developed) for many centuries before finally being committed to writing. Rather than being bound by a faith that demands that these and other stories and instructions be upheld as sacred truth, Progressive Judaism honours the efforts of our ancestors in identifying the key questions about human existence by revisiting them and applying to them the wisdom and knowledge of our own time. Thus we continue the process of which the production of the Five Books of Moses was an important part: to seek and work to implement God's true will for humanity.

29

THE MESSIANIC AGE

Rabbinic Judaism accepted the apocalyptic belief in a Messiah who would one day gather in the exiles and sit on the throne of a restored Davidic monarchy. We affirm the universalistic hope of the Prophets for a 'Messianic Age' brought about gradually, through the acceptance of God's will by all humanity.

The Messianic Age

Progressive Judaism believes that it is the divine will that humankind should live in harmony with itself and its Creator. This vision of a messianic age is one towards which all humanity should work and that should be the central goal of any religion that purports to speak in God's name. Orthodox Judaism's view of that future is rooted in the rabbinic vision of that messianic age, conceived two thousand years ago in a context that sought the return to political and religious conditions that had prevailed in the biblical kingdom of Judah, including a rebuilt Temple, priesthood and animal sacrifices. This is a view that Progressive Judaism cannot accept.

The rabbinic concept of a Messiah is probably one of the most misunderstood aspects of religion – not just in Judaism. The word is a translation of the Hebrew word *mashiach,* which means 'the anointed one'. Kings of Israel (and subsequently Judah) were welcomed to the throne in a ceremony where oil was poured over their heads. This was first done by the prophet Samuel to Saul[1] and then later to David[2]. A similar ceremony welcomed each of David's successors to the throne until the destruction of the city of Jerusalem and the end of the Davidic monarchy in 586 BCE. Since that time, there has been no monarch ruling over the Jews who was directly descended from King David – and in the eyes of the Jewish people, only such a person was qualified so to rule. This person would be the Messiah: the one who would be anointed as had all previous rulers of Judah, all members of the House of David.

The Messiah, then, must be a human being, not the supernatural or semi-divine figure that later myth has attributed to that title. At the time of Roman oppression, in the first century of the Common Era, anyone claiming to be the Messiah (and there were several) was making a political statement – namely that the oppressors would be overthrown

---

[1] I Samuel 10:1
[2] I Samuel 16:13

and independent Jewish rule re-established. The yardstick by which any would-be Messiah was measured was, therefore, self-evident: bringing relief from Roman oppression would constitute a legitimate claim to Messianic status. The destruction of the Temple in the year 70 CE and the subsequent dispersion of the Jews due to continued Roman oppression meant that the yearning for a Messiah went with the Jews into this new exile. The traditional belief developed that the arrival of this Messiah – the Jewish King who was a descendant of King David – would be heralded by the return of the prophet Elijah. The consequence of this Messianic return would be the rebuilding of the Temple and the re-introduction of sacrificial worship within it.[1]

Another aspect of this belief was that all Jews who had been exiled from their homeland would be gathered in to share this triumphant moment. This did not just apply to those who were alive at the time; every Jew who had died would be resurrected and brought back to the land of Israel. Belief in physical resurrection was a central element of rabbinic theology that is reflected in the second paragraph of the *T'filah* (which talks of God 'keeping faith with those who sleep in the dust') and *m'chayyeh ha-meitim* – (literally: who brings the dead back to life). This concept of physical resurrection and the ingathering of exiles is rejected by Progressive Judaism. The Progressive view of life after death is built around the concept of the eternity of the soul[2] which we like to believe in some undefined sense returns to the 'shelter of God's wings'.

---

[1] During the seventeenth century, there were several individuals who claimed to be the Messiah, raising the hopes of impoverished and persecuted Jews across Europe that redemption was at hand. The most notorious of these was Shabbetai Tzvi (1626-76) whose eventual conversion to Islam while imprisoned in Constantinople, shattered the dreams of many.

[2] This traditional belief in physical resurrection means that Orthodox Judaism does not permit cremation or any major interference with a body after death, such as autopsy and has been uncomfortable with most organ donation. See p. 150.

The Messianic Age

This messianic view, enshrined in traditional Jewish thought and prayer, also creates an ambiguity in the relationship of some Orthodox Jews to the modern State of Israel. The belief that a return to the land can only be brought about by the appearance of a descendant of David and associated divine intervention means that the modern state, created by human beings, is a contradiction that some ultra-Orthodox Jewish sects regard as an abomination. Thus one sees, in various improbable circumstances such as anti-Zionist demonstrations, *Chasidic* Jews in full seventeenth century Polish regalia bearing banners demanding the dismantling of the State of Israel. Even when serving orthodox synagogues or community organisations, you may note that some of the rabbis will not sing the words of Israel's national anthem *Hatikvah*.

The great medieval Rabbi Maimonides writes[1] that the 'Messianic age is when the Jews will regain their independence and all return to the land of Israel. The Messiah will be a very great king, who will achieve great fame, and his reputation among the gentile nations will be even greater than that of King Solomon. His great righteousness and the wonders that he will bring about will cause all peoples to make peace with him and all lands to serve him.... Nothing will change in the Messianic age, however, except that Jews will regain their independence. Rich and poor, strong and weak, will still exist. However it will be very easy for people to make a living, and with very little effort they will be able to accomplish very much... It will be a time when the number of wise men will increase...War shall not exist, and nation shall no longer lift up sword against nation...'

Despite Maimonides' words, the distinction between awaiting divine intervention to herald the coming of the Messiah and human action to change the political situation for the Jews represents the difference today between the traditional and

---

[1] Commentary on Mishna Sanhedrin 10:1

A Judaism for the Twenty-First Century

Progressive approaches to the messianic age. Progressive Judaism does not, however, regard the establishment of the State of Israel as a manifestation of the messianic age; along with the Prophets of ancient Israel, our view of that age is grander and more universal. As the prophet Isaiah declares, 'It is too small a task that you should be My servant only to raise up the tribes of Jacob and to restore the survivors of Israel; I will make you a light to the nations, that My salvation may reach to the end of the earth.'[1]

The exact nature of this messianic age is of course impossible to know or describe. There is a general sense that it will be a time to which various of the Prophets of Ancient Israel have alluded in their visions: Micah's view of a world where all weapons are turned into agricultural tools and everyone lives without fear under their own vine and fig tree[2] or Amos's yearning for a world where 'justice rolls down like water, righteousness like an everflowing stream'.[3]

Progressive Judaism fervently believes that such a world is the one that God wishes humanity to create for itself and that our divinely charged task is to do whatever we can, with God's guidance, to seek to bring it about. Sometimes the vision seems far away and efforts to assist with its realisation may appear futile. But Judaism has always cherished and nurtured the hope of such a future for humankind; much of Jewish liturgy reflects that hope. Our responsibility to work for it is reflected in the well known saying of the Rabbis: 'You are not required to complete the work but neither are you at liberty to abstain from it.'[4] Each of us has the duty to seek to bring God's will into our world, to do our part to bring the messianic age a little closer.

---

[1] Isaiah 49:6
[2] Micah 4:4
[3] Amos 5:24
[4] *Pirkei Avot* 2:16

30

THE SYNAGOGUE HAS PERMANENTLY REPLACED THE TEMPLE

*Rabbinic Judaism believed that with the coming of the Messiah, the Temple would be rebuilt and animal sacrifices would again be offered by priests. We affirm our belief that the Synagogue has permanently replaced the Temple. Accordingly, we recognise no distinction between persons of priestly descent (**kohanim**) and other Jews and we encourage the use of instrumental music in synagogue worship.*

A Judaism for the Twenty-First Century

At the heart of the rabbinic view of the messianic future that Judaism sought was the reintroduction of animal sacrifice. Detailed instructions for this ancient form of worship were contained in the biblical book of Leviticus, reflecting the fact that in the Ancient Near East several thousand years ago, the primary form of worship was the offering of sacrifices. This involved selecting a portion of that which had been received from the divine power and returning it to its provider by burning it (accompanied by appropriate ritual). This was believed to be the way to acknowledge the divine gifts of produce and livestock. As our ancestors' understanding of the nature of their relationship with the divine power grew more sophisticated (and so did the reasons for, and the nature of, their communication with it), there emerged the need for a particular group of people – priests – to oversee this most essential aspect of human life.

The emergence of specific groups responsible for managing the relationship between human beings and the deities of a particular society or tribe was not something that was unique to the ancient Israelites. Although their understanding of God as an invisible and omnipotent deity represented an enormous advance when measured against other nations' gods, the establishment of an elite group to undertake this task drew upon contemporary behaviour and custom. Thus there was a priestly elite – the sons of the first High Priest, Aaron – whose vital work was supported by other members of the tribe of Levi.

Clearly the priests *(kohanim)* and their assistants *(l'vi'im* – Levites) were an essential element of the Judaism that was being practised at the time of the Rabbis when the Temple still stood. Although there was hostility between the priestly and rabbinic groups[1], the latter recognised that, as many of the commandments in the Torah referred specifically to the role of

---

[1] Sadducees and Pharisees – see p. 158

The Synagogue has Permanently Replaced the Temple

the *kohanim* in sacrificial ritual, they were indispensable, no matter how corrupt and hostile they might be. Moreover, the need for the Temple, also mentioned in the Torah (as 'the place where the Eternal your God shall choose for the divine name to be established'[1]) meant that its destruction by the Romans in the year 70 CE heralded only a temporary absence and that it must be rebuilt in order for all the commandments in the Torah to be able to be carried out.

The destruction of the Temple brought an immediate end to the role of the priests. Nevertheless, the rabbinic belief that the Temple must be rebuilt meant that it was vital that the priestly role be maintained. This meant that, in their eyes, worship in the synagogue was only a temporary substitute for the Temple and some of the prayers uttered within it reflected the yearning for this return to the situation that prevailed in the first century of the Common Era. The traditional version of the seventeenth benediction of the *T'filah*, for example, recited three times daily by Orthodox Jews, includes the following request: 'Accept thy people Israel and their prayer; restore the service to the innermost part of thine house; receive in love and favour the fire-offerings of Israel and their prayer; and may the service of thy people Israel be ever acceptable to thee…' [2]

Moreover, one of the priestly roles, which was to bestow the priestly blessing[3] upon the people, was incorporated into the traditional recitation of the *T'filah*. This immediately preceded the final blessing, the theme of which is peace. Those who regard themselves as directly descended from Aaron leave the synagogue to have their feet washed by the Levites before returning, barefoot, to stand on the *bimah* to transmit God's blessing to the rest of the Israelite congregation – a ritual known as *duchening*.

---

[1] e.g. Deuteronomy 16:6, 11
[2] e.g. Singer's Prayerbook (1962 edition) p. 52
[3] Numbers 6:17-19

Other remnants of biblical rules relating to those purporting to be descended from the *kohanim* are to be found at Jewish cemeteries. According to rules in the Book of Leviticus, *kohanim* are not permitted to have any contact with the dead[1] and so there is a special room adjacent to the prayer hall and special paths within cemeteries to keep the *kohanim* at a prescribed safe distance from the dead body. *Kohanim* are also prohibited from marrying divorcees.

Progressive Judaism completely rejects the suggestion that the Temple will or should ever be rebuilt. Animal sacrifice is one of those elements of religion that belongs firmly in humanity's past, as does the notion that certain individuals have particular powers or duties based upon a hereditary connection (which, incidentally, is passed from father to son). The synagogue has completely replaced the Temple as the focal point of worship for Jews the world over – a reality acknowledged by the early Reformers of Judaism in the nineteenth century in Germany and America who actually called their places of worship 'Temples' – a tradition that can still be found in some of our congregations in Australia such as Temple David in Perth, Temple Beth Israel in Melbourne and North Shore Temple Emanuel in Sydney. There is no place in the liturgy offered within Progressive synagogues for any reference to the rebuilding of the Temple, the offering of sacrifices, or the coming of a Messiah to implement such practices. Nor indeed is there a place for any distinction between Jew and Jew based on hereditary connections or archaic priestly rituals of blessing.

The only element of Temple worship that Progressive Judaism has reintroduced into its synagogue worship is the inclusion of instrumental music, though not with any aim of reinstituting Temple practices. It is well documented (e.g. Psalm 150) that an

---

[1] e.g. Leviticus 21:11

array of different musical instruments accompanied the singing of psalms and other aspects of worship in the Temple. The Temple even included a *magrefah*, probably a water-powered organ.[1] Following the destruction of the Temple, such musical accompaniment was forbidden by the Rabbis[2]. Progressive Judaism, realising that the purpose of worship is the elevation of the spirit and that appropriate music can facilitate this, encourages the use of various instruments in its congregations' services. These might include, but are not restricted to, the organ, guitar, harp, flute or cello. The variety and the potential for meaningful worship has greatly increased with the inclusion of such accompaniment to our prayer within the place of worship that is now the focal point of Jewish prayer.

---

[1] Jerusalem Talmud *Sukkot* 5:6, 55c–d
[2] Talmud, *Gitin* 7a

31

SINCERITY IN WORSHIP

We affirm the paramount need for sincerity in worship: we may not say with our lips what we do not believe in our hearts. To that end, though we retain much of the traditional Jewish liturgy, we have revised it, with some omissions and modifications, and many amplifications. For the same reason, we use English as well as Hebrew in our services.

Sincerity in Worship

The general principle underlying worship in Progressive synagogues is that it should be uplifting for the worshipper. To the reintroduction of music is added the principle that in Progressive Judaism, the understanding of prayers is no less important than their recitation. Worship in ancient times was based on the belief that what was being done by humans was for the benefit of the divine power, that God saw, heard and – in the case of sacrifice, smelt and tasted – what was being offered and rewarded the worshippers. Progressive Jewish worship is directed more at the participants, intending to remind the worshippers' of their religious, ethical, moral and social responsibilities grounded in their Jewish heritage and to encourage future action.

As already noted, a significant proportion of Orthodox Jewish liturgy looks back to the time when sacrifice was central to Jewish worship and requests that it be restored in a rebuilt Temple in Jerusalem[1]. It also includes prayers that anticipate the re-establishment of the Davidic monarchy. Once the Messiah[2] has been restored as the King of the Jews, all his subjects (past and present) will be gathered from the places to which they have been exiled and brought to Jerusalem. These beliefs, central to the theology of the Rabbis following the destruction of the Second Temple in 70 CE, are the backbone of Orthodox Jewish liturgy. Whether or not those Jews, repeating those words, genuinely desire that the Temple be rebuilt in order that the smoke from sacrificial offerings can once again fill the air of Jerusalem as it did two thousand and more years ago, is for them to confirm. As far as Progressive Judaism is concerned, the offering of sacrifice belongs to a different time and place, to a phase of human development that has long since been left behind and to which any regular reference in prayer is felt to be unhelpful and inappropriate.

---

[1] See p. 190
[2] The anointed one; a descendant of King David. See p. 189

Accordingly, one of the first – and most important – tasks of Progressive Judaism was to revisit the Jewish liturgy with a view to ensuring that it reflected and expressed the aspirations of modern Progressive Jews, rather than those of the ancient Rabbis. Progressive Judaism accepts, admires and adopts much of Jewish liturgy. But some of the theological beliefs of the Rabbis and their visions of the ideal Jewish future have no place in a Progressive Jewish view of the world. Such visions and beliefs have, therefore, been modified or even removed entirely from Progressive Jewish liturgy.

The reforming of Jewish liturgy was one of the earliest and most defining elements of Progressive Judaism in Germany and America, and this trend has been enthusiastically embraced and continued across Progressive Judaism. It is worth a brief mention of British and American prayerbook development in part because our current liturgy is based on both traditions.

Early Progressive prayerbooks paid scant attention to the traditional structure of Jewish liturgy, preferring instead to concentrate on the aesthetic quality of the readings – almost entirely in the local language spoken – that made up the services. The 'Liberal Jewish Prayerbook' of 1926, produced by Rabbi Israel Mattuck was a classic example of this. It contained a choice of fifteen different Sabbath morning services, each of which contained a selection of passages from various strands of Jewish literature grouped according to theme rather than any traditional order; their reading would have lasted no more than an hour.

Forty-one years later a major re-evaluation of Progressive Jewish liturgy reached fruition. In 1967, 'Service of the Heart' was published as the new prayerbook of Liberal Judaism in Britain. This saw a return to more traditional service structures and a significant increase in the amount of Hebrew, though there were various alternative translations and other creative readings offered in its pages, and it was used as the basis of the then new American Reform prayerbook, *'Gates of Prayer'* which was also adopted by the Australian, New Zealand and South African Communities. The trend to use more traditional material has continued in the most recent British Progressive prayerbooks from the Liberal and Reform Movements. Here too the combination of traditional prayers are found alongside a selection of more creative readings and songs, and a similar structure has been adopted by the latest American Reform prayerbook, *'Mishkan T'filah'*, the World Union edition of which has been developed and adopted by the Australian, New Zealand and South African congregations.

In general, therefore, it could be said that there has been a trend in Progressive liturgy towards the traditional, with the development from what might be described as the 'anarchy' of the earlier prayerbooks through to the more traditionally structured new books, the creative readings of which are built around the traditional components of Jewish liturgy. The principles of Progressive Judaism remain, however: a desire to make worship a meaningful and enriching experience by ensuring that nothing that is uttered or read in Progressive Jewish worship runs contrary to the beliefs of Progressive Judaism. The regular revision of the liturgy and the production of new prayerbooks is a testimony to Progressive Judaism's desire to keep the words of its prayers in accord with its members' spiritual, emotional and intellectual needs.

Of course, the ideological content of the prayers is only a part of the worship experience. A key element of ensuring sincerity in worship is that prayers be understood. To this end, some of the prayers in Progressive synagogues will be read in English in an effort to help worshippers comprehend what they are actually reciting. To this must be added a note of explanation, however.

A Judaism for the Twenty-First Century

Much of what is read in our services is ancient poetry praising God and, as such, is not meant to be understood to be literally true. A good example of this is a short extract from the Book of Exodus that is traditionally sung on *Shabbat*. The full version of this passage reads 'The People of Israel shall keep *Shabbat*, observing *Shabbat* throughout the ages as a covenant for all time. It is a sign for all time between Me and the people of Israel. For in six days God made heaven and earth, and on the seventh day God ceased from work and was refreshed...'.[1] It has been quoted in full as it was felt that the reference to God creating the world in six days and resting on the seventh offered a poetic or midrashic explanation for the celebration of the Sabbath, which was not meant to be taken as a scientific statement regarding the origins of the world.

One significant change alluded to earlier is the introduction of the matriarchs, Sarah, Rebecca, Rachel and Leah to their male partners in the first blessing of the *T'filah*.[2] By doing so, we emphasise that the God to whom we still direct our prayers, and whose presence we feel or seek, is the same God known and experienced not only by our patriarchs but also by our matriarchs, who, a brief reading of the texts will demonstrate, were often pivotal in the unfolding of our story.

Another change to the key *T'filah* blessings is the recasting of the traditional mention of weather (wind, rain and dew), to act as a reminder to us of our dependence on the proper patterns of the global environment, and our reliance on it for our food and indeed for our very survival.[3]

Praying is not only about literal comprehension of the words that are being read. One of the limitations of what some might

---

[1] Exodus 31:16-17, see the World Union Edition of '*Mishkan T'filah,*' p.162
[2] E.g. see World Union Edition *Mishkan T'filah* p.324 and note
[3] E.g. see World Union Edition *Mishkan T'filah* p.246 and note

regard as the over-use of English in services is that a major feature of Jewish prayer, namely the use of the Hebrew language, is consequently limited. Considerably more Hebrew is used in Progressive synagogues at the beginning of the twenty-first century than was the case at the start of the last one. This does not necessarily reflect a greater level of Hebrew knowledge or ability on the part of congregants (though increased opportunities for study may have encouraged this). It is, rather, a recognition that prayer is as much about the creation of an appropriate atmosphere as it is to do with understanding. The reading of psalms and prayers in the original Hebrew allows their poetic quality to be appreciated as well as encouraging a link with Jewish communities all over the world who have, for generations, used those same words in their worship. It also links us to the past and to the future.

Finding a balance between ancient and current theological concepts, between the use of the vernacular and the ancient tongue of Hebrew, and traditional and modern prayers is an ongoing task that needs to be revisited in every generation. Progressive Jewish worship will continue to respond to changes in the needs of worshippers as well as to future technological developments that may, in time, see prayerbooks superseded by other methods of recording and reciting prayer. And, as in all cases, Progressive Judaism will seek to maintain the delicate balance between Jewish tradition and the demands of modernity.

32

THE EQUAL STATUS OF WOMEN AND MEN IN SYNAGOGUE LIFE

We affirm the equal status of women and men in synagogue life. The Progressive Jewish movement has been the pioneer in this regard. There is no sex segregation in our synagogues. Women and men may lead services, become Rabbis and hold any synagogue office.

The Equal Status of Women and Men in Synagogue Life

When, in March 1902, the Jewish Religious Union, the forerunner of Liberal Judaism, was seeking premises in which to hold its first religious service, it approached the then Chief Rabbi of the United Synagogue, Hermann Adler, to ask if it could use one of the United Synagogues to hold its first service on a Saturday afternoon. One of the grounds for the denial of the request was an objection to the proposal that men and women be allowed to sit together. The first service of the JRU took place in October of that year in the Wharncliffe Rooms of the Great Central Hotel in Marylebone Road in London. In his address, Claude Goldsmith Montefiore made several references to 'Jews and Jewesses'[1] – and one of the most famous of those Jewesses present that day was another founder of the movement, the Honourable Lily Montagu[2].

Because one of its founders was such a determined woman, Liberal and in its turn Progressive Judaism was always going to demand and practise equality for women. In fact, given the nature of its approach, equality for women in all aspects of synagogue and communal life was an integral part of its ethos that would have asserted itself in any event, even without the influence of Lily Montagu. As Rabbi Lawrence Rigal observes, '… right from the opening service the JRU made women feel welcome and encouraged them to participate.'[3]

It was also a woman, Ada Phillips, who in 1929 began to organise the formation of a Progressive Community in Melbourne Australia, following her various visits to London, having encountered and admired Lily Montagu and the Liberal Jewish Synagogue there. Within a year, the first American Reform Rabbi, Jerome Mark, had arrived, in time for the High Holydays, 1930, right at the start of the Great Depression.

---

[1] Lawrence Rigal and Rosita Rosenberg 'Liberal Judaism, The First Hundred Years.' (2004) p.23
[2] See p. 173
[3] Lawrence Rigal and Rosita Rosenberg 'Liberal Judaism…', *ibid*

Many challenges had to be overcome before eventually, under Rabbi Dr Hermann Sanger, himself persuaded to come to Melbourne by Lily Montagu, the congregation grew into the influential Temple Beth Israel, the alma mater of the entire Progressive Movement in Australia and New Zealand. Women have continued to be at the forefront of Progressive Judaism in Australia in every sphere since its first beginnings.

The difference in men's and women's religious roles in traditional Judaism dates back to the times of the Rabbis who decreed that women were not obligated to carry out time-bound positive *mitzvot* – that is, those active religious duties that could only take place at a specific time and in a public place.[1] The reason the Rabbis gave for not requiring women to observe these rules was based upon their numerous domestic roles, particularly in relation to children, which, the Rabbis felt, could not easily be set aside in order to fulfil so many individual religious obligations. In particular, these included *mitzvot* relating to worship – the lifestyles of men, apparently, being more flexible and adaptable to such demands. This distinction in roles is even mentioned in the traditional daily liturgy where a man recites a blessing thanking God for not making him a woman while the female equivalent thanks God for making her 'according to the divine will'.

Another factor in the desire to keep men and women apart derived from concerns relating to purity as defined in biblical times. Then, whenever a woman was menstruating, she was obliged to separate herself from the Israelite camp for a period of seven days until her 'uncleanliness' was ended. This fear of 'impurity' in relation to women, enshrined in the laws of the

---

[1] The lighting of candles, for example, is clearly a time-bound positive *mitzvah* and is defined by the Rabbis as being a woman's task, but it takes place in private. The place of women in Rabbinic Judaism is clearly limited to the private sphere.

The Equal Status of Women and Men in Synagogue Life

Torah and dressed up as a desire to uphold those laws, meant that although women were not actually prohibited from carrying out the *mitzvot* in relation to prayer, the custom was for them to be excluded. If women did wish to be part of the congregation during worship, it was deemed necessary to keep them separate from men (a tradition that had its roots in the Second Temple, which included a Court of the Women[1]). This separation eventually became accepted practice and was assumed to be the 'law'. Orthodox synagogues were constructed to ensure that men and women were kept apart – often by brick walls through which they could only observe proceedings through narrow slits, though in more recent times, this 'barrier' has been reduced in some synagogues to a low curtain or railing. A brief example will suffice to illustrate the inaccuracy of the misconception that women are prohibited from participating in synagogue worship. The daughters of the famous biblical commentator Rashi are reputed to have worn *t'fillin*. Though there have been objections to this practice, Orthodox scholars are forced to concede that there is nothing in any of the rabbinic sources that prohibits them from so doing.

Progressive Judaism would not, in any event, need justification from traditional sources to permit the inclusion of women in synagogue life. One of the most obvious consequences of its declared aim to incorporate modern trends into its practice of Judaism is the equal status accorded to women, reflecting the greater role played by women in society in general. Nevertheless, religion is often one of the most conservative areas of human behaviour and although no rational argument can be put forward as to why women should not be able to take part in synagogue ritual, lead services and even become rabbis, it was not until 1975 that the first woman rabbi was ordained by the Leo Baeck College in London and there are still some women in Progressive congregations who, when asked, are

---

[1] Described in the *Mishnah (Middot* 2:5)

reluctant to take an active role in synagogue worship (and a few Progressive synagogues who seem reluctant to employ women rabbis). Nevertheless, the participation of women in synagogue services and ritual is now an accepted element of Progressive Jewish practice. Women play their part in leading religious services and carrying out rituals in relation to the Torah (which, in Orthodox circles, are generally not touched or even approached by women). Mixed seating has been the norm in all Progressive synagogues since the movement was founded at the start of the twentieth century and the fact that families sit together is one of the most oft-quoted reasons for people preferring Progressive synagogue services to those in more traditional environments.

The role of women in lay leadership in synagogues has the same history as that of their role in its religious activities. Once again, Progressive Judaism has been at the forefront of involving women in this area of synagogue life. Women play an equal role on synagogue councils and committees and, following the example of Lily Montagu, have played major roles both within their own synagogue communities and in the Progressive Movement on a wider level. It is perhaps worth noting at this point that there is latterly a trend in orthodox communities to encourage such developments as women's prayer services and study groups. Without the pioneering work of Progressive Judaism in this field, it is unlikely that such innovations would have occurred – though it should also be acknowledged that the struggle to implement such practices will be far more hard-fought than was ever the case in the Progressive movement which, from the outset, regarded the equal treatment of women as one of its most basic principles.

33

THE EQUAL STATUS OF GIRLS AND BOYS IN RELIGIOUS EDUCATION

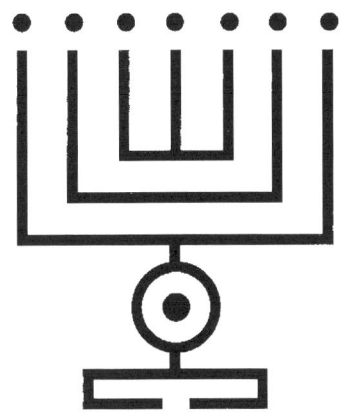

*We affirm the equal status of girls and boys in religious education. Accordingly, we have introduced the ceremony of **Bat-mitzvah** to complement the traditional **Bar-mitzvah** at the age of thirteen, and we encourage a further ceremony, such as **Kabbalat Torah** ('Acceptance of Torah' or 'Confirmation'), at fifteen or sixteen.*

Just as it discriminated between men and women in synagogue life, so traditional Judaism regarded the academic education of boys as essential while that of girls was at best a luxury but generally quite unnecessary. In the *shtetls*[1] of Eastern Europe, for example, boys went to school from an early age; they would learn to read and write Hebrew and then use that skill to learn and develop their understanding of Jewish literature, from Bible to *Mishnah*. If a boy showed particular aptitude, he might be considered eligible for further studies at *yeshivah*.[2]

A young girl in that same environment would receive a very different type of education. Typically, a daughter would be taught how to carry out various elements of household work by her mother – preparing food, laundry and even some of the more basic agricultural work. Although the world of the Eastern European *shtetl* has long since disappeared, within Orthodox Judaism the distinction between the educational opportunities for boys and girls often remains.

A boy marks his arrival at the age of thirteen by celebrating a *bar-mitzvah* ceremony as an individual, to denote his entry into the adult community. The literal translation, 'son of the commandment,' indicates a recognition that at this age a boy is deemed sufficiently mature to be responsible for fully carrying out his duties as a Jewish male. The *bar-mitzvah* 'ceremony' would occur on the first occasion when the Torah was read in public following the child's thirteenth birthday (according to Hebrew reckoning) and would serve a very specific purpose. Because of the intensity of the Jewish education that a boy received in an enclosed Jewish environment, a particularly gifted young boy might, from an early age, have read from the Torah or led some of the prayers in the synagogue service. He would not, however, have been called by name to come up and

---

[1] Yiddish word meaning 'small town'. See p. 42
[2] Academy for Jewish study.

The Equal Status of Girls and Boys in Religious Education

recite the blessings before and after the reading from the Torah. Being given an *aliyah*[1] was a privilege only granted to adult males in orthodox circles – that is, any male over the age of thirteen. Because of the traditional requirement that certain prayers can only be recited when ten men over the age of thirteen are present, a boy's thirteenth birthday was important because it meant that he could now be included in a *minyan*[2]. Consequently, calling him up to recite the Torah blessings was a way of announcing publicly that he could henceforth be counted as part of a *minyan*. It is worth mentioning that *bar-mitzvah* is a description of the young man who reaches the age of thirteen. One can be or become *bar-mitzvah*; one can celebrate this by having a *bar-mitzvah* ceremony; one cannot, despite common parlance, 'have' a *bar-mitzvah*. Indeed to be a Bar (or bat) mitzvah is the Jewish way to describe a teenager.

As detailed in the previous chapter, the development of Jewish law had, by and large, excluded women from any of the rituals relating to religious worship. Consequently it made no sense in Orthodox circles for the female equivalent of such a ceremony to be introduced. Moreover, the ancient Rabbis had recognised that girls tend to mature earlier than boys, and so had decreed that an equivalent level of maturity was reached by a girl when she attained twelve years. Those religious duties that applied to women were obligatory for girls aged twelve and over, but it was felt that no communal fanfare was required to mark this transition.

Some years ago, and perhaps in response to developments in Progressive Judaism, Orthodox synagogues introduced a ceremony, increasingly being called *Bat Mitzvah*, that takes place shortly after a girl's twelfth birthday. Usually it is a

---

[1] Being called to recite blessings before and after the reading of the Torah; see p. 105, note 1.
[2] See p. 94

group ceremony held on a Sunday or a weekday. They do not permit the celebrant(s) to have any contact with the Torah nor, indeed, to enter those areas of the synagogue that traditional Judaism regards as an exclusively male domain. As such, the gap between educational opportunities for boys and girls in a traditional Jewish environment has remained much as it has been throughout Jewish history. However, very recently a few modern Orthodox communities have started celebrating an individual girl's *Bat Mitzvah* on *Shabbat,* just after the service, and even inviting the girl to address the congregation about the content of the Torah portion, demonstrating that orthodoxy can eventually begin to respond to new understanding and the needs and demands of our time.

Progressive Judaism has long since recognised the importance of educating boys and girls together and to an equivalent level of knowledge. Our religion classes have always welcomed boys and girls (as indeed, it must be said, is now the case in the majority of Orthodox Jewish religion schools) and guided them towards the same educational goal: a full awareness of their Jewish heritage and, in particular, an appreciation of it from a Progressive perspective. When its founders first established this equality of educational opportunity for boys and girls, they also believed that the traditional idea of celebrating the transition into adulthood at the age of twelve (for girls) or thirteen years was no longer appropriate for two reasons: it was divisive, because it distinguished between boys and girls, and it was out of touch, because twelve or thirteen was not regarded as an age when a young person – male or female – was in a position to make a commitment to his or her Jewish heritage.

Accordingly, the founders of Progressive Judaism in Germany and America introduced a new ceremony for its young adults. Borrowing heavily from Protestantism, a ceremony of Confirmation was introduced. It was a form of graduation ceremony for an entire class of Jewish students reaching the end of their formal religious studies at the age of fifteen or sixteen. More recently it was given the Jewish title of *Kabbalat Torah* ('accepting the Torah'). In its early days, this group ceremony was held on the festival of *Shavu'ot*, which is traditionally celebrated as the time when the Israelites received the Torah at Mount Sinai. Nowadays, where they are observed, such ceremonies take place at various times of the year – *Sukkot* or *Chanukkah*, or at the end of the academic year, for example. A *Kabbalat Torah* ceremony typically involves all the students participating in the *Shabbat* or festival service and receiving a certificate and/or suitable gift (e.g. a prayerbook or a Hebrew Bible) at the conclusion of the ceremony.

Although the logic that led to the abandoning of *bar-mitzvah* in favour of a later ceremony is indisputable, religion rarely pays attention to logic. For reasons that were instinctive and emotional, Progressive Jews began to feel that their children – and their families – were somehow missing out by not having a ceremony at the age of thirteen. Consequently, in the mid-twentieth century, the *bar-mitzvah* ceremony was re-introduced and an exact equivalent for girls came into being alongside it – a *bat-mitzvah* ceremony. Aside from preparing for their *bar-* or *bat-mitzvah*, the children of modern Progressive Jews rarely have the experience of leading – or the skills to lead – parts of the service as might some male youngsters in a more Orthodox Jewish environment. Also, the fact that Progressive communities do not place so much emphasis on a *minyan* meant that the need to know the moment a boy reached the age of thirteen, and could then be counted, had less importance. So a *bar-* or *bat-mitzvah* ceremony has become an opportunity for a Jewish child to read from the scroll and perhaps lead some of the prayers in the service shortly after his or her thirteenth birthday, in the presence of family and friends, the community and of course, God. Usually the children celebrating this occasion are also expected to give a short speech, explaining the significance of their Torah portion and their *bar-* or *bat-mitzvah* ceremony. The participants will hopefully continue their Jewish education after this – though it is a source of regret that the percentage of our young people who continue their education beyond a *bar-* or *bat-mitzvah* ceremony is not as high as it might be. Nevertheless, Progressive Judaism is intent on seeking ways to attract more teenagers to continue to study and attend synagogue regularly, in order to assist and encourage them to make Judaism a part of their adult lives.

34

THE EQUAL STATUS OF WOMEN AND MEN IN MARRIAGE LAW AND RITUAL

We affirm the equal status of women and men in marriage law and ritual. With us, therefore, bride and bridegroom alike play an active role in the Jewish marriage service. Similarly, we object to the traditional **Gett** *(bill of divorce) by which the husband unilaterally 'sends away' his wife and have created instead a reciprocal* **Get**. *Moreover, recognising that there are loving, committed relationships other than marriage between a man and a woman, Progressive Judaism recognises the right of Jewish same-sex couples, with and without children, to receive equal treatment in all areas of congregational life, including the right to celebrate their partnerships with a Service of Commitment conducted by a rabbi.*

Historically, the union of a man and a woman has always been a significant moment in human society – not least because the role of the couple was to produce the next generation. A series of rituals, usually relating to the couple's fertility, invariably accompanies the marriage ceremony. Judaism is no exception to this and the roots of many of the rituals that are part of a Jewish wedding ceremony can be traced back to what was originally the primary purpose of marriage: the perpetuation of the family or tribal group.

In ancient – and not so ancient – times, great emphasis was placed upon marriage. In Jewish communities in the middle ages, marriages were invariably arranged by the parents of young people and the couple themselves often met for the first time under the wedding canopy, the *chuppah*. Nowadays, of course, the situation is very different. Although marriages are still arranged in a few ultra-Orthodox Jewish communities and although there are still some Jewish families who regard a child who marries someone non-Jewish (known as 'marrying out') as having died, the majority of Jews, in keeping with modern cultural developments, choose their own partners – often preferring not to commit themselves to marriage. The different types of partnership that exist and Progressive Judaism's attitude to them will be considered at the end of this chapter. Let us commence with the traditional rituals and regulations that apply to Jewish weddings.

In biblical times, women were regarded as possessions and effectively they were purchased by men. The traditional Jewish wedding ceremony, therefore, is a form of business transaction in which the man purchases the woman (by means of the ring) and utters the formula *'Har'ei at m'kudeshet li b'taba'at zo k'dat Moshe v'Yisra'el'* – 'Behold, you are betrothed to me according to the law of Moses and Israel.'[1] If this statement to the woman,

---

[1] Wedding service, eg see *Siddur Lev Chadash* p.598

accompanied by the giving of a ring, is witnessed by two competent Jewish male adults, then a document to this effect is signed *(k'tubbah)* and the woman belongs to the man. She can only be released from this legally binding agreement if the man grants her a bill of divorce *(get)*.

Such an attitude is unacceptable to Progressive Judaism. Men and women are regarded as equals, so marriage is a mutual contract. This is acknowledged in several ways in the Progressive wedding ceremony. There is usually an exchange of rings, and the woman recites a formula equivalent to the traditional one uttered by the man. Like the Orthodox document, the Progressive *k'tubbah* recording this exchange of vows contains details of the date and location of the marriage, as well as the names of the bride and groom. Whereas the Orthodox *k'tubbah* contains matters relating to property and finance as well as a list of the bride's dowry (in Aramaic), the Progressive one records (in Hebrew and English) that the bride and groom declared their love for one another and 'promised and undertook, through this holy covenant of love and respect, of peace and companionship, to establish a Jewish home, a sanctuary dedicated to godliness in accordance with the ideals of Jewish marriage.'[1]

Even though the Progressive emphasis on the equality of bride and groom in a marriage service makes its content and significance very different from an Orthodox wedding ceremony, the *k'tubbah* is one example of a practice being observed across the Jewish spectrum. This demonstrates the emotional attachment to traditional ritual and custom even in a modern age. Some customs (such as *bedeken* – see below) are clearly presented as options that can be used to enhance the couple's wedding experience. Progressive Judaism welcomes an attachment to Judaism's past but wishes to make clear the

---

[1] Quoted from the UPJ *k'tubbah*

likely origins of such practices and offers the bride and groom the choice of incorporating them in, or omitting them from, their wedding ceremony.

One such custom re-establishing its place in modern Progressive Jewish weddings is *bedeken*.[1] Immediately prior to the wedding ceremony, the bride and groom, along with both sets of parents (where possible) meet in an adjoining room where the groom lowers a veil over the bride's face. In arranged marriages in the past, this may well have been the first time the bride and groom have met and is therefore an opportunity for the groom's father to ascertain that the correct woman is being given. There are also reminders here of the incident in the Torah when Jacob was given Laban's older daughter, Leah, when he believed he was marrying the younger daughter, Rachel.[2] The idea today that the bride and groom are introduced to one another at this moment, when they have doubtless known each other for some time, is patently absurd. Nevertheless, this practice immediately prior to the public wedding ceremony can provide a moving private moment for the bride and groom to share. An exclusively *Ashkenazi* custom, for which no such practical explanation or justification can be offered, sees the bride circle seven times around the groom before taking her place alongside him. Though its origins are probably rooted in a superstitious anxiety relating to male fertility, some variation of this practice, such as the wife circling the husband three times and then the husband circling the wife three times, is occurring more frequently in Progressive weddings.

An enduring symbol of Jewish weddings is the *chuppah* (wedding canopy), beneath which the wedding ceremony takes

---

[1] *Bedeken* – a Yiddish word meaning 'covering'. This ceremony is not part of *Sephardi* wedding ritual.
[2] Genesis 29:31ff

place. The *chuppah* is popularly believed to represent the Jewish home that the couple will build together, though it may be meant to represent a four poster bed. As with so many things in Jewish tradition, the original reasons for ancient customs may have been replaced with explanations and interpretations that have symbolic or sentimental meaning. An example of this is the suggestion that the *chuppah* is open on all sides to remind us of Abraham's and Sarah's tent, which was open in order to welcome visitors.

The ceremony itself, conducted by the rabbi, traditionally has two parts: the betrothal *(kiddushin* or *erusin)* and the actual marriage *(nissu'in)*. In the Middle Ages, these two ceremonies took place at separate times – perhaps as much as a year apart. Nowadays both parts of the ceremony are combined beneath the *chuppah*. The bride and groom, along with all the guests, are welcomed in God's name and there then follows a blessing thanking God for the gift of marriage.

Then comes the exchange of rings described above, followed by the reading of the *k'tubbah*. There then follow seven blessings *(sheva b'rachot)* thanking God for the joy of marriage and asking for blessing upon the bride and groom. Following these blessings, from which Progressive Judaism has removed various references to the rebuilding of the Temple, the bride and groom share a glass of wine. Finally, in what is probably the best known feature of a Jewish wedding, the groom breaks a glass with his foot. Again, the reasons given for this custom are many and varied (the first – or last – time the husband gets to put his foot down!), but its origins are probably connected with the banishment of evil spirits that may affect the couple's fertility.

Although the ancient Rabbis (and biblical legislators) believed that the only permitted union was between man and woman, our modern age has developed a very different perspective.

Progressive Judaism's principles of inclusion and equality extend to lesbian and gay individuals, couples and families. Progressive Judaism rejects the biblical prohibition against sexual acts between members of the same sex[1] and may offer a Service of Commitment to same-sex couples. In accordance with the wishes of the couple concerned, a Service of Commitment may include some of the symbols and rituals associated with heterosexual marriage. In general terms, Progressive Judaism recognises that love between two people is a source of joy and is something that should be celebrated and for which God should be thanked.

Sadly, not all relationships endure, and Judaism has long recognised the need for appropriate legal structures to deal with the dissolution of a marriage. Unfortunately, just as the traditional marriage treated the woman as a possession, so too does the traditional process for divorce. If an Orthodox Jewish man who is civilly divorced wishes to remarry, he can. If an Orthodox Jewish woman wishes to remarry she cannot unless and until she receives from her ex-husband a bill of divorce, a *get*. A divorced woman whose husband refuses to issue her with a *gett* is known as an *agunah* – a chained woman.[2] Such a situation is unacceptable to Progressive Judaism: it will not tolerate any manipulation of ancient biblical law whereby a man seeks to penalise his ex-wife. Divorced couples are encouraged if possible to seek an Orthodox *gett* which should avoid any problems in the future, but alternatively can acquire a 'Document of Release' from a Progressive *beit din*[3] to confirm the dissolution of a marriage. However such a document is not recognised by Orthodox authorities. The idea is to have a religious ending to a relationship that started in a religious way.

---

[1] Leviticus 20:18
[2] If an *agunah* does remarry (this would not be permitted in an Orthodox synagogue), any children of that marriage are regarded in Orthodox Jewish law as *mamzerim* ('bastards', singular *mamzer*). See the next chapter.
[3] Rabbinic court: for more details, see p. 235

From the above, it should be clear that Progressive Judaism recognises that there have been many changes in family structures over the past 200 years. In keeping with its principles, this movement seeks to adapt its religious heritage to reflect these new realities and welcomes all Jews, whatever their family circumstances may be.

35

CHILDREN ARE NOT TO BE HELD RESPONSIBLE FOR THE ACTIONS OF THEIR PARENTS

We affirm the principle, forcefully stated in the 18th chapter of Ezekiel,[1] that children are not to be held responsible for the actions of their parents. We therefore reject the law of **mamzer** *('bastard') that penalises the offspring of unions prohibited by the biblical laws of consanguinity and affinity.*

---

[1] 'What do you people mean by quoting this proverb about the land of Israel: 'The fathers eat sour grapes, and the children's teeth are set on edge'? As surely as I live, declares the Sovereign God, you will no longer quote this proverb in Israel.' (Ezekiel 18:2-4). This chapter concerns itself with specific modern examples of children not being punished for their parents' actions.

Children are Not to be Held Responsible for the Actions of their Parents

According to tradtional Judaism, the offspring of an adulterous or incestuous relationship is referred to as a *mamzer*, which is often understood as 'bastard', but literally means 'spoilt'. Anyone in this unfortunate category is, according to the Torah 'forbidden to enter the congregation of the Eternal One.'[1] The rabbinic interpretation of this law was that a *mamzer* was not permitted to marry a Jewish person of 'untainted' stock. Thus, a person who was declared to be a *mamzer* could only marry another *mamzer* (though such individuals would be regarded as having Jewish status in all other regards).

It is patently unjust to punish children for the sins of their parents – a principle acknowledged in the Torah itself.[2] As such, the concept of *mamzer* is completely rejected by Progressive Judaism: those whose Jewish status might be questioned by Orthodox authorities on the basis of such biblical laws will find a welcome in a Progressive congregation. Ezekiel's comments, however, are general observations about the connection between the actions of parents and the effects on their children. 'A child shall not share the burden of a parent's guilt…'[3]. Progressive Judaism extends this principle so that it applies not only to the specific instance of forbidden unions but in a far more general sense, to the religious influences to which Jewish children are (or are not) exposed at the beginning of the twenty-first century. Progressive Judaism is more interested in the wishes and aspirations of the individual than in his or her parental or family background.

Nevertheless, parental influence plays an enormous part in the development of a child, not least a love of and a commitment to a religious heritage. Religion is in many cases not as prominent a feature of family life as it once was, but there are certain

---

[1] Deuteronomy 23:3
[2] Deuteronomy 24:6
[3] Ezekiel 18:20

stages, detailed elsewhere,[1] where pressure is felt by a family to observe Jewish customs or rituals. It may come from elderly relatives, the community or perhaps their own subconscious awareness that a life cycle stage needs to be marked in a traditional way.

A good example of this is when a child approaches the age of thirteen (particularly if the child is a boy). In a household where Judaism may have been conspicuously absent, it suddenly becomes a priority as discussions are held and preparations are made for a ceremony and celebration to welcome the child into a community of which he or she often has no knowledge. The effect of this can be bewildering for the next generation of Jews, and often does little to enhance or give substance to their Jewish identity.

It is equally possible that even should parents bring up their children in an idealised Jewish home, those children may rebel against their upbringing, or at least ask serious questions of it once they leave the home. Attending university or taking up employment in our multi-cultural society introduces young people to alternatives and possibilities that can be challenging and confusing. This is likely to happen not least because of the secular nature of the society we live in and the pressure to conform to those secular values (which may already have been implicit in the home and demonstrated by a child's parents). The suggestion here is not that parents are failing to equip their children for such challenges, rather that the way Judaism is presented to our children is, perhaps, not as useful in preparing them for the modern world as was the case in earlier times when the home and the world were in closer harmony.

This situation can be compounded in households where the parents are of a different religion. Progressive Judaism regards

---

[1] e.g. birth, p. 145ff, coming of age, p. 210, marriage, p. 216, or death, p. 148ff

Children are Not to be Held Responsible for the Actions of their Parents

the Jewish upbringing and education as being the key factor in determining a child's Jewish status[1], but the very fact that one of the parents is not Jewish creates the possibility of confusion. Even the most well-meaning non-Jewish grandparents can introduce doubts into the minds of children. One of the solutions that some parents in such situations decide upon is to bring up their children without any religion, saying that they will make their own decision when they are old enough to do so. Such an approach is also problematic: how are children going to be able to decide a religious path for themselves without a religious framework within which to make such decisions?

This brief glimpse into the reality of modern Jewish households is not meant to be critical of them or the values and religious options presented within them. Rather its purpose is to acknowledge the challenge that Judaism faces in holding on to or recapturing the next generation of Jews. In an age where individual choice holds more sway than any other societal factor, Judaism finds itself in competition with many other lifestyle possibilities.

As a consequence of this, young adult Jews may find themselves trying to rediscover their roots as they seek something solid upon which to build their identity in what often feels like a bewildering, anonymous world. An awareness of a Jewish background, however hazy, often propels them towards a synagogue in search of that identity. And this is where Progressive Judaism can put into practice the words of Ezekiel that make it clear that children should not be held responsible for the actions of their parents.

Progressive Judaism welcomes all those who enter the doors of its synagogues or make contact with it through its website or

---

[1] See next chapter.

other means[1] in search of a Jewish identity. It offers processes by which Jewish status can be conferred upon children who do not fit comfortably in the 'traditional' Jewish family structure. The important thing to be noted here is the willingness of Progressive Judaism to welcome all those who believe that Judaism has something to offer them. Whereas in a traditional Jewish environment the first question to be asked of anyone seeking membership of a synagogue would almost certainly relate to their parents (specifically the mother), a newcomer to a Progressive synagogue would be welcomed as an individual in his or her own right. The fact that a person has made their own decision to come to Judaism should be respected and acted upon without regard for the actions or influence of that person's parents. In this regard, Progressive Judaism has an important part to play in making Judaism open and available to people for whom such a possibility might otherwise not exist.

---

[1] www.upj.org.au. Telephone contact can also be made to +61 (0)2 9328 7644.

36
CHILDREN OF MIXED MARRIAGES ARE TO BE TREATED ALIKE

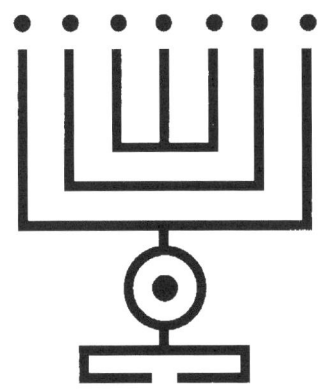

Since genetically children inherit alike from both parents, whereas culturally the influence of either may prove the stronger, the traditional law of matrilineality cannot be justified. Instead, we affirm the common-sense view that children of mixed marriages are to be treated alike, regardless of whether the mother or the father is the Jewish parent, and considered Jewish if so brought up. Moreover, we support the inclusion of couples and families with mixed backgrounds into the life of our congregations, and, where possible, that they may be buried together in our cemeteries when the time comes.

A Judaism for the Twenty-First Century

The question of who is a Jew – or rather, who decides who is a Jew – is perhaps one of the most controversial in Judaism today. Hardly a month passes by without an article appearing in the Jewish press about the Jewish status of a child being questioned by Orthodox authorities because of the child's mother's religious position. Such arguments are shameful, undignified and do a disservice to Judaism. They turn Judaism from being a four thousand year-old tradition of philosophy and ideas, questions and answers, customs and traditions into an accident of birth – something that can only be genetically transmitted. In the eyes of Orthodox Jewish authorities, Jewish status is quite simple to define: if a person's mother is Jewish, according to Orthodox Jewish law (*halachah*)[1], then so is her offspring. If this is not the case, or even if it simply cannot be proved by relevant documentation, then, in Orthodox Judaism, there is a problem.

This was not always the case. Although the relative roles of fathers and mothers in ancient Israelite society are not easy to clarify on the basis of biblical and extra-biblical texts, it seems reasonable to state that the determining factor in deciding a child's status was his or her father. The Bible is keen to point out that the twelve tribes of Israel could trace their ancestry directly back to Jacob – the fact that Jacob's wife Leah produced six of his sons and his other wife, Rachel, and two concubines, Bilhah and Zilpah (who were maids to Rachel and Leah respectively) each gave birth to two, is of no consequence.

It is quite clear that Jacob's favourite son Joseph married a non-Israelite, Potiphera, daughter of the priest of On, in Egypt,[2] and indeed their two children, Ephraim and Menasseh, become tribal heads and the role models we cite when we bless our sons on Friday night![3]

---

[1] *Halachah* = Jewish law: See footnote 1, p.171
[2] Genesis 41:50-52
[3] Page 121, *Mishkan T'filah*. Menasseh was the older, Ephraim the younger.

Furthermore, succession to the thrones of Israel – and particularly Judah – makes it quite clear that the father was the key figure in determining the next in line to the throne (though some mothers had a strong influence in that decision, as witnessed by Bathsheba's role in the succession of King Solomon following David's death!).[1]

What, then, was the factor that changed this very clearly patrilineal structure? It would seem that the Exile in Babylon following the destruction of the Second Temple – or, more specifically, the return from that Exile in the fifth century BCE – was the point at which the deciding factor for a child's religious status switched from the father to the mother. According to tradition, there were two key figures who influenced the development of Judaism at this critical period of its history: Ezra and Nehemiah. The biblical books relating the work of these two men in effectively re-establishing Judaism in Jerusalem and Judah contain many references to the mixed marriages that were prevalent at the time. According to the final chapter of the book of Ezra, the people were gathered in the square in front of the newly built Temple one wet winter's day and Ezra said to them: 'You have trespassed by bringing home foreign women, thus aggravating the guilt of Israel. So now, make confession to the Eternal One, the God of your ancestors, do God's will and separate yourselves from the peoples of the land and from the foreign women.'[2]

Although there is no direct historical reference to the establishment of matrilineality, it had clearly become the determining factor in deciding Jewish status by the time of the Rabbis, within a few centuries of the Babylonian Exile. The details relating to the transmission of Jewish status exclusively

---

[1] II Kings chapter 1
[2] Ezra 10:10-11

through the mother are well documented, particularly in the Talmudic tractate *Kiddushin* where the decision that has affected so many generations of Jews was formally recorded.

Progressive Judaism rejects this basis for deciding whether or not Jewish status should be granted to an individual. The absurdity of the suggestion that Judaism is something that is transmitted genetically requires no further discussion. Progressive Judaism recognises that an awareness and appreciation of a tradition that stretches back four thousand years is something that is absorbed culturally and instilled educationally and that these are the primary factors that should provide the basis for a person's identity.

Accordingly, most Progressive movements recognise as Jewish a child who has been brought up in a Jewish environment, has received a Jewish education and has celebrated key life cycle events confirming that Jewish status, even if only their father is Jewish. Typically, these events would be observing *Shabbat* and festivals and the ceremonies of *bar-* or *bat-mitzvah* and/or *Kabbalat Torah*, the occasion where young adults affirm their commitment to Judaism. In order for such an affirmation to be made, or to have any validity, the young person must clearly have an awareness of and a commitment to Judaism that must have been instilled both via a programme of formal education and, perhaps more importantly, exposure to Judaism in a domestic environment.

The religious atmosphere in a home where parents do not share the same religious faith presents a number of contradictions that might confuse a child growing up in that environment. (The same can, of course, be true of a household in which the parents do share the same religion but perhaps disagree about its practice or choose not to practice it at all. This emphasises Progressive Judaism's assertion that experience of Judaism is the basis of one's Jewish identity.) In order for a child of mixed faith parents to be brought up as Jewish, there must be an agreement between the parents that the child will receive a Jewish upbringing and the non-Jewish parent should endeavour to participate as far as possible in this, and that the child will only be considered as Jewish.

Progressive Judaism recognises that it has an important role and responsibility in fostering the Jewish influences on a non-Jewish parent. Non-Jewish partners are welcome in Progressive synagogues. Indeed, many now have an affiliation category specifically for 'Friends' of the synagogue, encouraging involvement and participation in most of the community's activities. Although there are some restrictions, and different synagogues have different regulations, non-Jewish parents can take part in their children's life-cycle events, such as baby blessings and *bar-* or *bat-mitzvah* ceremonies. The guiding principle is what makes 'Jewish sense' – it doesn't seem to make sense for someone who is not Jewish to say a blessing over the Torah, for example.

This attitude extends to the case where a Jew and non-Jew wish to marry. According to civil law in various places, a Rabbi cannot officiate at a wedding between a Jew and a non-Jew. However in some cases Progressive Judaism may permit its rabbis to officiate at an 'Act of Prayer' for a mixed faith couple. Rabbis have their own individual approach to such ceremonies. Many require an indication that the couple intend to make Judaism a part of their married life and, where appropriate, bring up any children as Jewish. In any event, a mixed faith blessing can only be offered if the couple are already married according to civil law or a civil marriage is imminent.

Concern is expressed by many mixed-faith couples over the prospect of their not being permitted to be buried in the same cemetery. Progressive Judaism recognises the importance of permitting this and, where it has exclusive use of a cemetery, has no difficulty in allowing mixed faith burials. Difficulties arise, however, in cemeteries shared with other Jewish organisations that do not agree with the inclusive Progressive attitude to non-Jewish partners. Progressive Judaism is currently working to make it possible for mixed faith couples to be buried together, believing that this will offer comfort at a difficult time to partners in, and children of, mixed faith relationships.

The intention and, in general, the consequence of such an approach, is that children of mixed marriages should feel comfortable with and welcomed by Progressive Judaism so that they are encouraged to want to continue to make it part of their adult lives and, in their turn, transmit it to their children, regardless of the genetic make-up of those children.

37

INCLUSIVE ATTITUDE TO JEWISH IDENTITY

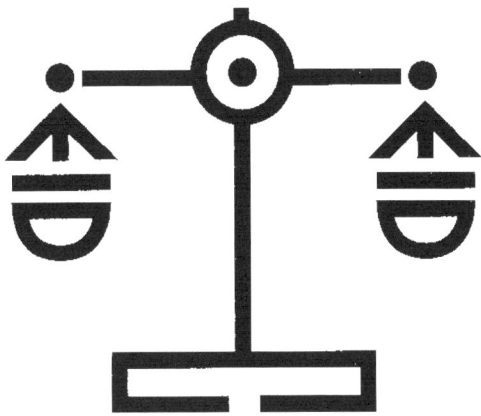

We affirm the need for an inclusive attitude to Jewish identity. We welcome sincere proselytes and make the process of conversion no more difficult than it needs to be. Likewise we welcome into our congregations all who have a good claim to be regarded as Jewish, regardless of marital status or sexual orientation.

A Judaism for the Twenty-First Century

As explained previously, according to Orthodox Judaism, Jewish status is transmitted directly and exclusively from a Jewish mother to her children[1]. Consequently, the document that is required to confirm a person's Jewish status in the eyes of Orthodox authorities is the mother's or maternal grandmother's *k'tubbah*[2]. Progressive Judaism recognises that sincerity and commitment are the most important elements of an individual's wish to adhere to Judaism and pays more regard to these than pieces of paper relating to religious ceremonies observed by their parents or grandparents.

This is as true of Jews who can claim to be Jewish according to Orthodox Jewish law (*halachah*[3]) as those who cannot. There is clearly an extent to which, in our modern age of individuality, all Jews attach themselves to Judaism as a matter of choice since the pressures to be part of the Jewish community recede with every passing generation. This reality only adds to the Progressive principle that sincerity is the most important measure of a person's commitment to Judaism and a Jewish identity.

Having said this, it requires more than just an indication of sincere commitment to the religion of Judaism for a person to be granted Jewish status. There is, as this book has indicated, an enormous history that underpins Judaism: traditions and literature, individuals and communities that a whole lifetime of study would not fully encompass. There is an assumption – possibly erroneous – that children of Jewish parents will have been introduced to some of this knowledge, and the ceremony of *bar-* or *bat-mitzvah* is meant, in some way, to acknowledge this. But the truth is that, even in Progressive Jewish communities, all that is required for a person to be welcomed as

---

[1] See previous chapter.
[2] Jewish marriage contract, see p. 217
[3] *Halachah* = Jewish law: See footnote 1, p.171

a member is evidence of previous synagogue membership or the above-mentioned marriage documents. As such, Progressive Judaism welcomes all those who have a Jewish background, and is open to all Jews, regardless of their marital status or sexual orientation. To those Jews who have technical Jewish status but no real experience or knowledge of Judaism, a course of study is offered, not as a requirement but as a suggested means of deepening their awareness and understanding of Judaism.

If a person does not have this Jewish background but wishes to become a member of the Jewish community, a process of conversion is necessary. At different stages of Jewish history, proselytisation has variously been enthusiastically encouraged and greatly frowned upon by Jewish authorities. Whatever the circumstances, the process has included and required a course of study, as the person wishing to convert acquaints him- or herself with Jewish tradition or practice. The course of study in Progressive Judaism tends to last for a minimum of a year, to enable the person converting to experience the full cycle of the Jewish calendar as well as to be introduced to elements of Jewish history, tradition, belief and practice – as laid out in this book. Different branches of Judaism require different lengths of time before the process of conversion is completed: some Orthodox authorities require as much as seven years before Jewish status is conferred.

Jewish status is confirmed by means of a panel of three rabbis[1] whose role is to examine the candidate and decide if he or she has demonstrated commitment to the process of conversion to Judaism and acquired a level of knowledge sufficient to live a Jewish life. Traditionally this panel is known as a *beit din* – a rabbinic court – the body whose members are assumed to have vast knowledge of Jewish law and practice. This court is given

---

[1] On occasion an elder of the community can be used

the responsibility of making *halachic*[1] decisions, including matters relating to Jewish status. The reason for having three rabbis on this panel is so that in the event of there being more than one opinion, a majority decision can always be reached.

As suggested above, some authorities are more stringent than others in their requirements for granting Jewish status to an intending convert. Progressive Judaism welcomes converts who have completed a course of study, usually run under the auspices of the synagogue or movement they wish to join, and who have regularly attended religious services and taken part in synagogue activities. Of course, the rabbis on the *beit din* do not subject a candidate to a testing examination. The expectation is that candidates will already have proved their knowledge and commitment to the rabbi who is sponsoring their conversion. In Progressive Judaism, they are usually asked to write short essays on different aspects of Judaism and on their reasons for wishing to convert, which they will then discuss with the *beit din*. Male candidates are expected to undergo circumcision, unless there is medical reason not to do so. In the end, the rabbis on the *beit din* are keen to establish the sincerity of a candidate's commitment as much as their knowledge of Judaism and the process of conversion to Progressive Judaism is intended to be as welcoming as possible to anyone wishing to commit themselves to it.

At the conclusion of the interview by the *beit din*, a certificate of Jewish status is read out and then passed to the rabbi of the new convert's community. A ritual immersion (*mikveh*) is required, and details of this are explained. A ceremony of admission is then arranged when the convert stands in synagogue before the open ark, declares his or her commitment to Judaism, and is then welcomed as a member of the Jewish community. This ceremony, after which the certificate of

---

[1] relating to *halachah*; See footnote 1, p.171

Jewish status is completed, can either be held in the presence of the congregation as part of a synagogue service or in private, accompanied by family members.

After this, converts are welcomed into the community and encouraged to take an active role in its activities. Traditional Judaism requires that once a person has converted to Judaism, no further reference should be made to their non-Jewish origins. The reality, sadly, is rather different. Although someone who has been a member of any of our communities is fully recognised within the wider non-Orthodox community, those who have converted under the auspices of non-Orthodox movements are not regarded as Jewish by Orthodox authorities, including those responsible for marriages and funerals in Israel. Nevertheless, the Israeli Law of Return means that such converts would be regarded as Jewish for the purposes of immigration (*aliyah*) to become citizens of the State of Israel. This unfortunate situation has particular ramifications for the children of mothers who have converted to Judaism via a non-Orthodox route: even if they are brought up as Jews, their Jewish status is not recognised by the Orthodox, though, as they consider them as non-Jews, the option of converting to Orthodox Judaism may theoretically be available.

Sadly, Jewish status will continue to be a contentious issue in the Jewish community for the foreseeable future.

38

ETHICAL EMPHASIS OF THE PROPHETS

We affirm the ethical emphasis of the Prophets: that what God chiefly requires of us is right conduct and the establishment of a just society. Religious observances are a means of cultivating holiness. As such, they are also important, but not of the same order of importance.

Ethical Emphasis of the Prophets

From its earliest days, Progressive Judaism regarded itself as inheriting the mantle of the Prophets of ancient Israel, who emphasised that religious ritual had little purpose unless it inspired action that accorded with the Prophets' view of the divine will. Progressive Judaism believed that this mantle had slipped and even perhaps disappeared from Judaism during the Middle Ages, when, as described elsewhere, exclusion from the outside world led to an obsession with ritual at the expense of the quest for righteousness and justice.

The Prophets of ancient Israel made their feelings about empty ritual quite clear to the people who, they believed, were placing too much emphasis on the quality of their sacrificial worship whilst ignoring the injustices in their society. The prophet Isaiah challenged the people of Judah as they made their offerings at the Temple in Jerusalem, putting these words into God's mouth:

> 'That you come to appear before Me – who asked that of you?
> Trample My courts no more;
> Bringing offerings is futile, incense is offensive to Me.
> New Moon and Sabbath, proclaiming of solemnities, assemblies with iniquity
> I cannot abide.
> Your new moons and fixed seasons fill Me with loathing;
> They are become a burden to Me, I cannot endure them.
> And when you lift up your hands, I will turn My eyes away from you;
> Though you pray at length, I will not listen.
> Your hands are stained with crime – wash yourselves clean;
> Put away your evil deeds from my sight.
> Cease to do evil, learn to do good.
> Devote yourselves to justice: aid the wronged.

Uphold the rights of the orphan; defend the cause of the widow.'[1]

His identification of the true purpose of worship echoed the words of an earlier Prophet, Amos, who had coined the image of a God who would decline to accept the people's offerings as long as injustice remained addressed:

'I loathe, I spurn your festivals, I am not appeased by your solemn assemblies.
If you offer Me burnt offerings, or your meal offerings, I will not accept them;
I will pay no heed to your gifts of fatlings.
Spare me the sound of your hymns,
And let me not hear the music of your lutes.
But let justice roll down like water,
Righteousness like an everflowing stream.'[2]

This might lead one to imagine that the Prophets were opposed to Temple ritual and that, by extension, Progressive Judaism should reject ritual and worship in favour of a life exclusively dedicated to social action and ethical personal conduct. Indeed, in the early days of reforming Judaism, this might well be regarded as having been the case: many rituals and practices were abandoned with apparent glee by the earliest reformers of Judaism as they sought to focus on ethical behaviour as the sole purpose of the religion they sought to make relevant to modern Jews.

There can be no doubt that the Prophets placed an enormous emphasis on human behaviour in relation to God and to fellow human beings as the true measure of the effectiveness of religion. The same can surely be said of Progressive Judaism –

---

[1] Isaiah 1:12-17
[2] Amos 5:21-24

and it is as true today as it was in the earliest days of our movement. But it should not be assumed from this that the Prophets of three thousand years ago were somehow hostile to the idea of or the need for worship. They regarded sacrificial worship – correctly presented and offered – as being a worthy and essential exercise in establishing and developing the relationship between individuals and tribes on the one hand and the God of Israel on the other. What they objected to was the hypocrisy that seemed almost inevitably to manifest itself in a society that quickly became more concerned with appearances than with substance. The writings of the Prophets make it clear that ancient Israelite society was rife with the exploitation of the poor, for example. While some of the biblical instructions, perhaps fashioned by those same Prophets or their followers, sought to ameliorate such injustice, its continued existence is clearly attested to in prophetic writings. Amos, for example, chastises the wealthy Israelites who would '…sell the poor for silver, the needy for a pair of sandals',[1] while Isaiah declares, 'Woe to you who add house to house, field to field.'[2]

It is fair to say that the earliest reformers of Judaism saw in these prophetic writings and utterances an invitation to dispense with any aspect of Jewish practice that did not accord with their nineteenth and early twentieth century views. A series of developments in Germany and later in the United States, led to the radical Pittsburgh Platform,[3] which spoke dismissively of 'Mosaic tradition' and rejected so much Jewish ritual and practice that, in some instances, it became difficult to distinguish the most liberal forms of Judaism from, say, a humanist or socialist organisation.

---

[1] Amos 2:6
[2] Isaiah 5:8
[3] Adopted 1885

Nowhere was this more clearly demonstrated than in the various liberal prayerbooks that appeared in Germany during the Nineteenth and early Twentieth Centuries. Because of the autonomy of the Jewish communities in major Jewish centres (a product of Germany's fragmented states and the attitude of their rulers to religion), communities produced their own prayerbooks. Beginning in Hamburg in 1819, a succession of prayerbooks, the object of which was to offer a modern Judaism to their worshippers, adapted or completely dispensed with more and more of the traditional elements of the *siddur*. This steady erosion of the traditional liturgy culminated in the Berlin prayerbook, produced in the 1920s. It was a prayerbook for the Jewish year, containing services for all the major festivals, weekdays and Sabbath and was a mere sixty-four pages long!

Although the Prophets might appear to have been opposed to worship in the Temple, their opposition was, in fact, aimed at worship that was not sincere, where wealthy Israelites made grandiose gestures while paying no attention to the social injustices that blighted their society – and for which, indeed, they were often responsible. The Prophets recognised that ritual had a value, insofar as it encouraged people to acknowledge the presence of God and establish their relationship with the divine power. Their concern, however, was that the key element of that relationship – the divine requirement that human beings establish justice in their lives and in their societies – came a very poor second to the ritual. The concern for ritual precision and purity quickly changed the function of ritual from being a means to encourage and inspire righteous action to become an end in itself. Priests and their latter day descendants became so concerned with the details of holiness that they forgot its original purpose.

It is worth taking a moment here to consider the nature of holiness. The Hebrew word of which 'holy' is a (rather poor) translation is *kadosh*. This word appears in a number of forms in Jewish tradition and practice: the *kiddush* wine, with which we welcome special days and occasions, the *kaddish* that is recited at a time of mourning, and a word for the sanctuary, *mik'dash*, are all drawn from the same Hebrew root. The original, biblical meaning of the word has a sense of something separate, set apart or special. Something that was *kadosh* was set aside for God: it was separated from the everyday life of the congregation of Israel. Although the common practice is for the word *kadosh* to be translated as 'holy', consider the following translation of these famous verses from Leviticus 19 (known as the Holiness Code): 'The Eternal God spoke to Moses saying 'Speak to the whole congregation of Israel and say to them: "You shall be special because I the Eternal, your God, am special."'[1] Holiness, then, means the recognition of the distinct nature of God and of the need to set aside items, places and times that are to be dedicated to God.

Religious ritual, whether Temple sacrifice in ancient times or synagogue worship in our age, is meant to provide a distinct or separate environment in which we might encounter God. Ritual was only ever designed as an aid to assist with the endeavour; it was never intended to subsume it. The ancient Prophets realised this and Progressive Judaism seeks to build upon their example and their insight. The Prophets needed enormous courage and took great risks when they entered the Temple and berated the worshipping Israelites for the insincerity of their offering and reminded them of their obligation to bring justice to their society. One wonders how a modern day Isaiah might be welcomed were he to burst into a crowded synagogue and launch a twenty-first century version of his biblical assault on the futility of worship and ritual that does not lead to action. Indeed this is a role for Progressive rabbis, amongst others. But no matter how the message is

---

[1] Leviticus 19:1-2

imparted, it states a fundamental principle that goes to the heart of the venture that is Progressive Judaism: that ritual, although important, is of little consequence unless it inspires worshippers to engage in activities the aim of which is to bring justice and harmony to the world.

Given the current nature of that world, there is no shortage of just causes to which the Progressive Jew can devote him- or herself. Many and varied are the items on any modern-day agenda of injustices that urgently need to be addressed. That these are acknowledged in Progressive Jewish worship can be clearly seen by glancing at the topics of the 'Themes and Readings' that are a feature of our prayerbooks. Often based on verses from the Torah, these include readings and reflections on topics such as peace, justice, conservation, tolerance, righteousness and love of neighbour. By directing worshippers to such causes, Progressive Judaism can truly claim to have adopted the mantle worn by Judaism's ancient Prophets.

39

SINCERITY IN OBSERVANCE

*As we affirm the need for sincerity in belief and worship, so we affirm the need for sincerity in observance. Therefore observances must be in accord with our beliefs and individual Jews must be free in this area to exercise informed, conscientious choice. That applies, among other things, to the details of Sabbath observance (***sh'mirat Shabbat***) and the Dietary Laws (***kashrut***).*

One of the basic principles underpinning Progressive Judaism is that of informed choice. The expectation is that Progressive Jews will consider the possibilities that are available to them as a result of the transmission and adaptation of Jewish customs and laws, some of which date back several centuries into the past, measure them against the reality of the modern world and reach their own conclusion. They will conscientiously decide which customs still apply or are no longer relevant, or will perhaps turn to an appropriate person or guide to assist until they are ready to make informed decisions for themselves.

Nowhere does this approach manifest itself more clearly than in the Progressive Jewish observance of *Shabbat* and of Judaism's dietary rules. The minutiae of these well-known Jewish customs are not set out in the Hebrew Bible. The Rabbis developed them two thousand years ago, operating within a specific theological framework. Their insistence that the text of the Torah was divine meant that they needed to create safeguards that would prevent a breach of divine law. With regard to *Shabbat,* their main aim was to uphold the biblical prohibition against work. In order that Jews might refrain from it, the Rabbis needed to define what constituted work.[1] They drew up a list of thirty-nine prohibited activities, including sowing, ploughing, reaping, grinding, baking, weaving, writing, building, lighting a fire and carrying items from one domain to another. These categories have been redefined to include modern activities that Orthodox authorities regard as falling within their definition of work, such as driving a vehicle or using electricity, even though such activities were unknown in the time that produced the Torah. As always, Progressive Judaism seeks to focus more on the positive spiritual potential offered by an observance of *Shabbat* rather than by becoming entangled in its biblically inspired restrictions.

---

[1] The 39 types of work prohibited on *Shabbat* are listed in the Talmud, *Shabbat* 49b

One of the best-known features of an Orthodox observance of *Shabbat* is the prohibition against driving. In the close-knit Jewish communities of the Middle Ages (and earlier), the question of using a form of transport was never raised: the synagogue was easily accessible to all. Modern demographic trends mean that people often live some distance from their place of worship, raising several new issues. Sometimes those who wish to observe the Orthodox restriction relating to travel on *Shabbat* have the option to live close enough to the synagogue that they do not need to travel. Alternatively (and this is mentioned because it is a common practice, not simply because it is illogical and inconsistent) worshippers can drive, park around the corner and walk the remainder of the distance. Or it can be acknowledged that if the choice is between people driving or not being able to attend at all, the preference must be for people to attend and therefore there should be no objection to congregants driving or using public transport. Progressive synagogues provide car parks for worshippers and some may organise rotas or taxis to assist those of their members who would otherwise not be able to get to synagogue.

The ruling that prohibits travel is based on a Talmudic discussion regarding riding a horse on *Shabbat*, a summary of which is as follows: if a person rides a horse on the Sabbath, he may accidentally drop the stick that he needs to hit the horse in order to guide it. As a result of this, he may reach up to a tree to pull down a branch to use as a replacement. This act would constitute a form of harvesting – an action that is specifically prohibited based on the Rabbis' interpretation of the biblical definition of work not permitted on the Sabbath. So in order to prevent the possibility of this horse rider 'harvesting', he is prohibited from mounting his horse in the first place.[1]

---

[1] Talmud, *Beitzah* 36b

This rabbinic principle, known in Jewish tradition as 'building a fence around the Torah'[1], is a feature of Jewish law. In order to avoid the risk of even coming close to breaking a commandment in the Torah, the Rabbis built in a series of safeguards. Another example of this is the prohibition of the use of musical instruments. There is, for example, no law against playing a guitar on *Shabbat* but if a string breaks, the player might be tempted to repair it. This would constitute work, a prohibited activity – so in order to avoid that possibility, a guitar may not be played.[2] Progressive Jews could legitimately argue that a guitarist might promise not to repair a broken string should one break, or suggest that the benefit to worship of musical accompaniment outweighs the risk of transgressing a law that is, in any event, a two thousand year old interpretation of some three thousand year old biblical verses.

The same principle can be applied to a whole host of *Shabbat* activities that are technically prohibited by a traditional approach to Judaism. An Orthodox approach might legitimise some Sabbath activities by relying on automatic timers, set before the arrival of *Shabbat*, to switch on certain electrical items whose use would otherwise be prohibited by traditional Sabbath laws. Another traditional way of dealing with 'troublesome' biblical laws is to create a legal fiction to get around the difficulty. An example is the prohibition against carrying items beyond one's own personal domain on the Sabbath (based on Exodus 16:29), a rule that restricts the movement of Orthodox Jews and prevents, for example, a pram from being pushed. The way to get around this is to establish an *eruv*, an artificial boundary enclosing a larger area that is declared to belong temporarily to the whole community, thus allowing greater freedom of movement within it.

---

[1] *Pirkei Avot* 1:1
[2] Talmud *Eruvin* 102b

Such legal intricacies are of little consequence to Progressive Judaism, which regards the Torah as a product of its time, containing various regulations that have no place in the twenty-first century. It seeks to rediscover the motivation that lay behind the biblical laws and the rabbinic interpretation of them and re-apply that motivation to the modern world.

A further example of this can be seen in the Progressive approach to *kashrut*. There are three aspects to what is perhaps regarded as one of the most integral elements of Judaism both by its adherents and observers, which we will first explain from an orthodox perspective. The first aspect of *kashrut* is the prohibition, outlined in chapter 11 of the Book of Leviticus, of eating certain animals. Whatever the basis, only animals that have a cloven hoof and chew the cud are traditionally allowed to be eaten. Among creatures living in the water, only fish with fins and scales are permitted and only some birds are specified as being suitable to eat. All insects and reptiles are forbidden, with the surprising, though perhaps unnecessary, exception of some types of locust.

Secondly, the biblical prohibition against the eating of meat that still contains blood[1] has implications for the methods by which it is prepared. This means that an animal whose meat is permitted to be consumed must still be killed in a prescribed manner to ensure that it is fit to eat (*kasher* – usually pronounced *kosher* – means 'fit'). So those Jews who observe strict traditional '*kashrut*' must only eat meat prepared in this way. This method, called *sh'chitah* (which means 'slaughtering') involves a swift cut of the animal's throat by a skilled butcher with an exceptionally sharp knife, allowing the blood to be quickly drained. Once the animal is killed, there are certain further restrictions that apply: if a carcass is seen to be damaged

---

[1] Leviticus 7:26, Leviticus 17:10-14

in any way when it is inspected after slaughter, it is declared *t'reifah* – unfit (literally 'torn') and sometimes shortened to *'treif'*. Moreover, certain parts of the animal are not allowed to be eaten and are removed. Finally, for the strictly observant, the raw meat must be soaked in water, salted and then rinsed before it can be cooked; the intention being to ensure the complete removal of all remaining blood.

The third aspect of *kashrut* is the requirement that milk and meat be kept separate. This is based upon another biblical law – which is repeated three times – forbidding the ancient Israelites from boiling a kid in its mother's milk.[1] The rabbinic interpretation of this is another example of the metaphorical 'fence' that was built around the Torah. The whole raft of legislation that has been constructed to ensure the separation of milk and meat exists solely to protect against the possibility that the cream poured on one's dessert, for example, might have come from the mother of whatever ended up as the meat in one's main course and, by eating them as part of the same meal, the two may have unwittingly been combined. Successive generations of Rabbis and scholars have added layer upon layer to this 'fence', imposing the same restrictions on poultry, for example, (in case one was served meat but was wrongly advised that it was poultry, and ate milk products with or after it). They also tried to calculate the time the human body requires to digest meat (often known by the Yiddish word *fleishig*) and dairy products (*milchig*). For example, some say that one can consume a meat product half an hour after eating something dairy but three hours must elapse before the converse is permitted, though customs on timings vary.

A Progressive approach to *kashrut* might take a variety of stances. Firstly, if one wishes to welcome Orthodox Jewish guests to one's home, one needs to recognise their dietary

---

[1] Exodus 23:19, 34:26; Deuteronomy 14:21.

requirements. Certainly one of the justifications for – and consequences of – the laws of *kashrut* was that it prevented Jews from eating, and thereby socialising, with non-Jews. Such a justification may not be appropriate or relevant to our modern age, but a failure to recognise the important part *kashrut* plays in the lives of many Jews would lead to Jews not being able to eat with other Jews. For this reason, many Progressive synagogues have kitchens that are dairy only – the safest way to avoid causing offence – even though the majority of the synagogue's members may have a different view of the importance of *kashrut*. For example, they may regard the Levitical lists of prohibited animals as ancient health and safety regulations based on knowledge available three thousand years ago. As such, modern health criteria may be applied to the distinction between goat's meat (permitted) and meat from a pig (forbidden) – and the modern Progressive Jew may make different choices from those in Leviticus. Indeed, many Jews, conscious of the dietary rules that their fellow Jews adhere to in varying degrees and perhaps alarmed by recent health scares in relation to the consumption of any meat, choose to become vegetarian.

The Progressive approach to *sh'chitah* provides a further example of the processes involved in informed choice. When the Rabbis laid down the rules of *sh'chitah*, it was believed to be the most humane method of killing an animal, and the probable intention was to minimise the animal's suffering. There is currently some dispute as to whether or not the modern technique of pre-stunning an animal is a more humane method of slaughter. A Progressive approach should recognise that if *sh'chitah* was categorically proven to no longer be the most humane method, then it should be superseded by the most humane. Progressive Jews should not cling to a 'tradition' whose basic intent no longer applies, particularly if it is shown to be contrary to the probable initial intent.

Another crucial feature of Progressive Judaism is its willingness to find new meanings in ancient customs and regulations. A recognition of the inequities that exist in the laws governing trade between developed and developing economies has led to the recent establishment of the Fair Trade movement. Recognising the emphasis that Judaism has always placed on food and its duty to seek to bring justice to areas where injustice prevails, Progressive Judaism encourages its constituent synagogues and individual members to purchase only 'fairly traded' products. This commitment to what we might call *ethical eating,* and which has been termed *'eco-kashrut',* can be regarded as a modern variation on the themes implicit in the laws of *kashrut*: the importance of recognising that what we do on a daily basis can have profound significance for our lives and the lives of others in our world.

In this way, Progressive Judaism applies the same principles to *kashrut* as to *Shabbat*: namely to seek out the spirit of the laws relating to eating. If the purpose of *kashrut* is to encourage human beings to eat healthily, or to exercise self-discipline in their choices of food, or to ensure the humane treatment of animals that are used for food, or to assist the world's poorer farmers to support themselves, then this is the spirit that should be applied at least as much as the traditional regulations. For example, we would consider that battery farming causes avoidable cruelty and hence its products cannot be suitable for us to consume, even though the majority of kosher chickens and eggs are produced in this manner. This same approach can be applied to all areas of Jewish life to ensure that this ancient heritage remains relevant and meaningful to those who seek to make Progressive Judaism a part of their lives.

40

INDIVIDUAL AUTONOMY

Because we affirm the importance of individual autonomy, therefore we do not legislate except in so far as it is necessary to do so. Nevertheless, individuals need guidance, and communal life requires rules. Both in the guidance we offer and in the rules we make, we endeavour to reconcile tradition with modernity.

Progressive Judaism walks something of a tightrope in trying to affirm the rights of the individual to make choices regarding individual practice and at the same time establishing a communal structure within which those choices can be exercised. This difficulty is rarely, if ever, faced by Orthodox Jewish communities, since the rules and regulations governing both individual and communal behaviour are basically accepted as being divinely ordained. Such regulations are either rigidly adhered to or, at least, members of Orthodox Jewish congregations have a sense of what is demanded of them. By its very definition, Progressive Judaism encourages individuals to decide for themselves their level of observance and belief.

Progressive Jews are encouraged to make choices about the range of possibilities in Jewish tradition that will enrich their experience of Judaism. It could be argued (and often is by Orthodox critics of Progressive Judaism) that this amounts to little more than an opportunity to pick and choose those elements of Judaism that are appealing and to reject those that are not. However, the genuine Progressive approach to Judaism is for Progressive Jews to inform themselves about the origin, development and intention of a given Jewish law or custom and then make a choice as to whether or not to incorporate that custom into their way of life at this time.

Given the Jewish propensity for disagreement and divergence, the balance between personal choice and Jewish tradition is likely to vary from Progressive Jew to Progressive Jew. A good example of this might be the area of Passover observance. One Progressive Jew might, for reasons of family tradition, wish to ensure that every item of food in his or her home is marked with a *kasher l'Pesach*[1] label to ensure that it meets with the

---

[1] A label (known as a *'hechsher'* – from the same Hebrew root as *kasher*) attached to foods whose preparation has been supervised by a qualified

Individual Autonomy

strictest dietary requirements for the festival. Another Progressive Jew might show great disdain for what he or she might regard as this annual price increase appended to everyday items that cannot breach the laws of Passover (such as sugar), and prefer to continue to purchase regular goods for the seven days of the festival, perhaps donating the money 'saved' to a charity relating to human freedom (which is, after all, the theme of *Pesach*). In terms of their own homes, this does not present an issue (depending upon the level of observance of those who might eat there during the festival). But a whole new series of questions is raised when a synagogue organises a communal *seder* for its members or wishes to serve food in the synagogue during *Pesach*. There may be some members of the community for whom the idea of serving food that was not specifically kosher for *Pesach* would be inappropriate, and so there has to be a consensus within the congregation as to what levels of *kashrut* should be observed within the synagogue building. This is an example of the point where individual autonomy meets communal life head on and creates a situation where sensitivity and compromise are needed. It is, of course, such matters that often fuel divisions within synagogue communities and can even lead to the establishment of new groups, each following a marginally different practice.

So it is, then, that compromise is invariably required as we seek to strike that balance between individual autonomy and communal requirements, set against a background of trying to balance tradition and modernity. Every synagogue is likely to have a committee that is responsible for establishing the rituals and customs that are practised by its own members. The role of such a committee might include (but not be limited to) agreeing upon the timings of *Shabbat* and festival services, the use and

---

Jewish official (*shomer*) to ensure they are kosher, and in the case of '*kasher l'pesach*', to warrant that no leavened material has been in contact with them (these foods usually cost considerably more than the equivalents that do not bear this *hechsher*. See p. 126)

type of instrumental music to accompany worship in those services and which readings and songs might be incorporated as part of the worship. Clearly, individual members can exercise their democratic right to influence and even change such decisions and in this way, it is hoped, communal practice will, in general, satisfy the majority, if not all, of the community.

Then, of course, there are decisions to be made that affect the Progressive Jewish community as a whole: decisions that cannot be left to individual choice. For example, issues relating to Jewish marriages and status or the production of liturgy, require a level of knowledge that must inevitably remain the provenance of the leaders of the movement: its lay leaders and particularly its rabbis. Examples of such decisions would be an agreement by the Rabbis of Progressive Judaism in our region to permit its members to conduct ceremonies of celebration and commitment for same-sex couples,[1] or on the possibility of permitting non-Jews to be buried alongside their Jewish spouses in cemeteries where the authorities will allow this. There is a democratic process that enables individual Progressive synagogues to make their opinions on such matters known and, where appropriate or necessary, exert their influence to bring about changes in policy.

The balance between individual autonomy and communal requirements considered thus far has concerned aspects of practice. While Progressive Judaism does not require or expect its adherents to subscribe to a particular set of theological beliefs, there is an ever-increasing number of areas of ethical choice with which we are confronted in our modern world that demand a religious response. Rapid advances in science and

---

[1] though not to use all of the familiar rituals, nor to call the ceremony *'kiddushin'*, to differentiate it from heterosexual marriage within Jewish tradition.

technology have often left us bewildered. Religion has an important contribution to make to the debate on such issues as abortion, euthanasia and genetic engineering. Here also, using Mordechai Kaplan's[1] aphorism 'tradition has a vote but not a veto', Progressive Judaism would not consider itself bound by ancient regulations but would rather endeavour to apply relevant Jewish teachings and wisdom to such issues along with the knowledge and understanding of our own time. Quite clearly, individual Progressive Jews will hold their own views on these and other matters, and one of the roles of Progressive Judaism is to provide a forum within which these individual views can be presented and discussed set against a background of Jewish knowledge and tradition. In this way, Progressive Judaism will maintain its role at the cutting edge of Judaism, seeking to balance four thousand years of Jewish tradition with our modern world.

---

[1] Rabbi Mordechai Kaplan (1881-1983) was the founder of the Reconstructionist Movement, now itself a part of the World Union for Progressive Judaism.

41

RABBINIC LAW AND THE MODERN WORLD

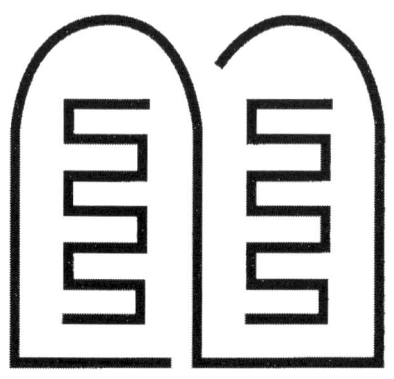

*In particular we affirm the need to harmonise Rabbinic Law (**halachah**) with the social realities and ethical perceptions of the modern world. For instance, we reject the antiquated ceremony of **chalitzah** ('Taking off the Shoe') releasing a brother-in-law from a no longer permitted levirate marriage, and we observe the Festivals according to their biblically prescribed duration, without the 'extra day' instituted in post-biblical times for reasons which have long since ceased to apply.*

Rabbinic Law and the Modern World

The task of reconciling ancient laws with the societies in which Jews lived was begun by the Rabbis. A further two thousand years on from their days – not to mention the vast physical distances that Judaism and its adherents have travelled during that time - the need to adapt rabbinic law to the realities of this age becomes obvious.

In biblical times, for example, it was a matter of honour that a man should ensure the continuation of his family name through producing offspring. If a man, having married, should pass away without having fathered any children, a surviving brother was obliged to marry his widow in order to protect and perpetuate the family name. This practice was known as *yibum*. If the brother-in-law declined the opportunity to marry his dead brother's widow, the ritual of *chalitzah* would take place. This involved the widow reciting various verses from the Torah decrying her brother-in-law's reluctance to marry her, following which she would remove a sandal from his foot and spit in his direction. According to an Orthodox Jewish source[1], such an occurrence today is exceptionally rare, but the fact that it – and many other clearly obscure and out-of-date ceremonies and rituals are still discussed and considered in Jewish circles – emphasises the need for a revision of rabbinic law if a Progressive perspective is to be applied and maintained.

To be fair to the Rabbis, in their time, they were in some respects trying to establish their own version of a developing Judaism. When faced with the alarming biblical requirement to punish a stubborn and rebellious son by having him stoned to death,[2] the Rabbis made the list of transgressions so lengthy for a son to qualify as 'stubborn and rebellious' that, according to the Talmud, not a single boy was ever the victim of this

---

[1] http://www.askmoses.com/article.html?h=167&o=177 where the rarity of *chalitzah* is emphasised – and the ceremony explained in more detail.
[2] Deuteronomy 21:18-21

regulation[1]. Similar criteria were introduced in order to prevent capital punishment, which was demanded for a number of offences in the Torah, from being carried out.

Although the Rabbis are, perhaps, to be admired for their ingenuity in circumnavigating many of the Torah's requirements, the implementation of which they deemed to be impractical or unacceptable, the need for such changes conflicted with the belief in its infallibility and divine origin. Some of their attempts to avoid infringing laws in the Torah have created legal fictions that are unlikely to reflect the intention of the original legislator, whether human or divine. Therefore Progressive Judaism feels entirely justified in making changes to, or setting aside completely, those aspects of rabbinic law that quite clearly belong to a different time and place and whose contribution to living a meaningful Jewish life today is at best negligible and at worst counterproductive.

There are many instances where the Rabbis, in attempting to protect the Jews from transgressing a law in the Torah, have added restrictions that have long since ceased to be necessary. An example of this is the second day that was, in rabbinic times, added to the biblical festivals of *Sukkot*, *Pesach*, *Shavu'ot* and *Rosh ha-Shanah*.

As explained earlier,[2] the Jewish calendar is based on the cycle of the moon, which orbits the earth in 29½ days. In ancient times, a new month would be declared when the sighting of the new moon was reported to the Sanhedrin (the Jewish Supreme Court) in Jerusalem by two independent witnesses. From there, emissaries would be despatched to the Jewish communities in the Diaspora (mainly in Babylon) with news that the new month had begun. (This information had previously been sent

---

[1] Talmud *Sanhedrin* 71a
[2] See page 115

by means of fires being lit along the hilltops of Samaria but the Samaritans – bitter rivals of the Rabbis – confounded this practice by lighting fires at the wrong time.) The news often reached the outlying communities after sunset, and too late for the new month to be declared. So communities in the Diaspora developed the custom of adding an extra day for each of the biblical festivals (except *Yom Kippur*) to compensate for any possible delay in reporting the sighting of the new moon. This inclusion of an extra day for biblical festivals still occurs in Orthodox communities outside Israel. Progressive Judaism, recognising that this old system became obsolete in the fourth century CE, when it was superseded by a new, mathematically computed calendar, has long since abolished these extra days and reverted to the original biblical duration of festivals, as is the case in the land of Israel (except for the observance even there of 2 days of Rosh Hashanah, which is not biblically required and which some of our communities do not observe).

These are two brief examples of how Progressive Judaism recognises that there is much in rabbinic law that may have had meaning and relevance two thousand years ago but whose place in a modern Judaism is difficult to justify. There are, of course, many other areas in which Progressive Judaism, acknowledging changes in our social environment and ethical perceptions, has brought its own modern interpretations to bear upon our ancient faith. Jewish law, *halachah*, has always been a dynamic and developing structure, adapting and changing to meet the needs of individual Jews and their communities in different times and places. Progressive Judaism is playing its part in this continuing evolution of Judaism's ancient heritage, keeping it vibrant, alive and relevant for future generations of Jews. The rabbis of our own time continue to meet regularly to discuss and recommend appropriate responses or ranges of responses for Progressive Jewish observance, and they are published and distributed to guide our members and communities.

42

RESPECT FOR OTHER RELIGIONS

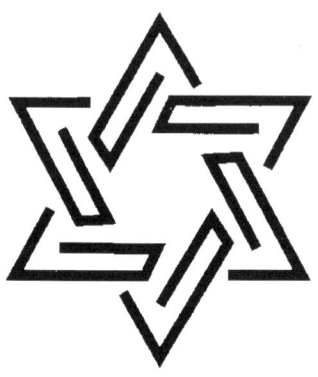

Committed though we are to Judaism, and profoundly convinced of its unsurpassed excellence, we nevertheless recognise that ultimate truth is mysterious and manifold, and that other traditions sincerely seek and find it in different ways. We therefore affirm the need to respect other religions and, through dialogue with them, especially Christianity and Islam, to promote mutual understanding, friendship and enrichment.

This book began with the suggestion that Judaism was and is the attempt to provide answers to life's eternal questions. It concludes with a chapter that acknowledges that life poses questions not just to Jews but to all humanity, and that Judaism therefore is only one answer of many. Religion *per se* represents humanity's attempt to understand its place in the world, to give meaning to life and, in particular, to provide a framework within which individuals can establish and develop a relationship with the Creator of all life.

It is to the shame of humankind that this project, whatever guise it may have taken, has on so many occasions been used as a pretext for war and persecution, hatred, prejudice and genocide. The biblical story of the Tower of Babel[1] may indeed have represented some kind of divine test for humankind: could it find its way back to that age where a single language was spoken and all peoples would work together, in partnership with God rather than as a challenge to the Divine? If this is so, then we have surely failed the test with dismal and disastrous consequences.

It is an alarming and depressing reality that religion, which in theory should have at its heart the desire to implement the divine will that humanity live in peace and harmony, should be the source of so much bitterness and bloodshed. The irony here cannot be overstated, nor can the extent of the hatred that religion has fostered. It seems highly improbable that the founders of any religious faith, seeking to comprehend the divine will and bring the people they represented closer to that understanding, would make the destruction of all other faiths a precondition or an aspect of such understanding. Even more absurd is the suggestion that the divine will actually demands such actions.

---

[1] Genesis 11:1-9

A Judaism for the Twenty-First Century

It is the subsequent historical interpretation of the work of the founders of faiths, mixed with the tribalism and latent aggression that are a feature of human society, that has introduced such ideas to so-called religious philosophies. As has already been observed,[1] the writings of the Torah, imbued with the potential for human growth in chapters such as Leviticus chapter 19, also contain the ghastly instructions for the conquering Israelites to wipe out the idol-worshippers of Canaan[2] or to blot out the name of Amalek from under the sky.[3] Demands to seek the annihilation of people of other faiths cannot be by divine command: they are human ambitions given authority and apparent authenticity by the assertion that they emanate from a divine source.

Progressive Judaism recognises that the Torah reflects the brutality of its age. The requirement to obliterate those who worship other gods is clearly a militaristic, political imperative that cannot be taken literally or seriously in our day. We live in a world that knows more about itself and the wide variety of cultures and religions that fill it than has been the case at any time in the past. This often bewildering landscape of beliefs and practices can offer us possibilities for co-operation and growth where our once limited view brought only conflict. The opportunity – and necessity – for inter-faith dialogue has never been greater.

One of the difficulties of inter-faith work lies in the very nature of religious faith itself. Often, adherents to a particular religious tradition believe in the sole authenticity of their faith, and if so, the authenticity of other faiths must, it would seem, be questioned. The challenge for our modern age is to recognise that no one religion has a monopoly on truth and that every

---

[1] See p. 187
[2] Deuteronomy 11
[3] Deuteronomy 25:17-19

Respect For Other Religions

religious heritage is an interpretation of an experience of the divine that is influenced by social, geographical and many other local factors. Without such an acknowledgement, the ability to accept the validity of another's faith is diminished to the point where meaningful dialogue is impossible and inter-faith work becomes mere tokenism.

Progressive Judaism has always been at the forefront of efforts to forge links with other religious faiths. It is another irony of religion that inter-faith work is a task that is often easier than making peace within one's own faith. It is common knowledge that Orthodox rabbis are permitted to share a platform with Christian and other clergy but have difficulties in entering a non-Orthodox synagogue. Be that as it may, the progress that has been made in the field of inter-faith dialogue in recent years suggests that, however belatedly, humanity is beginning to rediscover the true nature and purpose of religion.

That it has taken so long for this to become a possibility is due to generations of intolerance. It was only in 1965, in a document known as *Nostra Aetate*, that the Catholic Church officially stated that it did not hold the Jews responsible for killing Jesus – a belief that for almost two thousand years had fuelled so much Christian anti-Semitism. The document also stated that the Catholic Church: 'deplores feelings of hatred, persecutions and demonstrations of anti-Semitism directed against the Jews at whatever time and by whomsoever' and 'condemns as foreign to the mind of Christ any kind of discrimination whatsoever between people, or harassment of them, done by reason of race or colour, class or religion.' This statement came almost a quarter of a century after the establishment in Britain of the Council of Christians and Jews, an organisation whose declared aim is '…to bring together the Christian and Jewish communities in a common effort to fight the evils of prejudice, intolerance and discrimination between people of different religions, races and ethnic backgrounds, and to work for the betterment of human relations, based on mutual respect, understanding and goodwill.'[1] The International Council of Christians and Jews followed in the 1950s and is a constructive forum for dialogue and discussion between the two groups in countries all over the world.

Similar dialogue including Muslim organisations – or, technically, 'trialogue' – is a more recent development. The Council for Christians and Jews has undertaken various programs including Muslims, while the aim of the 'Jewish Christian Muslim Association of Australia' is '…to encourage friendship, goodwill and understanding amongst people of the three Abrahamic monotheistic faiths',[2] and most of our communities are involved with local interfaith activities. The common roots of Judaism, Christianity and Islam, and the bitter rivalries that have emerged despite (or perhaps because of) those common roots, emphasise the opportunity, and the need, for these particular faiths to work together.

There are, of course, many other faiths in the world. Progressive Judaism acknowledges that the beliefs and practices of each individual and each group have the right to be recognised as a genuine path to discovering and implementing the divine will for humankind. Progressive Jews believe firmly that any religious faith that has as its goals the betterment of humankind and the establishment of peace among all peoples is worthy of respect. The guiding principle for Progressive Judaism is not so much that 'our religion is right, so everyone else's must be wrong', but rather that 'our religion, our Jewish religion and our Progressive interpretation and implementation of it, is right for us; other people and other cultures have different ways of reaching a similar destination.' Progressive

---

[1] The Council for Christians and Jews was established in 1942, with similarities to the 1927 London Society for Jews and Christians – see p.174.
[2] See website: www.jcma.org.au

Jews look back with pride at four millennia of human history that have produced and shaped the religion we call Judaism, which was adapted and modified to ask questions of itself and face new challenges at every turn. Recognising that our religious duty to our heritage and to our Creator is to seek to bring meaning and harmony to our world as it continues to grow towards a greater understanding of itself, Progressive Judaism can justifiably claim to be a religion that is indeed committed to and worthy of that task. A modern adaptation of an ancient faith, it is a Judaism developed from its past to be relevant for today and to offer challenge, hope and inspiration for tomorrow.

Progressive Judaism: A Judaism for the Twenty-First Century.

GLOSSARY OF SOME TERMS USED IN THIS BOOK

afikoman	Piece of *matzah* (unleavened bread) hidden during the *seder* (special Passover meal).
Aleinu	One of the concluding prayers of the synagogue service.
aliyah	Lit. 'going up' – to be called up to recite the blessings before and after the reading of the Torah. Also means to immigrate to Israel.
T'filah	Lit. 'standing' – refers to the central prayer of Jewish synagogue service (also known as *ha-t'fillah* – 'the prayer).
Ashkenaz/ Ashkenazi	Germany, German – used to describe central European Jewish origins
BCE	Before the Common Era – Jewish way of counting years - equivalent dates to B.C.
Bar'chu	Lit. 'Let us praise' – the opening words of the prayer that starts the main section of a synagogue service.
bar-mitzvah	Lit. 'son of the commandment' – a boy who has passed the age at which he is obliged to observe the ritual laws of Judaism (13 years old).
bat-mitzvah	Lit. 'daughter of the commandment' – a girl who has passed the age at which she is obliged to observe the ritual laws of Judaism (12 years old in Orthodox tradition, sometimes referred to as *bat chayil* – daughter of worth).
bimah	Raised platform from which the synagogue service is conducted.
b'rachah (pl.*b'rachot*)	Blessing.
b'rit	Covenant.
b'rit milah	Lit. 'covenant of cutting'; the ritual of circumcision.
CE	Common Era – Jewish way of counting years - equivalent dates to A.D.
chag	Festival.

Glossary

challah (pl.*challot*)	Plaited bread loaf, often glazed with egg, used to welcome *Shabbat* and festivals.
Chanukkah	Lit. 'dedication' - 8-day winter festival commemorating rededication of Jerusalem Temple by the Maccabees in 165 BCE.
Chasidim	Members of the Jewish sect of Chasidism.
Chasidism	An ultra-Orthodox sect of Judaism originating in 17th century Poland.
chanukkiyah	A candleholder with 9 branches used for celebrating the 8 days of *Chanukkah*.
chevra kaddishah	Lit. 'holy group' – Burial Society
chuppah	Wedding canopy.
Diaspora	Collective title usually used for Jews living outside the land of Israel.
erev	Lit. 'evening' – when preceding a festival or event (e.g. *Erev Shabbat*) refers to its commencement at sunset.
etrog	Citron – one of the four species used at *Sukkot*.
get	Divorce document
g'milut chassadim	Deeds of lovingkindness.
Gemara	Commentary on the *Mishnah* written between 200 and 500 CE. The *Mishnah* and *Gemara* together form the *Talmud.*
haftarah	The 'concluding reading' which follows the reading of Torah on *Shabbat* and festivals.
haggadah (pl.*haggadot*)	Lit. 'telling' – the liturgical text used at the *seder* meal at *Pesach* (Passover).
halachah	Lit. 'the way of going.' Rabbinic law based on interpretation of biblical and subsequent texts and commentaries.
Hallel	Lit. 'praise' – refers to a series of psalms (Psalm 113-118) that are recited at festivals.
Haskalah	Enlightenment.
havdalah	Lit. 'separation' – ceremony to conclude *Shabbat* or festival.
k'tubbah	Wedding contract.
K'tuvim	Lit. 'Writings' – third section of the Hebrew Bible. In the acronym *tanaCH*, becomes 'ch'.

Glossary

Kabbalat Torah	Lit. 'acceptance of Torah' – Progressive Jewish ceremony of confirmation for older teenagers.
Kaddish	Prayer glorifying God, often associated with funerals and mourning, though it appears in several other versions, such as Hatzi Kaddish.
kasher	Literally 'fit' or 'suitable' – normally used with reference to food being ritually permitted (often pronounced *'kosher'*).
kashrut	Noun from *kasher*.
k'hillah k'doshah	Literally 'holy congregation' – title usually applied to a congregation, often preceding its specific Hebrew name.
kiddush	Blessings to sanctify *Shabbat* or festival with wine and bread; can also refer to other food served to accompany these blessings.
Kippah	Skullcap; also referred to as *yarmulke* or *cappel*.
Kohen (pl.*Kohanim*)	Priest – refers today to men whose lineage can be traced from Aaron and his sons.
Kosher l'Pesach	Fit to be eaten during Passover.
Liberal Jews	A part of the Progressive Jewish umbrella.
lulav	Palm branch used at festival of *Sukkot*; as a collective term it also incorporates the branches of willow and myrtle.
M'gillah (pl. *m'gillot*)	Lit 'scroll' – 5 biblical books are referred to as *m'gillot* – Song of Songs, Ruth, Lamentations, Ecclesiastes and, perhaps the one most often called a *m'gillah* – Esther.
Mah nishtanah	Lit. 'What is different' – the opening words of the section of the Passover *seder* usually known as 'the Four Questions.'
Masorti	Lit. 'traditional' – another name for the Conservative Jewish movement.
matzah (pl.*matzot*)	Unleavened bread.
Midrash (pl. *midrashim*)	Creative interpretation of biblical verse or passage (or collection of such interpretations).
minyan	Literally 'quorum' – ten people (traditionally men) required in order for certain prayers to be recited in public.

Glossary

Mishnah	Literally 'repeating' – collection of early rabbinic material, mainly ritual regulations, compiled about 220 CE.
mitzvah (pl.*mitzvot*)	Commandment.
mohel	Person qualified to carry out circumcision.
m'zuzah	Lit. 'doorpost' but refers to a small container on the doorpost containing biblical verses.
N'vi'im	Prophets – the second of the three sections of the Hebrew Bible, or the '*tanach*'.
ner tamid	Eternal light – permanent light shining above the ark in a synagogue.
Omer	A sheaf of grain, also a measure of grain; title given to the seven-week period between *Pesach* and *Shavu'ot*.
parashah (pl.*parashiyyot*)	Weekly section of the Torah – there are 54 *parashiyyot*.
Pesach	Passover.
Pharisees	Group of sages, predecessors of the Rabbis, who were responsible for interpreting the Torah in Greek and Roman times.
pidyon ha-ben	Redemption of the firstborn – archaic ceremony for firstborn sons aged 31 days (not usually practised in Progressive Judaism).
Pirkei Avot	'Verses of the fathers' – a part of the Mishna comprising collection of rabbinic aphorisms.
piyyut (pl.*piyyutim*)	Religious poetry.
Progressive Jews	An umbrella term for Jews who believe in Progressive Revelation rather than the literal giving of Torah from God at Mount Sinai.
Progressive Revelation	The belief that we continue to discover and understand God's wishes better (or God continues to reveal them to us) day by day as humanity develops and understands more about ourselves, our world and the universe.
Purim	Festival commemorating and celebrating the story told in the biblical book of Esther.
Reconstructionist Jews	A part of the Progressive Jewish umbrella.
Reform Jews	A part of the Progressive Jewish umbrella.

Glossary

Rosh ha-Shanah	1st day (new moon) of the seventh Hebrew month; the Jewish New Year.
Sadducees	Priestly group responsible for organising and conducting Temple worship in Greek and Roman times.
seder	Lit. 'order' – the name usually given to the Passover meal on the first (and second) night.
Sepharad/ Sephardi	Spain/Spanish – used to describe Jews with Spanish origins (often from Arab countries).
Sh'ma	Lit. 'hear' or 'listen' – opening word and title of section of Deuteronomy (6:4-9) traditionally recited twice daily, evening and morning.
Shabbat	Sabbath: from sunset on Friday until sunset on Saturday.
Shavu'ot	Lit. 'weeks' – festival falling seven weeks after the second day of Passover.
sh'chitah	Ritual slaughter of animals according to traditional Jewish law.
shiv'ah	Lit. 'seven' – 7 day period of mourning immediately following a Jewish funeral.
Sho'ah	Lit. 'destruction' – Hebrew name for the Nazi Holocaust.
shofar	Ram's horn.
shtetl	Yiddish word meaning small town or village.
siddur	Prayerbook.
Simchat Torah	Lit. 'Joy of the Torah', festival of celebration on restarting Torah following the end of *Sukkot*.
sukkah	Lit. 'booth' – temporary shelter decorated with branches and fruit for the festival of *Sukkot*.
Sukkot	Festival of booths – 7-day harvest celebration.
T'fillah	Lit. 'prayer' – alternative title for the *T'filah*, the central prayer in Judaism.
t'shuvah	Lit. 'returning' – repentance.
taharah	Lit. 'purification' – cleaning of a corpse in preparation for burial.
tallit	Prayer shawl.
Talmud	Collection of rabbinic law and commentary; a combination of *Mishnah* and *Gemara*.
Talmud Torah	*Elementary school for Jewish study.*

Glossary

Tanach	Hebrew Bible; acronym of its 3 sections: Torah, **N**'*vi'im* and **K**'*tuvim*.
Tish'ah b'Av	Fast day of 9th *Av*.
Torah	Lit. 'teaching' – the first section of the Hebrew Bible, also known as the 5 Books of Moses.
Tosefta	Lit. 'additional' - collection of rabbinic ritual regulations omitted from the *Mishnah*.
tz'dakah	Lit. 'righteousness' – usually translated as charity – either money or in kind.
Y'hudah	Hebrew for Judah – Jacob's third son, the name of the biblical kingdom and the name from which 'Jews' *(Y'hudim)* is derived.
Yamim Nora'im	Days of Awe – *Rosh ha-Shanah* and *Yom Kipppur*.
Yeshivah	Academy for advanced Jewish study – particularly of Talmud.
Yom ha-Atzma'ut	Israel's Independence Day – 4th *Iyar* (May).
Yom ha-Sho'ah	Holocaust Memorial Day (in Jewish tradition) 27th *Nisan* (May).
Yom Kippur	Day of Atonement.

INDEX

A

Aaron, 105, 194, 195, 270
abortion, 256
Abraham, 5, 7, 8, 14, 15, 27, 37, 38, 39, 55, 56, 92, 100, 146, 153, 169, 171, 185, 219
Adler, 46, 205
Adon Olam, 14
adult education, 73
afikoman, 127, 268
Agag, 138
afterlife. *See* life after death
Aleinu, 102, 268
aliyah, 105, 211, 237, 268
America, 42, 46, 171, 172, 174, 175, 180, 196, 200, 212, *See also* United States
American Reform, 97, 110, 172, 181, 183, 200
Amidah, 100 *and see* T'filah
Amos, 30, 76, 78, 118, 155, 191, 240, 241
Amalek, 138
animals
    eating, 249, 252
    humane treatment, 74, 78
    prohibited, 251
    ritual slaughter, 272
    sacrifice, 92
anti-Semitism, 141, 142, 164, 265
Apocrypha, 53
Aramaic, 55, 102, 104, 105, 121, 217
ark, 86, 95, 99, 105, 118, 121, 147, 236, 271
Ark of the Covenant, 93
Ashkenazi, 57, 105, 147, 160, 161, 218, 268
Australia, 1, 140, 175, 181, 266

B

b'rit, 27, 147, 268
Babylonian Talmud, 40, 76
baby-naming, 144
bar Yochai, 29, 57
Bar'chu, 99, 101, 268

bar-mitzvah, 210, 213, 268
bat chayil, 268
Bat-mitzvah, 209
beit din, 220, 235, 236
beit ha-knesset, 85, 87, *See also* synagogue
ben Gurion, 45, 47, 48
ben Zakkai, 119
bereavement, 102
Bible, iv, 12, 22, 27, 37, 38, 51, 52, 54, 56, 60, 71, 72, 75, 83, 92, 93, 96, 104, 105, 146, 153, 154, 159, 167, 173, 184, 185, 186, 210, 213, 228, 246, 269, 271, 272, 273, *See* Tanach
biblical laws, 3, 75, 222, 223, 248, 249, *See* Ten Commandments
bimah, 106, 147, 195, 268
birth, 47, 125, 144, 145, 146, 147, 224, 228
blessing, 65, 66, 91, 105, 112, 113, 195, 196, 206, 219, 231
blood libel. *See* ritual murder
Book of Life, 117, 118, 122
b'rachah, 91, 268, *See also* blessings
b'rit (Covenant), 26ff
b'rit milah, (circumcision) 146
burial, 57, 149, 272

C

calendar. *See* Jewish Calendar
Canaanites, 27, 187
candle lighting, 112
Chag ha-bikkurim, 129, See *Shavu'ot*
Chag ha-Matzot, 125, See *Pesach*
chalitzah, 258, 259
challot, 112, 269
Chanukkah (Rededication), iv, 83, 88, 116, 134, 135, 136, 213, 269
chanukkiyah (8-branched candelabra), 83, 136
Chasidism, 161, 179, 269
chevrah kadishah, 149
children, v, 69, 70, 71, 72, 73, 75, 81, 84, 88, 92, 122, 127, 128, 133, 137, 147, 206, 213, 215, 222-227, 231, 232, 234, 237, 259

274

Index

'chosen', 29, 30, 87, 174
Christianity, 165, 167, 173, 262, 266
chuppah, (wedding canopy),216, 218, 219, 269
circumcision. *See* B'rit Milah
commandment. *See* mitzvah
consecration of the home, 145
Consecration (of grave), 151
conservation, 74, 244
Conservative Judaism, 178, 181, 182
conversion, 190, 233, 235, 236
Council of Christians and Jews (CCJ), 265
Covenant. See b'rit
creation, 11, 13, 14, 17, 37, 62, 78, 101, 109, 111, 186, 202
cremation, 150, 190
cup of Miriam, 128
customs, 3, 54, 57, 81, 82, 91, 96, 106, 109, 111-2, 118, 122, 125-6, 128-9, 131-2, 136, 141, 145-6, 148-151, 154, 160, 165, 182, 194, 206, 217-9, 224, 228, 246, 250, 251, 254-5, 261

D

Day of Atonement. See Yom Kippur
Days of awe, 114
death, ii, 39, 103, 110, 117, 118, 144, 145, 148, 149, 150, 151, 190, 224, 228, 259
Declaration of Independence, 44, 45, 50
Deuteronomy, 28, 29, 41, 52, 56, 60, 70, 75, 76, 82, 96, 99, 101, 109, 117, 118, 122, 132, 133, 154, 185, 186, 187, 195, 223, 250, 259, 264, 272
Diaspora, 140, 142, 164, 260, 269
dietary laws. *See kashrut*
divine authorship, 52, 61, 62, 166, 187
divorce, 215, 217, 220
Documentary Hypothesis, 52, 186
duty
    towards God, 30, 67, 78, 94, 107, 125, 192, 267
    towards our fellows, 19, 31, 44, 49, 70, 79, 107, 125, 127, 128, 251

E

Eastern Europe, 33, 142, 173, 210
Ecclesiastes, 53, 270
eco-kashrut, 252
education, v, 45, 47, 69, 70, 71, 72, 73, 87, 88, 165, 166, 171, 173, 209, 210, 213, 224, 230
Einhorn, Rabbi David, 169, 171, 172
Eliezer, Rabbi Israel ben, 161
Elijah, 128, 190
Emancipation, 163, 164, 166, 168, 170, 178, 180, 182, 185
Enlightenment. *See Haskalah*
environment, 10, 39, 62, 71, 77, 78, 84, 94, 95, 137, 145, 165, 166, 167, 168, 171, 176, 179, 183, 210, 213, 226, 230, 243, 261
equality, 45, 205, 212, 217, 219
Erev Shabbat, 88, 112, 269
Esther, 53, 137, 138, 270, 271
Eternal light. *See* Ner Tamid
Ethical values, iv
Etrog, 131
euthanasia, 256
evil inclination, 18
exile, 39, 40, 130, 153, 154, 155, 156, 179, 190
Exodus, 52
Exodus (book of), 38, 52, 60, 109, 126, 187
exodus from Egypt, 12, 38, 52, 124, 126
Ezekiel, 52, 222, 223, 225
Ezra, 130, 229

F

Fair Trade, 251
Festivals, 115, 116, 123, 258, *See* also Named Festivals
Five Books of Moses, 28, 52, 60, 62, 66, 86, 91, 104, 135, 170, 185, 186, 187, *See* also Torah
food, 65, 81, 83, 125, 138, 210, 251, 252, 254, 270, *See* also kashrut
Four Species, 131
fourth commandment, 109, 185
free will, 16, 17, 18, 20
funerals, 50, 237, 270

275

Index

G

g'milut chasadim, 74
Gates of Prayer (prayerbook), 176, 200
Geiger, Rabbi Abraham, 169, 171
Gemara, 55, 71, 269, 272
Genesis, 7, 8, 11, 14, 18, 22, 23, 27, 37, 38, 52, 56, 60, 62, 75, 92, 104, 109, 111, 118, 133, 146, 186, 218, 263
genetic engineering, 256
genocide, 24, 141, 263
Germany, 24, 33, 57, 166, 176
   Progressive Judaism in Germany, 2, 24, 156, 164, 170, 172, 174, 175, 181, 196, 200, 212, 241
get, 215, 220
ghetto, 139, 140, 156, 164, 165, 171, 180
girls, v, 165, 210, 211, 212
   Bat-Mitzvah, 213
   Education, 209
God, iv, 5, 8, 9, 10, 11, 12, 13, 14, 15, 17, 18, 19, 20, 21, 22, 26, 27, 28, 29, 30, 37, 38, 41, 52, 53, 56, 59, 60, 62, 65, 66, 75, 76, 78, 90, 91, 92, 93, 94, 96, 97, 100, 101, 102, 106, 109, 117, 118, 119, 120, 122, 125, 130, 139, 147, 148, 153, 154, 155, 159, 182, 185, 187, 188, 189, 190, 192, 194, 195, 199, 201, 206, 213, 219, 220, 222, 229, 238, 239, 240, 242, 243, 263, 270, 271
good inclination. See *yeitzer ha-tov*
Great Britain, 174, 181, *See* also United Kingdom

H

haftarah, 105, 106, 118, 122, 139, 269
haggadah ('telling'), 125, 128, 269
Haggai, 53
halachah (Jewish law), 171, 228, 234, 235, 258, 261, 269, *See* also *beit din*
Hallel, 124, 131, 269
ha-motzi (blessing for bread), 112
Haman, 138
ha-Nasi, Rabbi Judah, 54, 55, 58
Haskalah (Enlightenment), 164, 269
Hatikvah, 191
ha-t'fillah. See *T'filah*
Havdalah, 108, 113
Head covering. See *Kippah*

Hebrew Bible. *See Tanach, Torah*
Hebrew language, 69, 72, 202
Hebrew Union College, 172, 181
Herzl, Theodor, 46
High Holydays, 34, 106, 118, 121, 122, *See* also Rosh Ha-shanah, Yom Kippur
Hillel, 46, 76, 77, 115, 158
Hitler, 34, 156
Holiness Code, 122, 243
Holocaust, 24, 42, 47, 71, 115, 134, 139, 140, 141, 142, 272, 273
Holocaust Memorial Day. See Yom ha-Sho'ah
home, iv, 7, 15, 37, 39, 40, 56, 80, 81, 82, 83, 84, 112, 118, 144, 145, 150, 156, 165, 172, 175, 180, 181, 217, 218, 224, 229, 230, 250, 254
homeland, 42, 45, 46, 47, 156, 167, 190, *See* also State of Israel
homosexuals, 75, *see also* same sex couples
Hosea, 155
Human fallibility, 20
human rights, 49, 79
humanity, iv, 16, 17, 18, 20, 22, 23, 24, 37, 61, 141, 149, 172, 179, 183, 187, 188, 189, 192, 196, 263, 265, 271

I

ibn Ezra, 55
ibn Ezra, Rabbi Abraham, 185
identity, v, 56, 84, 145, 147, 156, 178, 224, 225, 230, 233, 234
informed choice, 111, 246, 251
interfaith, 266
Isaiah, 14, 29, 52, 76, 78, 110, 119, 122, 139, 155, 191, 239, 240, 241, 243, *See* also haftarah
Islam, 190, 262, 266
Israel
   Children of, 13
   Israelite, 92, 93, 186, 189, 191, 239
   Jacob is renamed, 8
   Jewish people, 81, 101, 102, 109, 120, 195, 201, 216, 229, 243
   Land of, 45, 131, 137

Index

Northern kingdom, 39, 153, 154, 158, 186, 228
Northern Kingdom, 153
Progressive Judaism, 49, 50
religion, 27
State of, 42, 44, 45, 46, 47, 48, 49, 71, 115, 134, 138, 160, 182, 191, 237
Israelites, 26-8, 30, 38, 39, 56, 66, 75, 78, 81, 91, 92, 95, 105, 109-10, 112, 120, 124, 126-9, 130, 131-2, 135, 145, 153, 194, 196, 206, 213, 228, 241, 242, 243, 250, 264

J

Jacob, 8, 14, 15, 26, 38, 39, 81, 92, 100, 191, 218, 228, 273
Jeremiah, 52, 78, 92, 155
Jerusalem, 2, 6, 39, 48, 66, 82, 86, 92, 93, 94, 115, 119, 124, 129, 131, 135, 139, 153, 155, 161, 186, 189, 197, 199, 229, 239, 260, 269, *See also* Temple
Jewish calendar, 104, 111, 120, 122, 135, 235, 260
Jewish history, iv, 8, 36, 37, 38, 39, 40, 42, 45, 69, 72, 83, 139, 141, 155, 161, 164, 212, 235
Jewish law. *See Halacha*
Jewish literature, iv, 8, 51, 52, 53, 57, 58, 60, 70, 200, 210, *See also* named works
Jewish National Fund, 137
Jewish people, 8, 26, 29, 30, 32, 33, 35, 45, 52, 57, 58, 61, 65, 77, 106, 133, 135, 139, 142, 146, 158, 159, 164, 170, 189, *See also* Jewish History
Jewish status, 32, 223, 225, 226, 228, 229, 230, 234, 235, 236, 237
Jewish tradition, iv, 27, 37, 52, 60, 72, 79, 87, 96, 97, 109, 111, 148, 150, 159, 161, 181, 203, 219, 235, 242, 248, 254, 257, 273, *See also* custom(s); ritual(s)
Joshua, 52, 93, 117, 154
Judah, 228, 273
Southern kingdom, 37, 39, 139, 153, 154, 155, 158, 189, 229, 239
Judges, 39, 52, 93, 130, 154

K

k'dushat ha-yom ('sanctification of the day'), 102
k'tubbah (marriage certificate), 217, 219, 234, 269
K'tuvim ('Writings'), 53, 269, 272
Kabbalat Torah ('acceptance of Torah'),209, 212, 213, 230, 270
kaddish (prayer), 151, 242
kadosh (holy), 141, 242, 243
kashrut (dietary laws), 83, 84, 245, 249, 250, 251, 252, 255, 270
k'hillah k'doshah ('holy congregation'), 87, 270
kiddush, 83, 112, 118, 242, 270
Kings, 52, 99, 154, 186, 189, 228
Kippah, (head covering), 96, 171, 270
kittel (white gown), 118
kohen (pl. *kohanim* - priest/s), 105
Kohler, Rabbi Kaufmann, 169, 172
Kol Nidrei (prayer), 121
kosher / kasher ('fit'), 56, 65, 83, 249, 252, 254, 255, 270

L

L'cha dodi, 185
Ladino, 160
Lamentations, 53, 139, 270
Law of Return, 237
laws. *See* biblical law, *halacha, kashrut*
Leo Baeck College, ii, 176, 177, 207
Leo Baeck, Rabbi Dr, ii, 176, 177, 207
lesbianism, 219
levirate marriage, 258
Levite(s), 105
Levites, 93, 99, 105, 147, 194, 195
Leviticus, 60, 75, 76, 92, 93, 117, 120, 122, 130, 131, 186, 194, 196, 220, 243, 249, 251, 264
Liberal, ii, 1, 2, 3, 173, 174, 176, 177, 180, 183, 200, 205, 270
Liberal Jewish Prayerbook, 174, 200
Liberal Jewish Synagogue, ii, 174, 176
Liberal Judaism, 2, 3, 173, 174, 176, *See also* Progressive Judaism
life after death, 190

Index

life cycle events, 82, 111, 230, *See* birth; b'rit milah; coming of age; marriage; death
liturgy, iv, 10, 11, 12, 58, 83, 89, 92, 95, 98, 99, 100, 102, 103, 106, 117, 140, 174, 176, 180, 192, 196, 198, 199, 200, 201, 206, 242, 256
Lulav, 131

M

m'gillot, (scrolls), 53, 270
Maccabees, 53, 135, 136, 269
machzor (High Holyday prayerbook), 121
Malachi, 53, 118
mamzer, 220, 222, 223
marriage, v, 133, 144, 145, 166, 215, 216, 217, 219, 220, 224, 231, 234, 235
matrilineality, 227, 229
Mattuck, Rabbi Israel, 2, 169, 174, 177, 200
matzah (unleavened bread), 125, 127, 142, 268, 270
Mendelssohn, Moses, 164, 165
Meredith, George, 97
messianic age, 119, 189, 191
Micah, 76, 191
midrash, 51, 56, 202, 270
Minchah, 121, 122
minyan (quorum), 94, 99, 101, 103, 211, 213, 270
miracles, 12
Miriam, 128, *See also* Cup of Miriam
Mishnah, 51, 54, 55, 70, 71, 77, 103, 126, 137, 206, 210, 269, 271, 272, 273
mitzvah, iv, 65, 67, 209, 271
mixed marriages, v, 227, 229, 232
mohel (ritual circumciser), 145, 146, 271
Montagu, Lily, iii, 1, 169, 173, 174, 175, 205, 208
Montefiore, Claude, 169, 173, 174, 205
morning blessings, 100
Moses, 38, 39, 52, 57, 58, 60, 61, 93, 154, 164, 165, 216, 243, 273, *See also* Five Books of Moses; Mount Sinai
Mount Sinai, 28, 52, 59, 60, 93, 129, 185, 213

mourning, iv, 134, 140, 144, 149, 150, 242, 270, 272
Musaf (additional) service, 121
music, 99, 193, 196, 199, 240, 255
m'zuzah ('doorpost'), 65, 82, 96, 101, 271

N

N'vi'im. *See* Prophets
Ne'ilah (concluding) service, 122
Nehemiah, 104, 229
ner tamid, 94, 95, 271
New Zealand, 175, 177, 183, 200
New moon, 116
Numbers, 60, 92, 99, 110

O

observance, v, 32, 64, 65, 67, 72, 82, 110, 111, 124, 125, 132, 134, 154, 182, 245, 246, 247, 254, 261
Omer, 128, 129, 271
One God, 8
oral Torah, 54, 55, 62, 66, 99, 159
organ donation, 190, 197
Orthodox, 32, 52, 60, 61, 66, 72, 94, 95, 100, 102, 103, 105, 106, 109, 111, 119, 122, 125, 127, 128, 132, 133, 149, 150, 160, 161, 173, 174, 178, 179, 180, 181, 182, 185, 189, 190, 191, 195, 199, 206, 207, 210, 211, 212, 213, 217, 220, 223, 228, 234, 235, 237, 246, 247, 248, 250, 254, 259, 261, 265, 268, 269

P

p'sukei d'zimra (Songs of Praise), 100
Palestinian Talmud, 55
Palestinians, 48, 49, 50
Passover, 7, 83, 123, 126, 128, 137, 160, 254, 268, 269, 270, 271, 272, *See* Pesach
patrilineal, 229
Pentateuch, 52, 165, *See also* Five Books of Moses
Pentecost. *See* Shavu'ot
persecution, 36, 40, 41, 42, 46, 53, 79, 140, 141, 142, 176, 180, 263

Index

Pesach, 7, 53, 115, 116, 123, 124, 125, 126, 127, 128, 129, 142, 160, 254, 260, 269, 270, 271, See also Seder
Pharisees, 53, 86, 157, 158, 194, 271
Phillips, Ada, 205
phylacteries. See t'fillin
pidyon ha-ben ('redemption of the son'), 147, 271
Pirkei Avot (Sayings of the Sages), 77, 192, 248, 271
Pittsburgh Platform (1885), 172, 181, 241
piyyutim (religious poetry), 100, 271
poetry, 41, 58, 100, 174, 201, 271
Polish Jews, 161
prayerbooks, 102, 172, 174, 200, 201, 202, 241, 244
prayers, 2, 91, 94, 96, 98, 99, 100, 101, 102, 103, 121, 128, 140, 148, 150, 180, 195, 199, 201, 202, 210, 213, 268, 270
Priests, 242
Progressive Judaism, ii, 2, 3, 6, 12, 15, 33, 49, 50, 66, 72, 73, 78, 79, 95, 101, 110, 111, 127, 147, 148, 149, 150, 168, 169, 170, 173, 174, 176, 177, 178, 182, 183, 189, 197, 200, 201, 208, 220, 223, 226, 229, 231, 234, 235, 236, 239, 243, 246, 251, 252, 254, 257, 261, 266
Progressive Revelation, 61, 63, 271
prolonging of life, 79
Prophets (*N'vi'im*), v, 45, 52, 75, 78, 105, 155, 188, 191, 238, 239, 240, 241, 242, 243, 244, 271, See also named prophets
proselytes. See conversion
psalms, 97, 99, 124, 131, 150, 196, 202, 269, See also Hallel
punishment, 75, 110, 120, 139, 260
Purim, 53, 88, 116, 134, 138, 271
purity, 118, 206, 242

R

rabbinic dictum, 35, 70, 75
rabbinic interpretation, 27, 53, 82, 110, 185, 223, 249, 250
Rabbinic Judaism, 159
rabbinic tradition, 82, 117, 159

Rabbis, 17, 29, 40, 50, 53, 54, 55, 62, 66, 76, 77, 78, 88, 91, 94, 96, 101, 103, 117, 119, 128, 129, 130, 131, 155, 158, 159, 170, 171, 172, 177, 180, 185, 192, 194, 197, 199, 200, 204, 205, 211, 219, 229, 231, 246, 247, 248, 250, 251, 259, 260, 261, 271
Rashi, 55
Rayner, Rabbi John D, ii, 2, 3, 169, 176, 177
Reconstructionist Judaism, 183, 257
Reform Judaism, 172, 173
Reinhardt, Rabbi Harold, 34
religious education, 72, 87, 209, See also study; Talmud Torah
repentance, 16, 20, 114, 117, 120, 272, See also t'shuvah; Yom Kippur
Respect for conscientious options, iv
resurrection, 150, 190
revelation, 59, 62, 92, 129, 130, 170, 185, See also Mount Sinai; Progressive Revelation
ritual murder, 142
Ritual slaughter, 272, See also sh'chitah
rituals, 3, 39, 83, 92, 94, 95, 96, 110, 111, 112, 125, 127, 145, 148, 149, 171, 196, 207, 211, 216, 220, 224, 240, 255, 259
Rosh Chodesh, 116
Rosh ha-Shanah (Jewish New Year), 34, 37, 114, 116, 117, 118, 119, 120, 122, 127, 133, 260, 271, 273
Ruth, 53, 130, 270

S

Sabbath, iv, 7, 12, 32, 34, 65, 66, 81, 83, 88, 102, 108, 109, 110, 112, 160, 200, 202, 239, 242, 245, 247, 248, 272, See also Shabbat
sacrificial worship, 135, 190, 239, 241
Sadducees, 157, 158, 194, 272
same-sex couples, 215, 220, 256
Samaritans, 160, 261,
Samuel, 14, 52, 93, 154, 189
Sanger, Rabbi Herman, 46, 169, 175, 176
Sarah, 5, 7, 37, 38, 100, 153, 219
schools, 71, 158, 212
science, 10, 11, 47, 79, 145, 256

279

Index

scrolls (m'gillot), 270
Second World War, 33, 47
seder (Passover meal), 83, 127, 128, 137, 255, 268, 269, 270, 272
Seder Rav Amram, 100
separation. *See* havdalah
Sephardi, 57, 147, 160, 218, 272
Service of the Heart (prayerbook), 176, 200
services, 2, 14, 34, 50, 56, 81, 86, 96, 103, 112, 118, 121, 122, 124, 174, 197, 198, 200, 201, 202, 204, 207, 208, 236, 242, 255
S'fira, see *Omer*
S'firat HaOmer, see *Omer*
sh'chitah (ritual slaughter), 78, 249, 251
Shammai, 77, 158
Sh'ma (statement of affirmation), 10, 32, 70, 82, 95, 98, 99, 101, 102, 103, 272
sh'mirat Shabbat (Sabbath observance), 245
Shabbat, 7, 32, 56, 65, 77, 88, 96, 101, 103, 104, 105, 108, 109, 110, 111, 112, 113, 119, 135, 139, 146, 159, 160, 175, 185, 201, 212, 213, 230, 245, 246, 247, 248, 252, 255, 269, 270, 272
Shacharit (morning service), 121
Shavu'ot (Pentecost), 53, 116, 123, 124, 128, 129, 130, 213, 260, 271, 272
shiv'ah (mourning) prayers, 150, 272
Sho'ah, 139, 272, *See also* Holocaust
shofar (horn), 117, 119, 120, 122, 272
Shulchan Aruch ('Prepared Table'), 57, 58
siddur (prayerbook), 103, 242, 272, *See also* prayerbooks
Siddur Lev Chadash, 73, 147, 176, 216
Simchat Torah, 104, 116, 123, 132, 133, 135, 272
sincerity, 3, 130, 198, 201, 234, 236, 245
Six Day War, 47
social justice, 46, 49, 74, 78, 173
Song of Songs, 53, 270
Spain, 41, 42, 57, 139, 156, 160, 179, 272
Spinoza, Baruch, 185
standing prayer, 100 *and see* T'filah
State of Israel, iv, 44, 45, 49, 138, 191, 237, *See also* Israel, State of

status, v, 42, 48, 146, 190, 204, 207, 209, 215, 228, 229, 233, 234, 235, 236, 237, 256
Stone setting, 151
study, 62, 64, 65, 66, 67, 69, 70, 71, 75, 85, 86, 87, 88, 89, 91, 99, 103, 104, 108, 154, 165, 166, 171, 175, 179, 202, 208, 210, 214, 234, 235, 236, 272, 273
Sukkah, 130, 132
Sukkot (festival of 'Tabernacles'), 53, 115, 116, 117, 120, 123, 124, 130, 132, 133, 135, 197, 213, 260, 269, 270, 272
symbols, 94, 95, 96, 112, 126, 127, 128, 220

T

T'filah, 100, 101, 102, 105, 122, 190, 195, 268, 272
t'fillin (phylacteries), 95, 96, 101, 171, 207
t'shuvah (repentance), 16, 20, 117, 272
taharah (ritual cleansing of dead bodies), 149, 272
tallit (prayer shawl), 95, 106, 121, 149, 171, 272
Talmud, iv, 35, 51, 55, 61, 70, 76, 77, 126, 135, 159, 165, 179, 197, 246, 247, 248, 259, 260, 269, 272, 273
talmud torah ('Study of Torah'), 70
Tanach (Hebrew Bible), 53, 272
technology, 18, 47, 79, 256
Temple, iv, 39, 40, 66, 71, 82, 86, 87, 88, 92, 93, 99, 102, 103, 105, 117, 119, 121, 124, 129, 135, 136, 139, 147, 154, 155, 156, 158, 164, 167, 171, 172, 179, 180, 189, 190, 193, 194, 195, 196, 199, 206, 219, 229, 239, 240, 242, 243, 269, 272
Ten Commandments, 93, 99, 109, 129, 130
Ten Days of Repentance (*aseret y'mei t'shuvah*), 117
termination of life, 79, 148
Three Pilgrimage festivals, iv, *See also* Pesach; Shavu'ot; Sukkot
Tish'a b'Av ('Ninth of Av'), 134, 139, 140

Index

Torah ('Teaching'), iv, 13, 34, 52, 53, 55, 59, 60, 61, 62, 63, 65, 66, 69, 70, 71, 75, 76, 77, 86, 94, 98, 103, 104, 105, 106, 109, 112, 115, 116, 117, 118, 120, 122, 123, 129, 130, 132, 133, 135, 158, 170, 182, 185, 195, 206, 207, 209, 210, 211, 212, 213, 218, 223, 231, 244, 246, 248, 249, 250, 259, 260, 264, 268, 269, 270, 271, 272, 273, *See also* Kabbalat Torah; Simchat Torah; Talmud Torah
Tosefta ('additional'), 53, 54, 273
Tower of Babel, 22, 263
Tu biShvat (New Year for Trees), 137
twelve tribes of Israel, 228
tz'dakah, 74, 77, 273

U

ultra-Orthodox, 6, 49, 161, 182, 191, 216
United Kingdom. *See also* Great Britain
United States, 33, 174, 180, 181, 241, *See also* America
unleavened bread, 125, 126, 127, 142, 268, *See also* Matzah

W

war, 28, 33, 47, 139, 263
War of Independence (Israel), 47
wine, 81, 83, 112, 113, 127, 128, 146, 219, 242, 270
Wise, Nathan the, 164
Wise, Rabbi Isaac Mayer, 172
Wise, Rabbi Stephen, 172
women, v, 2, 14, 66, 94, 95, 133, 173, 181, 182, 204, 205, 206, 207, 210, 211, 215, 216, 217, 229
work, prohibition against, 65, 109, 110, 247
World Union for Progressive Judaism, ii, 2, 3, 169, 170, 174, 175

World War Two, 34
worship, iv, v, 10, 21, 30, 40, 45, 57, 86, 87, 88, 90, 91, 92, 93, 94, 95, 96, 97, 99, 100, 101, 103, 105, 108, 109, 112, 121, 153, 193, 194, 195, 196, 198, 199, 201, 202, 206, 207, 211, 240, 241, 242, 243, 244, 245, 247, 248, 255, 264, 272
written Torah, 52, 60, 61, *See also* Five Books of Moses; Torah

Y

Y'hudah, 37, 273, *See also* Judah
yahrzeit (anniversary of death), 151
Yamim Nora'im, 114, 122, 273, *See also* Days of Awe
yarmulke, 96, 270, *See also* kippah; head covering
yeitzer ha-ra (evil inclination), 18, 19
yeitzer ha-tov (good inclination), 18, 20
yeshivah (academy for Jewish study), 166, 210
Yiddish, 42, 72, 103, 160, 166, 210, 218, 250, 272
Yitzchak Rabin, 49
Yizkor (memorial) service, 121, 122
Yom ha-Atzma'ut (Israeli Independence Day), 50, 115, 134, 273
Yom ha-Sho'ah, 115, 134, 140, 273
Yom ha-Zikaron (Israeli Memorial Day), 138
Yom Kippur (Day of Atonement), 34, 47, 114, 116, 117, 120, 121, 122, 141, 261, 273
Yom Kippur War, 47

Z

z'man matan torateinu ('giving of Torah'), 129, *See also* Shavu'ot
Zechariah, 53, 118
Zionist movement, 46
Zohar ('Book of Splendour'), 57

OTHER RESOURCES TO INTRODUCE JUDAISM
from MHM Publications

You may be interested in

MOSAIC: FESTIVALS CD
Songs for the Jewish Year

14 catchy new songs in English which introduce and teach the basics of each festival – the easiest way to remember the details.

Complete with sing-along karaoke versions

You won't be able to stop singing them!

A great New Year, birthday or Chanukah gift for yourself and any Jewish children or grandchildren

HEBREW FROM ZERO

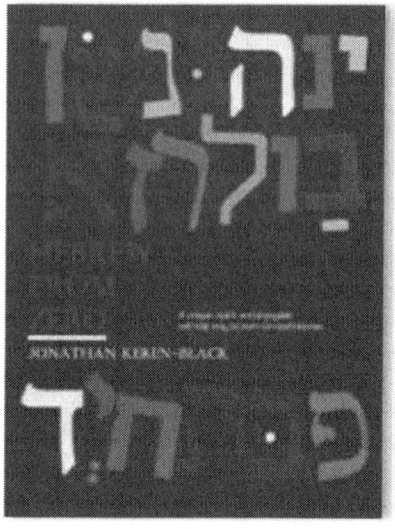

Finally, an innovative and effective quick course to learn and remember the Hebrew letters and vowels, developed for adults and older children.

Along the way, you'll learn plenty of useful vocabulary and some basic grammar, so you'll be able to confidently read the Prayerbook, the Torah, or any Hebrew, and start to understand some of its meaning!

DANIEL DERONDA'S JEWISH JOURNEY

George Eliot's final novel containsrich Jewish themes with regard to the conservative Jewish establishment and the 'new', liberal traditions, about what it means to be a Jew in Britain, and about 'proto-Zionism'. This very abridged version brings the Jewish stories and aspects into a short and readable form for your convenience and enjoyment.

THE JEWISH STATE THEODOR HERZL

A new and readable translation of Theodor Herzl's influential plan to create a Jewish State in Palestine. Indispensable for anyone interested in the establishment of a Jewish land after 1800 years, and of the history of Zionism. Complete with Herzl's original Introduction. 132 pages

Available on Amazon.com,
Fishpond.com.au
lbc.org.au or
direct from MHM Publications:
mhmpublications@dodo.com.au

Printed in Great Britain
by Amazon